Easy to Start, Fun to Run & Highly Profitable

HOME Businesses

EASY TO START, FUN TO RUN & HIGHLY PROFITABLE

HOME BUSINESSES

Katina Z. Jones

Adams Media Corporation
Holbrook, Massachusetts

Published by Adams Media Corporation
260 Center Street, Holbrook, MA 02343

ISBN: 1-55850-842-2

Printed in the United States of America.

J I H G F E D C

Library of Congress Cataloging-in-Publication Data
Jones, Katina Z.
Easy to start, fun to run & highly profitable home businesses / Katina Z. Jones.
p.   cm.
ISBN 1-55850-842-2
1. Home-based businesses—Management. 2. New business enterprises. I. Title.
HD62.38.J66   1998
658'.041—dc21   97-47528
CIP

This publication is designed to provide accurate and authoritative information with
regard to the subject matter covered. It is sold with the understanding that the
publisher is not engaged in rendering legal, accounting, or other professional advice.
If legal advice or other expert assistance is required, the services of a competent
professional person should be sought.
— From a *Declaration of Principles* jointly adopted by a Committee of the
American Bar Association and a Committee of Publishers and Associations

Cover art ©Stock Illustration Source, Inc.

This book is available at quantity discounts for bulk purchases.
For information, call 1-800-872-5627 (in Massachusetts 781-767-8100).

Visit our home page at http://www.adamsmedia.com

Table of Contents

Introduction

There has never been a more exciting time to start your own business. New businesses are springing up every day across the country, and the majority of them are started right at home. Whether these new ventures are inspired by stay-at-home moms looking to earn extra cash, young people starting their careers with their own businesses, previously employed middle managers, or just regular folks looking to increase their monthly income, everyone is finding themselves caught in the entrepreneurial spirit.

As companies are learning to be leaner and meaner, career-minded individuals are learning that the only place to find true job security is right in your own home. They already know that the best way to prevent an almost inevitable layoff is to open up shop for themselves. Changes in government programs and tax benefits for these entrepreneurs have created a market situation for which it has never been easier to start—and operate—a new business. It's almost as if you'd be foolish not to try your hand at running your own show!

Aside from government programs, new technology in both the communications and computer industries has made home offices the norm, instead of the exception. Many entrepreneurs have been able to start their own home ventures while still employed, thus increasing their capital and minimizing their day-to-day financial risk. With an answering machine, a second phone line, a computer, some letterhead, and business cards, many of these home-based businesses can literally run themselves while you keep your day job, leaving you to fill orders or talk to clients on your off time. And if you do choose to quit you day job and work at home full-time, a fax machine, modem, and Internet access can help keep you connected to the outside world during business hours, too.

This book emphasizes the potential for many businesses that might start out as hobbies, personal interests, or an expansion of a particular skill you might already have. Take time to read through all of the business opportunities we have selected to include. You'll find that there is a balanced mix of part-time and full-time opportunities. Many ideas are considered "white collar," but there are plenty of businesses listed that require a more hands-on approach and specific technical skills.

As you read each business description, you'll notice some specific statistical information at the beginning of each entry. It is organized as follows:

> **Start-up costs:** These costs are calculated by adding together all equipment, advertising, and operating capital costs. We have tried to consider every possible cost, and then asked the questions: "What's the least amount of money you would need to start this business the right way?"
> Potential earnings: This range is calculated by multiplying typical fees by a 40-hour work week. Obviously, this amount will change dramatically if you are only considering starting any new businesses part-time.

Typical fees: Each business idea has been thoroughly researched to find out what people who are actually in the business are charging their clients. For many entries, you might see a range instead of one flat fee. This is because your geographic location may influence your pricing strategy more than the actual demand for your goods or services.

Advertising: Here, we have listed all the possible ways you could promote your business, from methods that cost nothing, such as networking, to developing actual media campaigns that might cost thousands of dollars a year. These costs have been figured into the initial start-up cost.

Qualifications: This category contains everything you need to know about professional certifications, personality requirements, and other information pertinent to what it takes to enter a particular field.

Equipment needed: The equipment purchases you are likely to make to run your business efficiently.

Staff required: A high percentage of these businesses won't require anyone but yourself, but those needing additional staff are identified, often with a suggested number of employees.

Handicapped opportunity: You'll find that many home-based businesses are accessible to those with physical or developmental handicaps.

Hidden costs: This is probably the most important element of each entry. The costs that you don't think about are often the ones that drive your business into the ground. They include insurance coverage, worker's compensation, and even fluctuating material costs. Many of these are costs you simply can't predict—or might not have realized are incurred by state and federal government requirements. Some may be as simple as the cost of additional gasoline.

The rest of each entry provides a comprehensive guide to each individual business. With each, you'll get a total picture of what's involved in successfully running the kind of business that matches your skills.

What You Do: This section supplies the details of exactly what each business demands of its owner, what your daily activities will be, and who your customers are. This section also includes information on specific marketing opportunities.

What You Need: Here, you'll find an in-depth breakdown of your startup costs, including everything from office furniture, computer equipment, and advertising costs. You also find valuable information on how to arrive at specific earnings goals for each business.

Keys to Success: This section points out the positive and negative aspects of each business, so you'll know exactly what you're in for. Remember, there are positives and negatives for every opportunity.

In 1992, I started my own home business, a resume service, with about $500, a laptop computer, and some specialty paper that I bought from catalogs. Today, this business is still thriving, and still a home-based business. In the interim, I've written three books, got married, gave birth to a beautiful new daughter, and have had at least two other "full-time" jobs. No matter what life has brought me, this small business keeps going, profitably. I wouldn't have it any other way.

While this fast-paced, often crazy lifestyle is certainly not for everyone, you have already recognized the benefits of self-employment, even if it is part-time. I can tell you that there is no greater reward than working for yourself, at home (often without even getting dressed!). This book certainly does not provide all the answers, but lets you think about the many issues that will help you determine if your business idea matches your current ideals, and if an entrepreneur's lifestyle really is for you. Good luck as you embark on what will become the most interesting journey of your life!

KATINA Z. JONES
August, 1997

Accountant

Start-up cost:	$3,000-$6,000
Potential earnings:	20,000-$80,000
Typical fees:	$35 and up per hour
Advertising:	Membership and active participation in community groups, newspapers, ads in publications for local fund-raisers, referrals
Qualifications:	CPA, some experience in services on which you choose to focus
Equipment needed:	Office, furniture, computer, suite software, printer, business cards, letterhead, envelopes
Staff required:	No
Handicapped opportunity:	Yes
Hidden costs:	Errors and omissions insurance, subscriptions and membership dues, continuing education

What You Do

This is a service that virtually everyone needs. The challenge is to show potential clients how you can improve their lives by helping them manage their financial affairs better. The two major approaches chosen by solo accountants are to work with individuals on tax issues and personal financial planning, or to serve the burgeoning small business market with bookkeeping setup, payroll, tax planning, and all the other financial activities that enterprises require. You will need to be creative in distinguishing yourself from this rather crowded field. How are your accounting services better than those of the six other accountants who have called a business that week, looking for work? How can you show an individual that you can serve him better than the big storefront operations that prepare taxes for low fees during the winter and early spring?

What You Need

Will you meet clients in your office, or will you travel to their homes or businesses? These decisions will control your start-up costs (could be as little as $3,000). Potential earnings of $20,000 and more.

Keys to Success

Being an excellent accountant and being able to create a profitable business are two different things. The people skills required have probably been completely neglected in your education, and possibly in your experience if you have worked for a large firm. Gaining the confidence of potential clients is far more than simply having excellent accounting skills up your sleeve. You'll need to find a way to present your services in a way that appeals to people who want your help but don't really understand numbers and like to tell condescending accountant jokes at parties. On the downside, there is a seasonality to your services; you'll be busiest in December and March/April.

Expert Advice

What sets your business apart from others like it?

Personalized service and affordable rates are what set apart Kelly M. Zimmerman, CPA's business in Cuyahoga Falls, Ohio. "I take a genuine interest in my clients' businesses. I really care about whether or not they succeed."

Things you couldn't do without:

Zimmerman says she couldn't do without a computer, telephone, and calculator.

Marketing tips/advice:

"Get involved in an organization that you believe in personally and where you can also promote your business. Marketing for accountants is basically word of mouth, so be sure to do everything you can to keep your current clients happy. They'll send you more clients if they know you've gone out of your way for them."

If you had to do it all over again . . .

"I would try to be more organized and focused on the types of clients I really want to serve."

Adoption Search Service

Start-up cost:	$2,000-$3,000
Potential earnings:	25,000-$40,000
Typical fees:	$150-$250 per job or an hourly fee of $15-$25 per hour
Advertising:	Yellow Pages, referrals from social service agencies and associations
Qualifications:	Experience with the field, sensitivity, understanding of state laws, rules, and records regarding adoption, persistence
Equipment needed:	Computer, modem, printer office furniture, business cards, letterhead, envelopes
Staff required:	No
Handicapped opportunity:	Yes
Hidden costs:	On-line time, phone bills

What You Do

Adoption search services provide opportunities for birth children or birth parents to retrace the steps that separated them from their blood relatives. This is a challenging business, and it is still encircled with complex regulations that vary from state to state. Another source of challenge is the infinite variation of human nature. Some reunions are filled with joy, but not all discoveries are happy ones and some people would rather not be found. A vocal minority of the population strongly opposes the adoption search process. Overall, however, bridging the chasm caused by adoption decisions can be a viable service for a small business to offer.

What You Need

Some of the searching process may be done on-line (spend $2,000-$3,000 for a computer), but the telephone and shoe leather will be your major tools. You may opt to charge a flat rate ($150-$250) or an hourly fee of $15-$25 per hour. If the client has some information for you to go on, opt for the flat rate. If it looks like a wild-goose chase, you might seriously consider the hourly rate plus related expenses.

Keys to Success

Marketing will be a challenge. How will adoptees and birth parents come to know about your service? And since you will only work once for each client, marketing must be an ongoing part of your strategy. Linking people can heal old and painful wounds, so you will get more than monetary rewards from your successful searches. On the other hand, it could throw salt into a wound that was somewhat healed. How will turning someone's life around, for good or ill, affect you?

Advertising Agency

Start-up cost:	$7,000-$16,000
Potential earnings:	35,000-$75,000
Typical fees:	$75-$150 per hour, a monthly retainer, or a per-job basis
Advertising:	Networking, trade publications, teaching at a community college or adult school
Qualifications:	Knowledge of design, layout, and typography; writing skills; experience
Equipment needed:	Computer with modem and high-resolution printer, presentations, desktop publishing, and photo software, scanner, CD-ROM, fax, copy machine, business card, letterhead, envelopes
Staff required:	No
Handicapped opportunity:	Yes
Hidden costs:	Organizational dues and schmoozing may get costly

What You Do

You're probably not going to be doing the Cadillac ads for General Motors, but if you are motivated and highly skilled you can build up a home-based ad agency serving clients in a specialized area. To get a foothold, you'll need to have experience from a larger agency, or a source of clients who know you and respect your interest in what they do. Activities such as collecting or participating in a special sport could be your lead-in to a small but profitable market. Or you could specialize in one type of store, one product, or a type of service. You will get to know your client organizations well, and you will draw on all of your creativity, both verbal and graphic. New ways of getting a commercial message out to the public are revolutionizing the advertising field, so creativity extends into the nature of the business itself as well. Very few businesses can succeed without advertising in one way or another, so your creativity and awareness of market needs has many possible customers. You'll need to educate your clients about the value of advertising—even when things don't seem to be going very well for the company or when they are overbooked with too much business.

What You Need

High-end computers with the graphics and print-production software now available enable small agencies to produce ads that once required an entire art department. Setting up this equipment is expensive, though, and could cost from $3,000-$5,000. Bill out between $75-$150 per hour, or determine your rates on a per-job basis that takes into account how much work is actually involved in the project. Many ad agencies also work on monthly retainers of $500 or more; again, look at the workload and the time and expertise involved in each project.

Keys to Success

Advertising is a rewarding occupation because it relies so heavily on ideas and inspiration, connected directly to business results. Successful ad agency personnel (in this case, you) develop close relationships with their clients. You'll be serving an area or group that you know about and enjoy, and you'll be using all of your talents to do so. As a one-man (or -woman) band, you must be able to do all the facets of the advertising process, from sales to writing and paste-up. The pressure never lets up—and the competition for clients is sharklike.

Expert Advice

What sets your business apart from others like it?

For Carol Wilkerson, owner of Wilkerson Ltd., in Portland, Oregon, it's experience that sets her business apart. "I have over twenty-three years of experience in advertising and public relations, and I have dealt from the bottom up with any kind of promotional effort there is. Also, I'm small and selective about who I work with, because I want to make sure I can really provide the top-notch service the client's looking for, turning things around quickly enough to keep them coming back for more."

Things you couldn't do without:

Wilkerson's business depends on a computer, laser printer, fax, telephone, and overnight delivery services.

Marketing tips/advice:

"Before you start, determine what your strengths are and identify them for your clients. You really run into problems when you start promising things you really can't do . . . you can't fake knowledge and experience. Farm out what you can't do to others who can, and you'll gain a lot more respect."

If you had to do it all over again . . .

"Oddly enough, I didn't promote myself well enough in the beginning . . . I wasn't a big enough cheerleader for my own business. It's so ironic!"

Advertising Sales Representative

Start-up cost:	$1,000-$1,500
Potential earnings:	40,000-$150,000
Typical fees:	Commission-only is standard and ranges from 5 to 25 percent
Advertising:	Direct mail, trade journals, referrals
Qualifications:	Experience with an advertising agency or periodical sales rep
Equipment needed:	Basic office equipment, business cards, letterhead, envelopes
Staff required:	No
Handicapped opportunity:	Yes
Hidden costs:	Expect high phone bills and mileage costs

What You Do

This business must be built on extensive experience in the field. Your expertise lies in matching the need to the availability. If you know how, you can sell advertising space in all magazines to the advertisers who need it. Your job is to find a buyer at a good price that might never have discovered this advertising venue unaided. You'll need contacts and experience to make a success of this enterprise, but room exists for the independent rep and many earn $100,000 or more. Much depends on the media you're selling ad space for; for instance, if you're selling ads in a trade journal or well-known national publication, your income will be quite high. However, if you're selling ads for a community newspaper, your income may reach its peak at $35,000.

What You Need

The telephone is your major tool, and you may discover a great need for a car phone (which brings with it monthly charges and high incoming-call fees). You'll need access to reference books listing periodicals, rates, and dates. Expect a $1,500 initial start-up cost for this business.

Keys to Success

If you love selling, this is selling in its purest form. No limitations bind you to one focus, one time, or one perspective. Businesses need to advertise, and finding space for their commercial messages can be a real challenge. Your services are the perfect answer to their needs. The same old way of doing things will be your biggest hindrance. Established agencies are your competitors, and you will need to market your services vigorously.

Airbrush Artist

Start-up cost:	$500-$1,000
Potential earnings:	25,000-$50,000
Typical fees:	Varies; could be as low as $125 and as high as several thousand per project
Advertising:	Local art galleries, art studios, art supply houses
Qualifications:	Graphic design, art background or degree
Equipment needed:	Airbrush, paints, hose, canvas, cloth, masks
Staff required:	No
Handicapped opportunity:	Yes
Hidden costs:	Ventilation system, rising materials costs

What You Do

Airbrush art is found in many different places, such as on billboards or T-shirts. An art background is a must for this job. It's essential that you can separate colors as well as mix them. The ability to think in fine detail and visualize is also essential. Build your reputation as an artist wherever you can find work (try magazines, ad agencies, and public relations firms). There are several ways to do this; the most simple is to enter a contest or show or try to get your work exhibited locally. The icing on the cake would be to get your work commissioned for private or public display. Either way, this shows that someone (hopefully with big money) has noticed your work and is willing to pay for it. You're well on your way.

What You Need

Most of your initial investment will be in trying to enter your work in contests and art galleries. Some charge a fee for this. You should already have the tools you need because of your background training (start-up could be as little as $500). Be prepared to start out slowly until you build your reputation. If you hit some craft shows and are lucky enough to get into an exhibit, your monthly income could be approximately $1,000-$3,000 per month. But don't quit your day job just yet, since your income is bound to be unpredictable. It's the nature of the creative beast to live paycheck to paycheck.

Keys to Success

If you live for creativity, the sky is the limit. You can airbrush on all types of materials: wood, shirts, brick, film—you name it. Sure, it will take a while before you'll make really big money, but in the meantime you can console yourself with the fact that this is a growing industry and you will have repeat business once you've done at least a few good projects for your clients.

Animal Broker/Dealer

Start-up cost:	$10,000-$15,000
Potential earnings:	45,000-$70,000
Typical fees:	Often $200 per animal
Advertising:	Trade journals, direct mail, referrals, networking
Qualifications:	Familiarity with CITES, the international treaty on the movement of plants and animals, contacts with zoo personnel, animal parks, and importers
Equipment needed:	Computer, modem, fax, printer, office furniture, business card, letterhead, envelopes
Staff required:	No
Handicapped opportunity:	No
Hidden costs:	Travel and conference fees

What You Do

Zoos increasingly have breeding programs and tend to trade animals amongst themselves. Not all the needed exhibit animals can be obtained by this means, however, and brokers and dealers must fill the rest of the bill. Many animals are bred in private parks and later become available for display in a zoo. There is still some international trade in animals as well, regulated by CITES and various national laws and regulations. To make a go of being an animal broker, you will need many close contacts in the zoo world so you will hear when a particular species is needed. Sources of animals can be even harder to find, and your ability to link the creature with the zoo needing it will set you apart from the competition. Be certain that you like animals and don't mind caring for them in interim situations when they are between places to live. On a smaller scale, you can locate purebred puppies.

What You Need

The telephone will probably be your most important piece of office equipment, along with some method (probably Internet) of communicating with distant sources.

Keys to Success

This is not the fast-growing fad business of the '90s. Nor is it open to just anyone who has completed a course or two in zoology at the local community college. But if you have a friend in every zoo in the country, and if you care enough about the welfare of animals to plan their new homes successfully, you can establish yourself as an animal broker. Don't expect to grow rich overnight, though. Like the many animals you'll represent, this one will take time to grow.

Antiques Dealer

Start-up cost:	$20,000-$40,000 (depending on how large your inventory is)
Potential earnings:	35,000-$65,000
Typical fees:	Varied; your pieces will sell anywhere from $10-$10,000
Advertising:	Yellow Pages, community newspapers, direct mail, show participation, location
Qualifications:	Should be knowledgeable about antiques and pricing
Equipment needed:	Storefront with cash register, computer for accounting/inventory purposes, printer, fax, retail display equipment
Staff required:	Not initially
Handicapped opportunity:	Yes
Hidden costs:	Insurance, warehousing

What You Do

The lure of the old and priceless draws many a sentimental customer into an antique store, and you could start such a business with a dozen or so nice pieces of furniture, some antique china, and lots of old books and toys. All of these items tend to sell well, as they are collectible and worth increasingly more with each passing year. You'll need to develop a sizable stock or inventory of pieces to sell, and that can best be accomplished by combing thrift shops, flea markets, and estate auctions for the best and most interesting old items you can find. Watch the newspaper for garage sales, too—sometimes people will unknowingly unload a fabulous antique dresser at a steal of a price.

Basically, you should keep in mind that your business will need to be run just like any other retail establishment—and that means you'll need to price yourself well enough to cover your operating expenses in addition to building a profit. Tricky work, because folks will want to barter with you on price.

What You Need

You'll need at least $20,000 and probably closer to $50,000 to get this business started properly, mainly because you need to have a significant inventory and a storefront to display and sell your products. Look to earn $35,000-$65,000, depending on three things: location, quality of product line, and price. Obviously, if you're in a quaint New England town, you might fare better than an antique shop in the middle of Kentucky.

Keys to Success

It's a competitive market, and too many well-intended entrepreneurs make the mistake of thinking this will be an easy ride. If you've got sufficient working capital to buy the kinds of pieces that will build your reputation for the finer things, then you'll have little problem making a living. If you're undercapitalized, you'll be out of business before you know it, because you'll probably have bought way more than your operations can support.

Apartment Preparation Service

Start-up cost:	$500
Potential earnings:	20,000–$30,000
Typical fees:	$50 and up per apartment
Advertising:	Yellow pages, direct contact with apartment owners
Qualifications:	Knowledge of cleaning procedures and painting skills
Equipment needed:	Cleaning supplies, sweeper, mops, buckets, painting equipment
Staff required:	No
Handicapped opportunity:	No
Hidden costs:	Insurance, equipment maintenance

What You Do

You add the finishing touches to apartment buildings before the next tenant moves in. To increase your marketability, offer several services, including carpet cleaning, wall washing, painting and wallpaper repair, and overall cleaning services. Set fee schedules appropriately depending on individual services (or offer an all-inclusive package price). Advertise your services to many apartment complexes. To cut down on driving, try to get a contract with a multi-unit apartment complex offering short-term lease options.

What You Need

Invest in good quality cleaning equipment, including a sweeper and carpet cleaner. Start-up costs can be as low or as high as you want, depending on what services you are going to offer and the quality of equipment you purchase. This business can be started for a relatively low cost with high return on investment.

Keys to Success

This business is not for someone who is afraid of good hard elbow grease. Be prepared to encounter some messy situations. An apartment preparer might spend quite a bit of time on their hands and knees cleaning baseboards and floors—consider the health of your back and always wear a back corset. In addition, invest in a good pair of knee pads and rubber gloves.

Art Broker/
Corporate Art Consultant

Start-up cost:	$1,000 plus
Potential earnings:	35,000-$100,000
Typical fees:	$50 per hour
Advertising:	Trade publications, business periodicals, service on boards or in community charitable organizations, networking, referrals
Qualifications:	Degree in art or related field, extensive gallery or museum experience, interior design credentials
Equipment needed:	Business cards, letterhead, envelopes, phone
Staff required:	No
Handicapped opportunity:	No
Hidden costs:	Membership dues, subscriptions to art periodicals, travel

What You Do

The corporate art consulting business is where connoisseurship and corporate image issues come together. It's a rarified combination, and you'll need a strong eye for art and a reputation for awareness of business requirements to create a successful enterprise. The art world often has trouble communicating with business people. Your ability to move in both worlds is a major factor in your success. To a large degree you will be selling yourself, and you will do this by listening well, grasping the needs of the corporate culture of your client, and presenting each organization with choices that will enhance their workplaces and their image. You will transform your own appreciation for art into a service that adds value to your clients' enterprises.

The ability to locate the perfect piece of art for the corporate environment is rare. You'll need to visit every art show or trade convention you can, and collect catalogs from dealers worldwide. Then, you'll negotiate fair prices—as an expert, you can help the newly discovered artist price to sell.

What You Need

You'll be working at your clients' premises, in galleries, etc., not at your own office, which only needs to support your business needs, not to impress (as little as $1,000 to start). Depending on your clients, you could easily earn up to $100,000.

Keys to Success

Establishing yourself as an art broker or corporate art consultant will take time, determination, and persistence. Your location will control your avenues of approach; probably operating independently will be possible only in one of the major U.S. cities. Elsewhere, you'll need to be associated with a commercial interior design firm or an art gallery.

Art/Photo Representative

Start-up cost:	$5,000-$15,000
Potential earnings:	25,000-$50,000
Typical fees:	20 percent commission on each sale
Advertising:	Trade publications for artists and photographers, listings in Photographers Market and Guide to Literary Agents/Art Photo Reps, direct mail to related associations
Qualifications:	Ideally, an artistic and/or sales background
Equipment needed:	Computer, printer, fax/modem, copier, phone
Staff required:	No
Handicapped opportunity:	Yes
Hidden costs:	Insurance, bad risks (artists whom you care about but who aren't really very marketable)

What You Do

Behind every successful artist or photographer is an agent who carts around resumes and slides from market to market, seeking the best opportunity to sell works of art to everyone from gallery owners to art catalog publishers and distributors. The key is to juggle several artists and photographers at once, and to spread their work as far out as possible in the hopes that offers will come rolling in. To grow your stable of candidates to represent, advertise in the publications that artistic types generally read. Invite them to respond to your "cattle call" by sending in a detailed resume and plenty of slides; if you should decide to represent someone, provide a contract that clearly spells out what is expected in the give and take of the business relationship; for instance, if you expect to get 20 percent commission on each sale, state it clearly in the contract so that the artist doesn't get snooty with you after you help him become famous.

What You Need

You'll need to promote your services in each of the respective professional trade publications, and that will likely cost you in the neighborhood of $3,000-$5,000 (some directories, however, allow you a free listing). Next, you'll need to have a set of dynamic, yet professional-looking promotional materials of your own and a basic office setup (computer, printer, fax/modem, copier and phone system) to keep it all running smoothly. With a commission of 20 percent on each deal you make, you should be able to earn an annual paycheck between $25,000-$50,000, depending on where you live and how many successful artists you represent.

Keys to Success

The art world is extremely narcissistic and tight-knit; cliques abound, and if your name isn't known as one of the "chosen" few, you may not succeed as much as you'd like. Work the art show openings and other functions; attend trade shows and the like if you really want to get your name out there fast. Above all else, be knowledgeable about art—if you're not, it will definitely show. The positive side is, there are far more talented artists than there are folks to represent them—so your income potential is quite high.

Marketing Trends of the Future

How your business will look in the future depends upon your changing consumer base. Here are just a few trends:

- **The Age Factor.** The number of Americans over 65 exceeds the total population of Canada. Aging bodies have distinct needs in everything from health care to cosmetics. Aging minds may be in search of nostalgia as well as retirement planning.

- **Alternative Lifestyles.** Notice this in health issues (aromatherapy, organic foods, wellness programs) and in the move to the home office, to a slower pace of life, to spiritual fulfillment.

- **Cocooning.** People are claiming control of their immediate environments. This shows itself in increasing gun-ownership (particularly among women), in the rise in home-schooling, in people's reluctance to go to a business. You may have to go to your customers.

- **Adventure.** People want excitement, but they want it safely. The trend is toward exotic foods, sports, and travel.

- **The Informed Consumer.** Access to information allows a consumer to research your product before speaking to you. Be ready to listen, to get to know your customer, to establish trust.

These are some of the broad trends. Get to know the narrower trends, too, in your neighborhood and business area.

Arts Festival Promoter

Start-up cost:	$500-$1,000
Potential earnings:	20,000-$45,000+
Typical fees:	40 percent of registration fees from artists; often, you'll also make a commission from each ticket sold
Advertising:	Word of mouth, ads in artists' newsletters and publications, direct mail to artists, newspaper/billboard ads for the event itself
Qualifications:	Strong organizational skills
Equipment needed:	Computer with desktop publishing software and laser printer
Staff required:	No (you can solicit volunteers to work at each festival)
Handicapped opportunity:	Possibly
Hidden costs:	Insurance and low attendance due to poor advertising or inclement weather

What You Do

Annual arts festivals abound in nearly every community, and you could cash in on the public's interest in the arts by sponsoring or promoting your own group of arts festivals. Give your events a flashy name so that you can win instant recognition with your buying public and among artists (who get barraged with requests to appear in shows all over the country). You'll need to promote your festivals two ways: first, to artists who might like to participate; second, to folks who might like to attend. So, your advertising budget must be split to cater to both "customers." Set your festivals apart somehow by inviting only particular types of artists/craftsmen or by attaching your festivals to some sort of theme (such as an Oktoberfest arts festival). That way, you've set an annual time for the show to be expected to recur; build your mailing list for the following year by requiring everyone to sign in (or, better yet, by offering a drawing for an exquisite work of art).

What You Need

You'll need $500-$1,000 to launch this interesting and artistic enterprise; this seed money will primarily cover your computer costs (printer, desktop publishing software) and a little advertising until you've got one or two shows under your belt. Once you've established a name for your arts festivals, you could have annual repeat business in certain areas and begin to make more than $45,000 per year doing something you truly enjoy.

Keys to Success

You love the arts, and know that others like artsy events. So what's the downside? The only real negative is that sometimes the weather rains on your parade of artists. You could avoid such mishaps if you hold all of your events indoors; even though it may raise your space rental cost, the payoff might be worth it.

Association Management Services

Start-up cost:	$2,000-$9,000
Potential earnings:	20,000-$50,000
Typical fees:	Monthly retainers of $1,000-$5,000 are not uncommon (directly dependent upon the association's size)
Advertising:	Network with professional and trade associations, advertise in related publications
Qualifications:	Good organizational, writing, marketing, communication, and motivation skills, an eye for detail, office management or administrative experience is helpful
Equipment needed:	Office and computer equipment, phone, fax, copier, business cards, letterhead, supplies
Staff required:	None
Handicapped opportunity:	Yes
Hidden costs:	Membership in associations; subscriptions to related publications

What You Do

From the Association for Association Management (yes, there really is an association for everyone) to the Association for Children for Enforcement of Support, most organizations need help in managing their operations. Especially well-suited to a management service are groups too big to rely solely on volunteers but not big enough to justify hiring someone to do it on a full-time basis. Your services for each client may vary, but may include maintaining membership lists, publishing a newsletter, mailing out information about the organization, keeping records, collecting dues, and handling meetings, events, and fund-raising activities. Not only can you work for an existing organization, you could also start an association of your own. Best bet: base it on your own profession or something else with which you have personal experience.

What You Need

Office and computer equipment are your biggest expenses (about $2,000). You may be able to get the organization(s) you represent to pay for some supplies, but that is not something to rely on at the business plan stage. Charge a monthly retainer of $1,000-$5,000 for your services to make sure you cover all of your expenses; since many of these associations work with volunteers, they may try to take advantage of your expertise, too. Don't let them.

Keys to Success

Association management provides a great variety of duties and an opportunity to interact with interesting people. You will also get opportunities to learn about an array of topics at meetings and conventions. This is a great opportunity for those with philanthropic tendencies.

Juggling Family and Work

Let's face it, raising a family and growing a business are each full-time jobs. So, how can you give 100 percent to each and still maintain your sanity?

First of all, set aside a special time each day or week that is designated "family time." During this time, you will accept no phone calls, set no appointments, and not even think about your business. You will probably not even want to stay near your office. Think about going out to dinner and sharing the three best things that happened to each family member during that week.

Or, if you feel you can incorporate your family into parts of your business, it might help them to better understand your needs and constraints. It's one thing for your spouse or children to see you completely stressed out; it's quite another for them to be in your office when that high-volume order comes in on short notice. Especially for children, it is a good idea to demonstrate your commitment to your work.

Smaller children, particularly females, need positive workplace role models—and who better to pave the way than Mom or Dad? Historically, children who are raised by entrepreneurs do tend to become entrepreneurs themselves.

What should you do in the event that a client or customer wants to meet during one of your special family times? You can handle it one of two ways: first, you could rearrange your family time. But the better solution might be to simply say, "I am already meeting with a client at that time . . . is there another time that works for you?" Others will respect your attention to commitments, and you never have to offer an explanation for whom you're meeting with, and why.

However you decide to work your children into your business, or your business into your family life, one thing is for sure: there will never be a time without challenges and disruptions.

You will need to develop the skill to work around any obstacle or challenge, and the best way to accomplish a good balance between work and home life is to learn to follow a time-management program. Scheduling your time is the best way to make sure everything gets done. The rest is just recognizing that it is possible to have two loves: your business and your family.

Auditing Specialist

Start-up cost:	$5,000-$8,000
Potential earnings:	50,000-$75,000
Typical fees:	Percentage of the savings you find for clients; often 50 percent for past savings and about 10 percent for two or more years into the future
Advertising:	Business and trade publications, direct mail, membership in business groups, networking, referrals
Qualifications:	Knowledge of area of specialty (utility bills, telephone options), excellent math skills, a detail orientation, good selling skills
Equipment needed:	Office furniture, computer, suite software, printer, calculator, business card, letterhead, envelopes, marketing materials
Staff required:	No
Handicapped opportunity:	Yes
Hidden costs:	Ongoing marketing time and materials, continuing education

What You Do

As bills become more complicated, the opportunity for finding errors and overcharges in them increases. For most businesses, though, the tedious, detail-oriented work necessary to check each bill and interpret all the data is just too time-consuming. An auditing specialist can work through all the paper records, uncover overcharges, collect a percentage of the money saved, and make an excellent living. To be very successful, you will need the ability to consider what lies behind the rows of figures on a utility bill. Something as basic as a misplaced decimal point can have a huge effect, but it's harder to spot incorrect rate assignments, double billing for small segments of the service, or opportunities to use a different rate structure.

What You Need

You'll need a good place to work. This is a lot of detailed reading, calculating, and thinking, so your equipment needs to fit you comfortably (around $3,000 to start). Earnings could be $50,000 annually.

Keys to Success

If you focus on utility bills, look for organizations that consume large quantities of electricity—businesses that are open all night, for example. Government, churches, and other institutions with big buildings and inadequate staffing are excellent prospects also. Some auditing services focus on insurance costs or telephone charges. In spite of the clear benefits you will offer, however, marketing is a challenge. People aren't used to the idea of auditing specialists, and they probably have no idea how much money they are pouring down the drain each month in their businesses. In other words, they undoubtedly need your service, but they don't realize it. You will succeed when you find a way to help them understand the benefit you offer.

Expert Advice

What sets your business apart from others like it?

"I don't just punch numbers into a computer . . . I delve deeper to find out more about the customer and how I can help them on a long-term basis," says Dianna Stahl, President & CEO of E.R.S., Inc., in Akron, Ohio.

Things you couldn't do without:

Stahl says she absolutely couldn't do without a computer and a phone.

Marketing tips/advice:

"Find a good mentor in whatever area you're weak in. I was weak in sales, so I found myself a good sales mentor and it helped immeasurably."

If you had to do it all over again . . .

"Know the people you're going to go into business with well before you do it. I was starting my business based on someone else's promises, and they didn't come through. Fortunately, it worked out."

Automotive Detailing

Start-up cost:	$5,000-$10,000
Potential earnings:	30,000-$60,000
Typical fees:	$100-$500 per job
Advertising:	Newspaper, automotive publications, body shops, network with dealers
Qualifications:	A flair for the artistic
Equipment needed:	Cleaning equipment such as polish, rags, brushes, toothbrushes, cotton swabs; equipment such as airbrush, paint, sealer
Staff required:	No
Handicapped opportunity:	Possibly
Hidden costs:	Larger building as business grows, hourly wages of additional assistants

What You Do

Automotive detailing can be done anywhere and at your convenience. A relatively low initial investment will start you on your way. Although the number of auto detailers has grown significantly, you can remain competitive by creating a smart marketing plan, providing superior service, offering lower prices, and exhibiting sound management skills. Continually look for ways to provide services that your competition has overlooked.

What You Need

Aside from the cost of basic cleaning equipment, an airbrush and related art supplies will start at $2,500. It may be necessary to consider the location of your business. Expect a minimum monthly payment of $250 if you will require a small garage in which to work.

Keys to Success

If you have dreamed of working at your own pace and during the hours you choose, automotive detailing can be a rewarding occupation. Individuals with artistic flair and an appreciation for well-kept automobiles are always in demand as many automobile dealers continue to farm out their detail work. Creativity is the key to keeping the competition at bay. Consider a mobile detail shop as your business van allows on-site work, saving you and your customers valuable time. Your work is different everyday—so what's not to like?

Expert Advice

What sets your business apart from others like it?

Paul Taylor, owner of a Midas Muffler franchise in Lawrence, New York, says his business is set apart because it's run by him. "I believe in the highest standards of equipment and service, and my customers know that about me."

Things you couldn't do without:

"It really depends on the types of services you're providing. If it's just a muffler shop, you'll only need an air compressor, cutting torches, a MIG welder, and lifts; you'll need more equipment if you start adding brake services and other automotive repair services." Taylor says he couldn't do without multiline phones, an answering machine, fax, and printer in his office.

Marketing tips/advice:

"As an independent, you'll need to do more guerrilla-type marketing, going after wholesale work within a trade as a subcontractor for body shops or transmission services. If you're in a franchise operation, you should be getting all the marketing and technical support they can offer; after all, that's really the only reason for buying into a franchise."

If you had to do it all over again . . .

"I think I've done all the right things, but the climate is awfully discouraging for newcomers due to heavy environmental and government regulations. If I had to do it all over again, I'd probably think twice."

Automotive Loan Broker

Start-up cost:	$500-$1,000
Potential earnings:	50,000-$70,000
Typical fees:	Percentage of loan amount, from lender or borrower
Advertising:	Classified ads in local and national newspapers and magazines
Qualifications:	Finance background would be helpful
Equipment needed:	Office furniture, computer, suite software, printer, fax, modem, business card, letterhead, envelopes
Staff required:	No
Handicapped opportunity:	Yes
Hidden costs:	Utility bills

What You Do

A loan broker brings together the people who need money with the institutions that are in the business of lending it. As an automotive loan broker you will be specializing in a type of loan applicable to almost every household in the country. There are roughly 1.8 vehicles per household in the U.S., and most of the new vehicles sold are purchased through loans. That's a huge potential market. How can you become a part of this picture? You have a list of lenders, a long list. You have obtained their trust with a well-organized business plan. You advertise for borrowers. It is possible that local auto dealerships might be good referral sources for you. But you don't have to restrict yourself to your own geographical area; much of this business can be done by phone. It is important to have a written agreement before you begin the loan search process, as most of your clients will use your service over a bank for credit reasons (i.e., they've had trouble securing credit in a more traditional way).

What You Need

The borrowers will visit the lenders, not your office. Your only start-up costs are your advertising and the equipment to support your paperwork and communications; all of these should be under $1,000. Considering that, if you have marketing savvy, you could earn as much as $70,000. In short, the potential for success in this business is high. All you need is the ability to produce.

Keys to Success

Clarity on goals and expectations is vital to the professional, ethical conduct of a loan brokering business. You make it clear to the potential borrower what expenses are to be reimbursed, and you take a fee only as a commission on a completed loan. Skill at bringing the two sides of the automotive transaction together can enable you to earn a very high income once you are established. Persistence pays off here, as it so often does in the world of small business.

Automotive Maintenance

Start-up cost:	$2,000-$5,000
Potential earnings:	25,000-$50,000
Typical fees:	$25 and up per job (usually an hourly rate of $45 plus parts costs)
Advertising:	Newspaper, radio, billboards, neighborhood flyers, direct mail, location
Qualifications:	Certified Automobile Mechanic
Equipment needed:	Automotive repair tools, inventory of wipers, motor oil, garage space (rented or owned)
Staff required:	No
Handicapped opportunity:	No
Hidden costs:	Inventory, insurance, ongoing advertising

What You Do

On average, each American spends half of one year's wages on his or her car. To put it another way, we value our autos very highly, and we want excellent care for them. An auto maintenance service can be a wonderful way to reach this large group of customers, most of whom are keeping their cars years longer than they did in the past. You can focus your business just on maintenance and leave the complicated computer diagnosis and repairs, and the big parts inventory, to the dealers and garages. You'll have a limited, repeated set of procedures to follow, and you can build a loyal clientele if you keep people's cars running well, and do it in a way that is convenient for their drivers.

What You Need

Costs will be fairly high to equip your business, unless you can buy a set of tools from another business for a reasonable sum. It will take some expensive marketing to launch your enterprise, and you will need to keep a certain level of advertising going throughout each year. If you are good, word of mouth could get you at least $25,000 the first year.

Keys to Success

So, what makes you think you can compete with Minit-Lube? The answer, of course, is personal service. You're not just a well-trained teenager in a clean uniform, you're an experienced, well-organized, customer-oriented maintenance person. You're the answer to the dreams of the little old lady on the corner who relies on her car for safe travel, of the incredibly busy executive who demands rapid, accurate service, and of the car nuts who drop in and want to "talk cars" with someone else who cares about them as much as they do.

Automotive Paint Touch-Up Professional

Start-up cost:	$500-$1,000
Potential earnings:	15,00-$25,000
Typical fees:	$30-$50 per job
Advertising:	Memberships and active participation at car enthusiast events, direct mail, flyers, referrals from dealers and auto repair stores, radio spots, classified ad in auto sales section of newspaper
Qualifications:	Some experience with auto paint work, sales skills
Equipment needed:	Inventory of popular paint colors, sander, brush
Staff required:	No
Handicapped opportunity:	No
Hidden costs:	Inventory and disposal of used chemicals

What You Do

It's not the big things that drive us crazy, sometimes, it's the dings in our car doors and the chips off the hood. For an entirely new paint job, or the replacement of a crumpled fender, plenty of sources are available in most communities. But how can people keep those little scratches and chips from slowly ruining the appearance and resale value of their cars? That's where your service comes in. You can fix the small stuff, which is important nowadays just to keep a car's body panel warranty in effect. Your business meets the need for a smaller, less expensive way to maintain the smooth surface that your customers' vehicles had when new.

What You Need

Costs are low (about $500 for materials); your skill in doing neat-looking paint touch-ups is your main product. On a part-time basis alone you could earn in excess of $15,000.

Keys to Success

Can you find a way to combine customers? Would it work to fix the scratches in every car in the parking garage or lot of a huge company? Can you be an add-in to the work of a local detailer, car wash, or used car lot? You decide—and market yourself accordingly, perhaps offering group discounts.

Balloon Delivery Service

Start-up cost:	$5,000-$10,000
Potential earnings:	25,000-$35,000
Typical fees:	$10-$15 per balloon (some add a delivery fee)
Advertising:	Yellow Pages, classified ads, coupon books
Qualifications:	Valid driver's license
Equipment needed:	Transportation, helium tank supplier, assorted ribbons, and a good range of balloon styles
Staff required:	No
Handicapped opportunity:	Possibly
Hidden costs:	Mileage and discount offers (be sure you're still covering costs when you offer specials)

What You Do

This simple, straightforward service is popular for children's parties, welcome home parties, get well wishes, and birthday surprises. You'll advertise in the Yellow Pages or in local newspapers, take orders more often than not over the phone (be sure you're set up to process credit cards) and then deliver the balloons to the happy recipients. Not too difficult, except when you consider that you'll be competing with florists, who can provide the same services and extras such as flowers and mugs filled with candy. So, how do you set yourself apart? Start with a creative name for your company, one that people will identify with or maybe even chuckle at. The funnier the better, since this is a fun business. Figure out what extras you can provide: is it a singing balloon delivery service, where your delivery people perform a special (and often silly) song when handing over balloons to the intended targets? Or, can you offer them balloons tied to gift items such as a coffee tin filled with gourmet blends? Decide what you can afford to use as a differentiator, then get to work!

What You Need

You will need reliable transportation, most likely a van or truck to haul helium tanks and supplies. That's why your start-up costs are in the $5,000-$10,000 range. But your helium tank won't be very expensive (around $150 or so) and your orders should bring in about $10-$15 per customer (unless you add on special services or products), so the potential to make money is there if you are clever enough to stand apart from the crowd.

Keys to Success

Network with local party supply retailers and wedding shops; ask them if you can leave pamphlets or business cards for customers. Advertising is critical to the success of this business. This is a competitive business; if you can't find your own niche, you'll have a hard time surviving.

Band Manager

Start-up cost:	$500-$1,000
Potential earnings:	15,000-$25,000
Typical fees:	10 percent to 25 percent of a gig
Advertising:	Industry trades, local paper, direct mail, nightclubs, bulletin boards, musicians' associations
Qualifications:	An ear for what will sell, management skills
Equipment needed:	Computer, laser printer, phone, letterhead, business cards
Staff required:	No
Handicapped opportunity:	Yes
Hidden costs:	Band could fire you without notice; it might be a good idea to represent several

What You Do

You're into the club scene; you know instinctively what's hot and what's not. You see a few up-and-coming bands who need representation (because, truthfully, most musicians lack business skills). If you've got the ability to convince musicians that you can really sell them and make their jobs easier by handling all of the business details they'd probably rather not think of anyway, you could make a decent living. You'll need to be well-connected on the club scene, and if you are clued in on where to plug your band(s), you could successfully book them for regular gigs and earn a steady flow of income for yourself in the meantime. Of course, you need to really believe in your band, because if you don't, you won't be able to develop and promote them properly and it will show in your presentation. Good negotiation skills are a must.

What You Need

You'll need some initial capital ($500-$1,000) to help get the band off the ground and lay the ground for some publicity. The ability to negotiate good contracts is important not only to the band, but to you because you get roughly 10 to 25 percent of what they make. With percentages like that, you could make $15,000-$25,000 (depending on how many bands you represent).

Keys to Success

Expect to spend long hours on the phone trying to get bookings. At the start, you'll probably still have a day job, so expect your evenings and weekends to be tied up. Start out at small clubs and work your way to bigger ones as your band(s) get more confident.

Bankruptcy Services

Start-up cost:	$500-$1,000
Potential earnings:	25,000-$40,000
Typical fees:	$350 per client; sometimes an additional percentage (5 to 10 percent) from the creditors
Advertising:	Classified ads, local newspapers, seminars, and public service speaking engagements
Qualifications:	Financial planning expertise, good people skills
Equipment needed:	Office furniture suitable for client conferences, business card, letterhead, envelopes, marketing materials
Staff required:	No
Handicapped opportunity:	Yes
Hidden costs:	Errors and omissions insurance

What You Do

Overextended is one thing; completely out of financial control is another. Your clients are the people who realize that they can't manage the debt they've accumulated, and they can't manage the bankruptcy process either. You assist them in developing a clear picture of their financial problem, filing for bankruptcy, and planning for the consequences. In today's world of easy credit, many people find themselves in bankruptcy without quite realizing what hit them. They're distressed, humiliated, and probably very confused as well. Your assistance with the painful process of sorting out the facts from the feelings is a very significant benefit.

What You Need

Costs can be low ($500-$1,000), depending on the furniture and space you already have. If you're good at what you do, you could earn between $25,000-$40,000.

Keys to Success

You are meeting your clients at a real low point in their lives, but you are the first step on their way back up. So the emotional temperature of your workday is going to be fluctuating wildly. Keeping a good psychological balance will be as important as getting the paperwork filled out correctly. Some of your clients will just have been irresponsible, but other have been dealt an impossible hand by fate. Historically the bankruptcy process has been designed to help these people by wiping the slate more or less clean. Nevertheless, people facing bankruptcy are not generally easy to work with. Your skill in dealing with the human side of your business will be essential.

Bartending Services

Start-up cost:	Under $1,000
Potential earnings:	10,000-$20,000
Typical fees:	$15-$30 per hour, or a flat per-event rate
Advertising:	Classified ads, bulletin boards, community newspapers
Qualifications:	Must be legal age (and should know how to make drinks without looking them up)
Equipment needed:	None
Staff required:	Might be a good idea to have one or two other bartenders
Handicapped opportunity:	Possibly
Hidden costs:	None apparent, so just watch your mileage

What You Do

Being a traveling bartender service for private parties is an exciting way to meet people and make money at the same time. You'll mix libations for everyone from wealthy executives to people at a family celebration, and the time will always pass quickly. You'll need to make sure that if you are expected to bring the beverages, you secure funds for that ahead of time to avoid excessive outlay of your own cash. Be sure to add in the cost of delivering the goods as well. The best way to get started is to produce professional-looking business cards and leave them prominently displayed at a few of your first jobs. In fact, you may want to do your first five jobs for free (if you feel you'll get a lot of attention)—that may be a great way to start the highballs rolling!

What You Need

With virtually nothing to lose but your time, you could do far worse than start a bartending service. Invest in a few good mixology handbooks and you're off to a great start! You also may want to visit the more progressive bars in your area to see if the bartenders know of any interesting new drinks—the more you can offer your clients, the happier they will be.

Keys to Success

You'll really absorb the energy and variety of bartending work, but it can be tiring to stand on your feet in one place for too long. Remember to bring a bar stool for yourself—and invest in a good pair of shoes with soothing inserts!

Barter Systems

Start-up cost:	$500-$1,000
Potential earnings:	15,000 and up
Typical fees:	$15 or more per transaction
Advertising:	Penny savers, community newspaper classifieds, bulletin boards, flyers, networking, participation in community activities related to recycling, cooperative grocery stores
Qualifications:	Friendliness, detail orientation
Equipment needed:	A computer would help you keep track of the information, but you could use a paper system as well
Staff required:	No
Handicapped opportunity:	Yes
Hidden costs:	Phone bill may be higher than expected

What You Do

You know everyone. You never waste a penny. You love to solve problems, and to help other people solve theirs. That's why you will derive great satisfaction from your barter system business. It's really just putting two and two together: what someone has, with what someone needs, and vice versa. Making it all work as a profitable business will be a bit more challenging than just this (which you have probably been doing on an amateur basis most of your life). Many barter systems are warehouse operations, with individuals buying bulk odd lots and then trying to trade them. You will need to become known, to gather the data, the offerings, and the needs, and to work continually at the matches. Creating some kind of valuation system for disparate objects and services may pose difficulties also: how does a car wash match up with a soccer ball? Trading small ski boots for larger ones is easier.

What You Need

Costs will be minimal (only about $500 to start). You'll need some way for your clientele to reach you, and some way to track what is bartered. Your thoughtfulness is your real product in this business. A part-time business should net you around $15,000.

Keys to Success

Barter systems appeal to people who try to live inexpensively and not wastefully—the cooperative market types, people in academic communities, and creative thinkers who are trying to step off the whirl of consumerism that keeps the rest of us in debt. You'll develop repeat customers if you can help people achieve their wants, and get rid of their don't-wants, without the exchange of large sums of money—just a small fee to you for the privilege. This business is a classic example of making something out of nothing. Virtually no investment, no training required, nothing but hard work on your part.

Bed & Breakfast

Start-up cost:	$60,000 (assuming you already own building)
Potential earnings:	35,000-$175,000
Typical fees:	$125+ per room, per night (depending on season)
Advertising:	Yellow Pages, B&B directories, direct mail to travel agencies
Qualifications:	None
Equipment needed:	Beds, towels, dining tables/chairs, stationery/brochures
Staff required:	Yes (but it could be comprised of family members)
Handicapped opportunity:	Unlikely (but not impossible)
Hidden costs:	Be sure your prices cover everything from electricity to food

What You Do

Large verandas for after-dinner strolls . . . billowy white curtains blowing in the wind . . . quiet meals by firelight. The sheer romance of owning and operating a Victorian-style B & B inn can be intoxicating enough to entice you into starting one of your own. If marketing trends are on target, more and more folks are looking for unusual escapes from city turmoil—and what better place to recuperate than a quiet little inn in the middle of nowhere (but within close driving distance to somewhere). You'll need anywhere from two to 12 extra rooms for guest accommodations, in addition to adequate kitchen and dining space. You will need to be meticulous in your cleaning and make sure that all prepared foods follow strict regulations. Also, be sure to educate yourself on all of the tourist attractions in your immediate area—you'll be surprised how often customers will count on your local expertise in devising their travel plans.

What You Need

You'll need at least $100,000-$400,000 if you purchase a building; you may also look into buying an existing B&B and simply taking over the business (turnover is relatively high, as many owners burn out after a period of ten years or so). If you already have a building, put aside extra cash ($5,000-$10,000) for repairs and updates, in addition to another $10,000 to cover your initial operating costs. You'll spend between $1,500-$5,000 on your first six months of advertising as well. But, considering that you'll charge clients $125 and up per night, you should be able to develop a steady cash flow within the first five years of your business plan's projections.

Keys to Success

You could easily be drawn in to the seemingly idyllic country inn lifestyle. But before you launder the sheets and open your doors to guests, give a lot of thought to the hard work ahead; most B&B owners will tell you that there are long hours of intense work (cooking, cleaning, and assisting guests in all of their needs). If you don't mind putting in a 60+ hour work week without the promise of grand riches, a bed & breakfast inn can be a great match.

Bicycle Rental

Start-up cost:	$7,500-$12,000
Potential earnings:	50,000-$80,000
Typical fees:	$12-$15 per half-hour rental
Advertising:	Flyers/brochures (give some to the Chamber of Commerce or travel agencies), Yellow Pages
Qualifications:	None
Equipment needed:	Fleet of bicycles and repair kits
Staff required:	No
Handicapped opportunity:	Possibly
Hidden costs:	Liability/theft insurance

What You Do

Remember the days of the bicycle built for two, when tourists rented bikes to explore island areas where cars either didn't exist or were blessedly limited? Those days are still here—but the majority of bicycle rental businesses are clustered around heavily trafficked tourist spots such as Michigan's Mackinac Island or Florida's sandy beaches. Many bicycle rental shops are now featuring Rollerblade rentals as well, especially in places like California. Regardless of what you decide to offer, you'll be amazed at how much money can be made in this relatively easy business. Each day, you'll take a fee for short-term rentals, offering the possibility of instant repeat business or a large number of daily rentals. And, since most bicycle rentals are cash transactions, you'll have instant money. What could be easier than that?

What You Need

Your main costs stem from the fact that you must buy a good fleet of bicycles, typically 20-25 of them at a cost of $300 or so each. If you invest in only used bicycles, your maintenance costs will be high. Considering that you'll be earning $12-$15 per half-hour rentals, you could make a sizable amount of money very quickly in this business if you're in a tourist area (especially one that doesn't allow many cars).

Keys to Success

Do your homework and choose the right location for this business. Obviously, it will only be seasonal in northern climates—is that all you want? Or would you rather make money from this relatively simple, straightforward business all year long? You decide. Either way, you're bound to make a decent piece of change.

Biofeedback Therapist

Start-up cost:	$20,000-$50,000
Potential earnings:	30,000-$45,000
Typical fees:	$150 per hour-long session
Advertising:	Yellow Pages, referrals from physicians and psychologists, advertising in community newspapers
Qualifications:	License or certification in your field
Equipment needed:	Biofeedback equipment (equipment for heart rate, pulse, breathing, and muscle movement)
Staff required:	No
Handicapped opportunity:	Not typically
Hidden costs:	Insurance (sometimes malpractice or liability insurance is suggested), equipment upgrades and maintenance

What You Do

Folks who suffer from chronic pain or complaints are often referred to biofeedback therapists who can connect sensitive pieces of equipment to various parts of the body to determine where pain is coming from and how to interpret stress. For instance, a heart rate monitor might tell what types of activities or conditions make a patient's heart rate rise, and what types lessen or eliminate body stress. The idea is to locate key centers in the body that are more sensitive than others to stress and high levels of activity. The results of each test are recorded and then interpreted by you or the referring physician or psychologist. Many times, you'll see that a patient is experiencing psychosomatic illness, and your test results will provide the proof of such imaginary illness. However, your services should not be used as a tool for committing the mentally unhealthy; rather, you provide a proactive service that helps people redirect their energies after being made aware of what stresses them out. They then have the opportunity to "teach" their bodies new ways of responding to stress; that is what the majority of your clients have been experiencing anyway (especially those with heart conditions).

What You Need

You will need $20,000-$50,000 for your highly sensitive equipment, which will also need regular maintenance due to the risk of inaccuracy. Speaking of risk, you'll need to make sure that you have adequate liability insurance, too. If you are well-connected with other health care professionals who can provide regular referrals, you could make $30,000-$45,000 per year in this specialized profession.

Keys to Success

If you enjoy working closely with people and in working with them to create more positive responses to stress, this business will give you everything you need (including a reasonable amount of financial security). On the other hand, getting insurance companies to cover your services might be trickier than you'd ever imagined; hire an administrator who knows the ins and outs of insurance claims.

10 Ways to Expand Your Business for Little Cash

1. Get on the Internet. For just a few dollars per month, you can market your services worldwide. Who can beat that?

2. Trade services with a franchisee prospect. You could work a deal where a potential franchisee's buy-in fee would be cut if they helped produce the operations manual; this way, you use one franchisee to get more franchisees. The payoff comes later.

3. Hire commission-only sales reps. You only need to pay them what they earn.

4. Hire interns from colleges and universities. They often work for free or next-to-nothing, and get college credit in return.

5. Participate in business organizations where you can network for free.

6. Find inexpensive ways to advertise your company on a regular basis (such as asking all family members with a car to sport your company logo).

7. Join forces with a compatible business. For instance, you could merge with a secretarial service if you are a resume service.

8. Put on seminars, charging a fee for teaching others your own skills.

9. Sponsor trade shows or other events.

10. Develop a program or system for your business that can be marketed and sold to others. You could write a book or develop a software program for mass production.

Blade-Sharpening Service

Start-up cost:	$500-$1,000
Potential earnings:	8,000-$15,000
Typical fees:	$5-$15 per blade
Advertising:	Yellow Pages, community newspapers, word of mouth, cold calls
Qualifications:	None
Equipment needed:	Blade sharpener
Staff required:	No
Handicapped opportunity:	Yes
Hidden costs:	Insurance, equipment maintenance

What You Do

Knives get dull, and most households and small businesses don't have the sharpeners or time to deal with such an inconvenience. You can market your service through the Yellow Pages and through cold calls to restaurants and other places where many knives are used on a regular basis. You could offer package deals (i.e., 12 knives for $25) or special promotions. You could network with kitchen and restaurant equipment suppliers to provide counterreferrals. Still, the work is quite simple and the hours few—you get the knives, put them through the sharpener, and return them in tip-top condition. It's an excellent retirement possibility or opportunity for supplemental income.

What You Need

You'll spend $500 or less on your blade sharpener and the rest on your Yellow Pages and other forms of minor advertising (such as business cards to leave at kitchen supply stores). Of course, this is a sporadic and highly specialized type of business, so your income potential is limited to $8,000-$15,000 per year (unless you somehow manage to work out regular contracts with large restaurants and restaurant supply houses).

Keys to Success

It's simple, it's straightforward—what's not to like? Well, the low-income potential could be troubling . . . but then, you probably chose this type of specialized service knowing it would only provide a supplemental income.

Boat Maintenance/
Cleaning Service

Start-up cost:	$2,000-$10,000
Potential earnings:	30,000-$60,000
Typical fees:	$55 per hour
Advertising:	Marinas, boat retailers, Yellow Pages, brochure
Qualifications:	Know the mechanics of a boat and the types of boats
Equipment needed:	Tools, cleaning supplies, dock, storage space
Staff required:	No
Handicapped opportunity:	No
Hidden costs:	Repairs, insurance

What You Do

Boat owners are nuts about their boats and while they enjoy being out on the open seas, they often hate keeping up with the maintenance end. After all, boating is about getting away from it all, right? Usually, your clients have a lot of disposable income, since they've invested a great deal of cash in the boat itself; that's how you can be sure of your own earning potential. On a more practical note, this business is for you if you don't mind a little grease under your nails and working out in the hot sun occasionally. Know your boat types (fiberglass, wood, steel, aluminum) and what type of chemicals you can use on each without causing any damage. Certification as a boat mechanic will be helpful but not required. Advertise where people buy dock space and at boat retailers. Try to get the businesses (such as restaurants) along the shore to carry your brochure.

What You Need

If you are a good mechanic to begin with and have your own tools, your start-up costs could be minimal (about $500). You'll need storage space, possibly a dock, and all types of cleaners, paint, and detergents. Your basic fee to do a tune-up would likely be $50 per hour; add another $25 per hour to clean. Your salary will be in the $30,000-$60,000 range.

Keys to Success

This is a big undertaking, as boat owners usually pamper their boats. You have to be truly committed. If you like working with your hands and tinkering with engines, this would be a great opportunity for you. The pay-off in the end could be great, too, as there are hundreds of thousands of registered boaters today. If you space your jobs out well, this could be a full-time job, and you could add staff before you know it.

Boat Operation Instructor

Start-up cost:	$25,000+ (depending on whether you own or lease a boat)
Potential earnings:	23,000-$45,000
Typical fees:	$75 per person for a one-time class of four hours
Advertising:	Marinas, flyers, Yellow Pages, boating publications
Qualifications:	Captain's license, CPR certification
Equipment needed:	Computer, boat, safety equipment
Staff required:	No
Handicapped opportunity:	Not typically
Hidden costs:	Insurance

What You Do

The water can be a very unsafe place these days. Most people who get behind the wheel of a boat are inexperienced and accidents are on the rise because of negligence. People are starting to hire boating operation instructors for their own personal safety. As an instructor, you need to know what the Coast Guard requires (life preservers, flares, fire extinguishers, etc.), boat safety regulations, chart-reading and meteorology. In addition, you'll need to have general seamanship knowledge and a good dose of common sense. Market yourself to local boat retailers with brochures and flyers—and get to know your water neighbors, so they can help spread your word with waves of referrals.

What You Need

It is possible to be a boat operations instructor without a boat, since you could use your client's boat, but it would probably be a good idea to have one of your own. You will need to carry some type of insurance and probably legal counsel to draw up necessary papers for the client to sign absolving you from any type of negligence. Depending on where you live, you could teach for a possible 13 to 26 weeks and make a minimum of $23,000-$45,000.

Keys to Success

Spring and summer will be your busiest seasons. If you love to teach without the confines of a classroom, then this water job is for you! Be prepared for some clients to not take you seriously, since people tend to be a little more relaxed with their leisure vehicles. Encourage them to stay with the program.

Book Indexer

Start-up cost:	$500-$1,000
Potential earnings:	15,000-$30,000
Typical fees:	$2.50-$4.00 per printed book page
Advertising:	Direct mail to book publishers, Yellow Pages, industry newsletters
Qualifications:	A strong eye for detail and subject matter; impeccable organizational skills
Equipment needed:	Computer with alphabetical sorting capability, printer
Staff required:	No
Handicapped opportunity:	Definitely
Hidden costs:	Your time—indexes are complex and time-consuming, and must be accurate

What You Do

When you're reading a book and you want to find information on a specific topic, you look in the index first. But it probably didn't occur to you that putting together an index is a job dependent upon painstaking accuracy and attention to detail. It's an area of specialization that sets professional indexers apart from other editorial types. These folks are typically not writers (although they can be), and they are not really editors, either. Their expertise is sought after the book is written and edited, but prior to publication; they provide readers with a service that enables them to conduct research or just locate topics of interest to them, saving them time in combing through the entire book. Obviously, indexers work with nonfiction books, but the subject matter can be extremely varied and could include everything from automotive manuals to business or self-help guides. A good place to start if you feel that your organizational skills are up to this kind of work is the American Society of Indexers in Phoenix AZ at 602-979-5514. Joining organizations such as this prestigious association could instantly raise your credibility level.

What You Need

Start-up costs are almost negligible for indexing. Begin with memberships in key organizations, then submit a letter of interest or resume to book publishers in and out of your area. Set aside at least $500-$1,000 for working capital; you may need it to furnish your office with a comfortable chair (a must). Charge anywhere from $2.50-$4.00 per printed book page; for example, a 200-page book will net you $500 minimum for your indexing work.

Keys to Success

Low initial investment makes this a win-win if you don't mind detail-oriented work. The hours may be long, the turnaround time may be quicker than you had hoped, but the ability to generate income is there for those with talent.

Book Packager

Start-up cost:	$1,000-$5,000
Potential earnings:	45,000-$80,000
Typical fees:	Sometimes a percentage of total production costs; often, a flat consultant's rate
Advertising:	Writers' publications, industry trade magazines, direct mail, word of mouth
Qualifications:	Editorial background and top-notch organizational skills; broad understanding of publishing process
Equipment needed:	Computer with printer, fax/modem, desktop publishing software, phone
Staff required:	No
Handicapped opportunity:	Yes
Hidden costs:	Insurance, cost of sales (it often takes a lot of socializing to get work)

What You Do

Book packagers are often hired by publishers whose staffs are too limited to work on a multitude of projects simultaneously; in other words, they are maxed out on projects and need outside help in handling additional ones. Some book packagers handle as much as 75 percent of a publishing house's projects, allowing the in-house staff to concentrate on future projects and expansion. You would do well as a book packager if you have an editorial background, a knack for organizing and pulling together all the details of a book project, and the foresight to set realistic goals about accomplishing publication. You will likely handle everything from hiring writers and photographers to production and sales/marketing management. You would do well to pick an area of expertise, such as high-quality illustrated books, since many publishers don't have that kind of in-house expertise and will gladly pay you for yours.

What You Need

Expect to spend between $1,000-$5,000 on your start-up, which will cover your initial advertising in addition to your complete computer setup (with printer, fax/modem, and desktop publishing software). You'll need to work hard to make $45,000-$75,000 or more in this field, but it isn't uncommon (especially for those in close proximity to the publishing capitals of New York and San Francisco).

Keys to Success

Things could easily get out of hand when you are pulling together many different creative forces for a special project; try to work out your worst-case scenarios early enough to form a game plan around them—and set deadlines that are in reality far ahead of when you actually need a project to be turned in. You'll see why after only one project.

Expert Advice

What sets your business apart from others like it?

Andy Mayer, President and co-owner (with Jim Becker) of becker & mayer ltd. in Seattle, Washington, says the ability to produce very complicated, production-intensive books is what sets his business apart from others like it. "My partner and I both have backgrounds in toy invention and design, and we can produce really interesting books as a result."

Things you couldn't do without:

"Our staff! We couldn't do anything without them . . . so many good ideas come from them. From an equipment standpoint, we couldn't do without a phone, a computer, and a color printer to produce mock-ups for publishers."

Marketing tips/advice:

"Bring a lot of who you are to your company. Find out what your passions are and try to put that into the things you produce. Also, don't listen to people who try to tell you there's only one way to do something. Freely break the rules and see what happens."

If you had to do it all over again . . .

"I would have focused the business on book packaging much earlier . . . we tried to do both book packaging and toy invention, and that didn't work as well."

Bookkeeping Service

Start-up cost:	$2,000-$9,000
Potential earnings:	Typically $20,000-$50,000 per year
Typical fees:	$25-$35 per hour; more for financial statements and other tasks. Certain clients may pay a flat monthly fee rather than hourly charges
Advertising:	Ads (phone book, trade publications), networking, referrals (from CPAs, for example)
Qualifications:	Knowledge of basic bookkeeping principles, some legal and tax knowledge, ability to use a computer, accounting/spreadsheet software, good eye for detail, honesty, good communications skills
Equipment needed:	Basic computer and office equipment, a financial calculator and accounting software
Staff required:	No
Handicapped opportunity:	Yes
Hidden costs:	Organizational dues, if applicable

What You Do

Small business owners, in particular, use bookkeeping services to keep up with the ever-changing tax laws and the constant flow of bookkeeping details they don't have time for. Clients need help with such tasks as making deposits, reconciliation of bank statements and preparing financial reports, payroll, billing, and accounts payable and receivable, to name a few. What's the difference between bookkeeping and accounting? Bookkeepers are the record keepers; an accountant's job is to analyze and audit the records. If you have a clear, logical mind and common sense, this may be a great business for you. It is recession-proof, essential work that can be challenging and fun.

What You Need

The required computer and office equipment can be acquired for as little as $2,000. Add another $500 or so for your first six months of advertising, and you'll be all set. You might consider joining business owners' associations or your local Chamber of Commerce to generate business. Charges for your services will vary according to the extent of the project, but the average fees are $25-$35 per hour.

Keys to Success

This work gives you a great opportunity to learn more about the business world—and about specific fields of business. The work requires close attention to each detail and necessitates your staying current about tax-law changes relating to payroll and record keeping. Mistakes may cause problems for your client with the government; clients may also blame you for mistakes that they made. If you like numbers and enjoy working independently to solve problems, bookkeeping may be a great career for you.

Bridal Consultant

Start-up cost:	$1,000-$3,500
Potential earnings:	25,000-$60,000 (depending on volume and location)
Advertising:	Bridal magazines (many areas have their own, local versions), bridal salons, newspapers, word of mouth
Qualifications:	An eye for detail and a cool head
Equipment needed:	Cellular phone, computer plus software for contacts and clients
Staff required:	Sometimes
Handicapped opportunity:	Yes
Hidden costs:	Keep accurate records of the time you spend with each client, or you could short-change yourself.

What You Do

Wedding planning can easily turn any reasonable family into a temporary war zone—and that's where bridal consultants have entered the picture. With most families spending anywhere from $10,000-$15,000 and up on the wedding extravaganza itself, what's a few extra dollars to take the headache out of the blessed event's planning? Your rates would range from $50 per hour to a flat fee of $1,000 or more for the entire wedding, so it is easy to see how you could earn a profitable amount of money in a short period of time. But don't think you won't work hard for it. As a bridal consultant, you will handle every minute detail, from the number of guests to invite to what kind of champagne to buy. You are essentially in the hotbed of the action, with total responsibility for every aspect of the wedding.

What You Need

You will need to develop strong word of mouth (try forging reciprocal referral arrangements with florists and bridal and hair salons) to build a good reputation. Also, since this is a people- and image-oriented business, you will need to make sure you look like you're worth it; dress professionally and carry yourself with poise and an air of diplomacy. But the bulk of your start-up will be in producing business cards and brochures in addition to placing newspaper and bridal magazine ads (count on forking over at least $1,000 for those items).

Keys to Success

The flash and excitement of impending nuptials can be intoxicating, as can the power involved in directing others to perform their best. Be careful not to offend anyone or step on their toes. Listen to what your customers tell you they want—and have the good sense to make them think all of the good ideas were theirs. While such ego-suppression is hard to accomplish in a high-profile job like this one, remember that the customer is always king.

Bridal Show Promotions

Start-up cost:	$5,000-$15,000
Potential earnings:	20,000-$40,000
Typical fees:	$125 per booth rental space
Advertising:	Flyers, radio ads, newspapers, bridal shops, mailings, billboards
Qualifications:	Exceptional organizational skills
Equipment needed:	Computer with mailing list program
Staff required:	Not initially
Handicapped opportunity:	Possibly
Hidden costs:	Radio ads are expensive; try to secure or split costs with sponsors

What You Do

Bridal shows are popular in every town—there are always young women who seek the best in wedding preparations. You should have no trouble securing an audience if you book in the right places (such as shopping malls, banquet halls, and hotels). Your biggest challenge will be to gain the attention, support, and dollars from participating vendors, who could be made up of businesses like caterers, florists, musicians, and cake decorators. You must be highly organized, however, to pull this one off convincingly. Lose sight of details and you'll instantly lose credibility with your audience as well as your vendors. The best advice is to secure your financial support up front to avoid any of your own out-of-pocket expenses—that way, in the event of a no-show vendor, you'll still have your cash.

What You Need

The $5,000-$10,000 you'll need to get this business off the ground properly will mainly cover your advertising and promotional costs. Remember that you'll need to have professional-looking materials to sell vendors on in the first place, let alone the flyers and billboards to attract your audience. Do it all correctly and you'll pull in between $20,000-$40,000 yourself, depending on how many shows you run per year.

Keys to Success

If you can't get at least 50 vendors for your first show, maybe you ought to rethink your marketing strategy. Try a novel approach, or try to get a well-known spokesperson or celebrity to appear. Do everything humanly possible to attract attention.

Building Maintenance Service

Start-up cost:	$20,000-$40,000
Potential earnings:	45,000-$75,000
Typical fees:	Monthly contract of $150-$350 per client/building per month
Advertising:	Yellow Pages, direct mail to building owners and rental property managers, networking, cold calls
Qualifications:	Handyman experience (preferably with some background in electrical work)
Equipment needed:	Van equipped with tools, chemicals/solvents, ladders and small power equipment
Staff required:	No (but you will need additional staff if your business gets too large for you to handle your workload alone)
Handicapped opportunity:	No
Hidden costs:	Insurance

What You Do

Nearly all of the apartment complexes, office buildings, and universities in your community need to be maintained by someone—and, if you have a technical, hands-on background in building maintenance (or even more generally, as a "Mr. Fix-It") you can parlay that talent into a building maintenance service quite nicely and logically. After all, whom would you trust with your fix-up needs: a small service with an expert at the top or a large company of transient employees? That's exactly how you'll need to position yourself in this competitive business: as a small-but-mighty industry leader with stability and a commitment to keeping everything running smoothly. Of course, you can't promise that every single light switch will always work perfectly, but you can offer a pager accessibility and 24-hour service so that your clients can rest comfortably knowing that you're in charge of those three-o'clock-in-the-morning emergencies (and isn't that the time most things go wrong?).

What You Need

Your costs to launch this business will be moderate ($20,000-$40,000) due to the fact that you'll need a good van filled with everything from wrenches and sockets to small pneumatic drills and large ladders. If you're a hard worker, as most maintenance folk are, you could make $45,000-$75,000 (depending on how many clients you serve). Of course, the more you make, the more likely you'll need additional staff, since one person can't simultaneously fix all the light switches and circuits in a dozen buildings.

Keys to Success

Be prepared to spend long hours doing the kind of work that tinkerers like to do most of all: figuring out what went wrong with that blower or electrical system, and being the hero when the problem is solved. It's not a bad way to end each day, even if it is long.

Expert Advice

What sets your business apart from others like it?

Lillian Lincoln, President of Centennial One, Inc., in Landover, Maryland, says her company distinguishes itself from others by emphasis on quality. "We place a great deal of emphasis on giving our clients a comfort level that assures them that their building maintenance requirements will be adequately addressed."

Things you couldn't do without:

Vacuums, buffers, scrubbing and shampooing machines. "No equipment is needed until some work has been secured. No lead time is needed unless the job requires specialized equipment, so purchase only the equipment needed for each job as they roll in."

Marketing tips/advice:

"Industry knowledge as well as business acumen is a great asset. Too many people have the mistaken impression that this industry is a 'mop and bucket' business. Far from true! It requires knowledge of chemical and equipment usage, time management, human relations, and a number of other skills. For anyone going into this business, I advise them to work in the industry (preferably in the field) for a minimum of six months."

If you had to do it all over again . . .

"I would spend more time working in the field to learn more about on-site operations. I made some mistakes early on because I was not as knowledgeable as I should have been about the basics of the business."

Bulletin Board Services

Start-up cost:	$1,000-$3,000
Potential earnings:	5,000-$15,000
Typical fees:	Monthly subscription fees start at $10; annual are $20-$50
Advertising:	On-line services
Qualifications:	On-line marketing skills
Equipment needed:	High-power computer with fax/modem, printer, phone
Staff required:	No
Handicapped opportunity:	Yes
Hidden costs:	On-line time can get expensive

What You Do

In the computer age, more and more folks are seeking special places to communicate with others who have similar interests. If there is no official on-line bulletin board on a subject such as baseball card collectors or movie buffs, your business can provide one. You would advertise the availability of such a bulletin board, then post as many pieces of related information as possible to generate the number of users tapping into your service. The more information you have on-line, the more you'll be able to charge individuals for getting to this data. A related service that is even more important is to check the messages frequently and remove outdated ones. You can see that messages are arranged neatly and any inappropriate material is removed on a regular basis. Check with major carriers to familiarize yourself with their bulletin board regulations—and any possible charges you may incur from them for use of their on-line services.

What You Need

All you will really need to start is a computer with a modem (about $2,000). Bulletin boards are widely available; check carefully to avoid duplicating another service or you may have some problems. What you earn is directly dependent upon how many people use your service, so make sure your topic is of wide-range interest.

Keys to Success

Selling skills and patience are the two vital ingredients here. To gain repeat business, you have to keep up with the bulletin boards under your care. A large clientele is needed to make an adequate profit overall—and remember that some competing BBS are offered for free.

Business Broker

Start-up cost:	$2,500-$7,000
Potential earnings:	100,000 (based on one sale a month for ten months of the year)
Typical fees:	Standard 10 to 12 percent of the selling price of the business
Advertising:	Direct mail, telemarketing, networking, referrals, ads in Yellow Pages and business publications
Qualifications:	Ability to understand financial reports, solid business background, considerable legal knowledge, good sales and "people" skills
Equipment needed:	Computer and office equipment, telephone, answering machine or voice mail
Staff required:	No
Handicapped opportunity:	Yes
Hidden costs:	Some states require a real estate broker's license

What You Do

Business brokers match clients interested in selling a business with others who want to buy—and many are home-based. This field is growing; many people think it's less risky to buy an existing business than to start a new one. Nearly all brokers represent the client who is selling a business, but a few choose to represent the buyer. Specializing in a particular size or type of business, or in a particular geographic area, brings success to many home-based brokers. Excellent communication skills are vital, particularly empathy and an ability to listen carefully. Strong sales skills, coupled with the essential legal knowledge and business background, will help you establish what may be a most lucrative business.

What You Need

Computer, printer, and software (some specialized) will cost an average of $3,500. Add to this at least $700 for office furniture, phone, letterhead, and supplies. Your earnings will hinge on whether you're able to strike a deal; if so, take a 10 to 12 percent cut on the selling price.

Keys to Success

Network, network, network! Talk to people who own businesses, figure out what associations they belong to, and join them. Take some adult education courses, if necessary, to help you learn more about the unfamiliar aspects of your new business. Get referrals from lawyers, accountants, and bankers. Getting businesses to sell is hard work (although specialization helps) and you don't get paid until you sell something, but it's fun to act as matchmaker and satisfying to help your clients succeed. Your expenses and start-up costs are low, and the opportunity to make a great living is excellent. Nothing succeeds like success, so once you make a great match, you'll have a basis on which to build future business.

Business Form Sales and Service

Start-up cost:	$20,000-$40,000
Potential earnings:	35,000-$60,000
Typical fees:	$25-$30 per form; more it's a complex custom design
Advertising:	Yellow Pages, classified ads, direct mail
Qualifications:	None
Equipment needed:	Printing equipment (or sub-contractor lined up), extensive color catalog of your goods, inventory
Staff required:	No
Handicapped opportunity:	Yes
Hidden costs:	Cold-calling can get expensive

What You Do

This type of business is so standardized and easy for others to learn that it is among the top franchise businesses on the market today. All you need to do is find out what potential customers are using for business forms (such as inventory records, receipts, invoices, and other important documents). Then, you sell them on your customized service, quick turnaround, and easy terms. Remember, though, that you will be competing heavily against some fairly large organizations (Office Depot and Office Max plus other independents like yourself); you will need super sales skills to stay on top of it all and make your regular goals. Cold-calling is your primary way of finding new business, and it is extremely uncertain in the beginning (not to mention costly). Still, the income potential is great for those who can stomach the competition—and if you capitalize on your strong points, you should be able to come up with forms that make every customer happy (and, ultimately, result in your own profitability).

What You Need

You'll need between $20,000-$40,000, particularly if you buy into a franchise operation. This investment will cover your catalogs, inventory, and training materials, and may also cover printing equipment (typically including specialized software). You'll charge $25-$30 per type of form; more if it's a complex custom design. In the end, you'll wind up making between $35,000-$65,000 per year—but that's only if you're working at this full-time and full-throttle.

Keys to Success

There is probably no more straightforward, easy business to learn than this—but do recognize that you're going to need to be well-connected to get regular, dependable business. Network with anyone who's anyone, and make the daily fifty of so phone calls it may take to get one fresh lead. After all, you're competing against major office store chains, and you need to tell people just what's different about your business (in this case, it's the customized service).

Business Plan Writer

Start-up cost:	$5,000-$10,000
Potential earnings:	30,000-$100,000
Typical fees:	$3,000-$6,000 per plan (about two weeks of work)
Advertising:	Teaching courses on business development, networking, business associations, referrals from bankers and entrepreneurship centers, advertising in local business newsletters
Qualifications:	Understanding of financial statements, savvy business sense, excellent oral and written communication skills, ability to get people to work together, experience writing business plans
Equipment needed:	Computer, fax/modem, laser printer, suite software, business-planning software, office furniture, business card, letterhead, envelopes, brochures
Staff required:	No
Handicapped opportunity:	Yes
Hidden costs:	Organizational dues, business periodical and newspaper subscriptions, insurance

What You Do

Businesses are being created all over the country at a phenomenal rate. All of these new enterprises can get two kinds of benefits from having a business plan. First, the plan structures the efforts of everyone involved, outlining what needs to be done and describing the means by which those goals will be achieved. It highlights the feasibility of the products or services the enterprise will be marketing. Most importantly, it estimates expenses and revenues, along with projections. If the revenues won't cover the expenses, it doesn't matter what wonderful things could happen down the road. The cash-starved business won't be able to get there to achieve them.

The second benefit of having a business plan is to obtain financing. A business plan is essential for the process of obtaining bank loans and most other types of outside financing. You can take your good sense of business and finance, your high-level business writing skills, and your ability to communicate with fledgling entrepreneurs and earn a hefty annual income writing business plans.

What You Need

The equipment and materials to present a reassuringly professional image are fairly costly (in the neighborhood of $3,000-$10,000). You'll need to be able to produce a very polished printout of the final plan, most likely using one of the better-quality business plan software packages available (about $150-$300). But, you can charge $3,000 and up for each package, with hourly fees of $45 and up (depending on your location).

Keys to Success

If you have developed the wide range of skills necessary to do this work, you undoubt-edly are the kind of person who loves it and can tolerate the tedious parts. What can be more rewarding than helping a new enterprise take wing and fly? It is very difficult to write an effective business plan, but that is the very reason your market exists. Each sit-uation is different; that means opportunities for constant learning on your part. Once you complete a plan, you will need to find another client, so your marketing must be ongoing. Some business start-ups are shaky, even sleazy, although most failures are due to poor marketing and undercapitalization rather than dishonesty. In any case, try to get at least half your fee up front. You will really be a combination counselor/consultant for the entrepreneurs.

Computer Equipment "Musts"

Here's a checklist for setting up your computer system with everything you will likely need:

- ❏ A Pentium or higher computer (preferably with a 15" color high-resolution monitor)
- ❏ 8MB RAM and hard disk with Windows 3.1 or Windows 95.
- ❏ A 2X CD-ROM drive for some of the more innovative (and comprehensive) new programs on the market
- ❏ Near-letter quality or laser-quality printer
- ❏ 3.5" diskettes for file storage and backup
- ❏ 14400 baud or higher modem (preferred 28,800 baud or higher)
- ❏ An accounting program (such as Quicken, QuickBooks, or one-write plus) to keep accurate records and manipulate data to create reports
- ❏ Word-processing software (such as WordPerfect or MS Word for Windows 6.0)
- ❏ Graphics or desktop publishing software (to create your own marketing materials, slides, and graphs)
- ❏ World Wide Web Site construction software (if you feel like creating your own Web page on the Internet)
- ❏ On-line services or Internet launch software
- ❏ Mouse, mousepad, and keyboard.

Cake Decorator

Start-up cost:	$100-$200
Potential earnings:	5,000-$25,000
Typical fees:	$10-$1,000 per cake
Advertising:	Word of mouth, newspaper ads, neighborhood bulletins
Qualifications:	Cake baking and decorating knowledge
Equipment needed:	Baking pans and utensils, decorating supplies, ingredients, oven
Staff required:	None
Handicapped opportunity:	Yes
Hidden costs:	Make sure you have enough kitchen space for finished cakes; may need a second oven or other facilities as business grows; need vehicle if you deliver

What You Do

People love home-baked goodies. All it takes to satisfy that need is an oven, some recipes, and a way (brochure, advertisement) to tell customers you're in business. Birthday cakes for children are especially popular; a home baker can customize and personalize them in countless ways to please the customer. Wedding cakes can be very lucrative but require more time and equipment than cakes for other occasions. Nowadays people want to choose from more than chocolate, vanilla, or yellow cakes—the sky's the limit!

What You Need

Start-up costs for a cake-baking business are minimal. Some great recipes, baking pans, decorating supplies, utensils, and an oven (your kitchen range will do just fine) are all that you need. If you can't easily learn to decorate cakes from a book or by trial-and-error, you may want to invest in an inexpensive cake decorating course. If you plan to deliver the cakes, you will need an appropriate vehicle.

Keys to Success

The potential market out there is huge, especially since most working women and men don't have time to bake, but still want homemade cakes. There are so many special occasions to celebrate, and most of them feature great cakes: graduations, birthdays, anniversaries, retirement parties, baby and wedding showers, weddings . . . the list is endless! A cake that can be made for as little as 60 cents can sell for as much as $9—a nice profit for your efforts! On the downside, it may take some practice to make beautiful cakes. You also need patience and good marketing skills to build your business.

Calendar Service

Start-up cost:	$3,000-$5,000
Potential earnings:	10,000-$25,000
Typical fees:	$150/year for each subscription
Advertising:	Business and trade periodicals, organization membership, networking, direct marketing
Qualifications:	Energy, a very high level of organization, an outgoing personality, good writing skills
Equipment needed:	Computer, office suite software with powerful database program, high-quality fax/modem, copier, printer, office furniture, business cards, letterhead, envelopes
Staff required:	No
Handicapped opportunity:	Yes
Hidden costs:	On-line time, attendance at functions, organization dues

What You Do

This business is among the newest emerging businesses. You'll create a master calendar of public events for your community, or an annual publication that is sent to your client list of hotels, motels, restaurants, and other high-traffic businesses. The excitement comes from the fax; each week you fax a reminder-and-update sheet to everyone on your list. As you become established, gathering the information will become easier, as planners, public relations people, and event sponsors will be sure to inform you about their dates and events. Why does this work? Many individuals and businesses need to know this information, and they appreciate the opportunity to have information to offer free of charge to their customers. Everyone from politicos to florists needs to have event dates at their fingertips, and your service will be faxing it to them weekly. In short, it is your business to make other businesses look "in the know."

What You Need

You will need the equipment to gather and print the information, and above all, the fax capability to broadcast it weekly. This should cost you between $5,000-$10,000; but, by billing $150 per year for a company's subscription to your service, you could easily earn back your investment in two to three years.

Keys to Success

Keeping track of dates is hard—that's why all those meeting planners and impresarios are going to pay you to do it. You'll need to be the kind of person whom bigwigs like to talk to, both for info-gathering and sales of your service. Writing it all up in an accurate, amusing manner is important, because you're competing against a myriad of free arts and entertainment newspapers and similar publications. Creating a service like this means a super marketing effort until you get established.

Calligrapher

Start-up cost:	$150-$500
Potential earnings:	10,000-$15,000
Typical fees:	$50-$75 per invitation, other items on a per-job basis
Advertising:	Classified ads, bridal magazines, bulletin boards
Qualifications:	A steady hand and a love for lettering
Equipment needed:	Calligraphy pens and ink, parchment or specialty paper
Staff required:	No
Handicapped opportunity:	Possibly
Hidden costs:	Don't spend too much on advertising until you're sure of your market

What You Do

The fine art of calligraphy began in medieval times, when monks joyously and labori-ously produced biblical text using intricate, artistic lettering. This regal writing appears today in items such as wedding invitations, birth notices, and certificates of merit. You could also produce suitable-for-framing family trees (the customer would, of course, need to supply the data). Without a huge initial investment, you can offer your ser-vices to schools (for diplomas), brides-to-be (for addressing invitations), athletic teams, and even corporations that are involved in recognition programs where cer-tificates are in order. The market is large, diverse, and challenging—because there are many paper companies that offer programs for producing certificates having the same look as a hand-produced one. Consider branching out and offering both hand-pro-duced and computer-generated calligraphy, and you'll stand a good chance of con-tinuing this fine and delicate tradition.

What You Need

Calligraphy pens and paper are all you need to start this business, although you will have to work hard to get the word out. Perhaps you could mail invitations to those who might need your service, inviting them in for a free consultation. Networking with bridal salons may also help build business. Charge at least $50 for your services, since they are specialized and time-consuming.

Keys to Success

The freedom and creative nature of this age-old art form is in demand by those who still place value on the handmade; but, with the ability to quickly generate calligraphic style on a computer, you may find the market challenging, at best. Also, being a profes-sional calligrapher isn't necessarily going to make you rich—but it's not a bad way to earn some extra pocket money, either.

Caning Specialist

Start-up cost:	$50-$150
Potential earnings:	1,000-$2,000 per month
Typical fees:	$25-$75+ per chair
Advertising:	Country magazines, furniture manufacturers, local paper, craft publications
Qualifications:	Should be an apprentice first
Equipment needed:	Cane, splints, rush, razor blades, scissors, tack hammer/puller
Staff required:	No
Handicapped opportunity:	Yes
Hidden costs:	Mileage for deliveries

What You Do

Before venturing into this profession on your own, you should be an apprentice, since caning is a time-honored tradition. It takes patience and an eye for detail to reweave wicker that has worn with time, or to add wicker to a piece of furniture that didn't have it to begin with. It helps if you are dedicated to the task at hand, because if you're good at what you do, you'll get lots of referrals, since there are so few caning specialists around these days. Still, caning is a slow process. Once you get an order, allow for soaking (about one day), drying (about two days), and making the chairs (approximately four hours per chair). You might want to partner with a chair maker to make your business more profitable; the two of you can copromote each other and provide a constant flow of referrals both ways.

What You Need

Cane is sold in hanks (1,000 feet)—enough to make four chairs. Plan to pay close to $10-$15 per hank, depending on where you buy it. Total cost for materials is so low that, if you market yourself well, you could make a decent living of around $15,000-$24,000 per year.

Keys to Success

This could be a high-risk venture if you haven't done your homework or let potential clients know about your services; expect to spend a great deal of time promoting yourself in the beginning. The best part is you are considered a craftsman and artist for the beautiful work you weave. For this, you'll need to like working by yourself and have enormous amounts of patience.

Career Counselor

Start-up cost:	$10,000-$15,000
Potential earnings:	30,000-$65,000
Typical fees:	$350 and up per session
Advertising:	Yellow Pages, classified ads, job fairs, human resource newsletters
Qualifications:	Many states require certification
Equipment needed:	Computer, assessment software programs, TV/VCR (for educational videos), cellular phone, answering service or pager
Staff required:	No
Handicapped opportunity:	Yes
Hidden costs:	Any type of counselor must keep an eye on the clock if he or she is billing by the hour. Remember that time is money; clients often need to be told when their time is up

What You Do

There are literally thousands of careers out there—and many people simply can't follow the road signs. As a career counselor, you can assist them first with personality assessment, then with matching your client's motivations and interests to a potential career. Next, map out a success plan for achieving that new job or business (yes, many people do discover through career counseling that they would really rather work for themselves). You can use formatted questionnaires or conduct personal interviews (or a combination of both) to arrive at some career-forming conclusions. But your counseling efforts don't have to stop there; you can also offer résumé services, viewing of motivational videos, cassette tape rental, and a library of resource books. The best part is, your business is recession-proof and corporations often contract with career counselors during periods of downsizing. The difficult part is reaching those who may need your services but are currently unaware that these services even exist.

What You Need

Your start-up costs primarily reflect your office furniture and assorted resource/testing materials ($10,000-$15,000 is about right if you don't already have a computer). But the going rate for career counseling services is $350+ (depending on whether you're in a metropolitan area). With at least one good corporate client and a few stragglers, you should be well on your way in your own career path!

Keys to Success

You will be working with many different types of people, but they do have one thing in common: they have no idea what direction to take their careers. This can be frustrating to them, and no doubt that will translate into work for you which is part information-giving, part hand-holding. If you're well-adjusted enough yourself to help others deal with a career catharsis, you'll probably get a lot professionally and personally from this type of service.

Carpet/Upholstery Cleaning

Start-up cost:	$1,000-$3,000 if leasing equipment initially; $4,000-$10,000 if buying equipment
Potential earnings:	35,000-$50,000
Typical fees:	20 cents per square foot first room; $40 each additional room
Advertising:	Direct mail, Yellow Pages, newspaper ads, coupon books
Qualifications:	Physically able to do manual labor, some prior experience
Equipment needed:	Cleaning machine, large quantity of chemical cleaners, some mode of transporting materials
Staff required:	No
Handicapped opportunity:	No
Hidden costs:	Fuel for vehicle

What You Do

If "Out, damned spot!" is your battle cry, getting others to enlist your services in the carpet/upholstery cleaning business shouldn't be too hard. After all, we've all spilled seemingly unremovable food or drink on at least one piece of furniture in our homes—and we've all thought of paying a professional every once in a while to freshen up the house with a clean-smelling carpet, right? That's why this is such a recession-proof business; the need for clean places to live never goes out of favor with consumers. You could offer your cleaning services to everyone from individuals to apartment complexes or even corporations, and the best way to get your name out there is through excellent, timely service and its resultant good word of mouth. You'll sweep the surface dirt from furniture and floors, perform an overall general cleaning, and use industrial-strength spot removers on tough stain areas. Since each room takes approximately an hour to service (if there are few stains requiring more attention), there is the potential for making lots of money once you learn to work quickly and efficiently while maintaining high-quality standards. One final note: Buying cleaning fluids will be slightly more expensive if environmentally safe products are chosen, but many people prefer "green" cleaning products, especially for health reasons. Customers will feel safer and more satisfied when they know there are no toxic residues in their house.

What You Need

Deciding whether to buy or lease equipment at first will depend upon how much capital is available to invest. A carpet cleaning machine itself will cost from $600-$3,500, while leasing will run about $300-$400 per month. Rotary shampooers and steam extractors are the two current types available, and each has its advantages and disadvantages, but rotary shampooers are the preferred method because they clean more deeply. A good, strong vacuum cleaner is the next most vital tool, and buying a sturdy canister model with a variety of attachments will cost $400-$600. The leasing option will be anywhere from $100-$200 per month. Access to a reliable vehicle large enough to tote around all equipment and supplies (and gasoline to run it) is another expense involved in this business, but really won't amount to much if you already have a station wagon/truck/van. Include advertising in your budget, which could run anywhere from $600-$3,000 for half a year. Coupon books seem to be fruitful ground for carpet cleaning businesses as a starting point for bringing in new customers. For carpets, fees are often 20 cents per square foot plus an additional $40 or more per each extra room depending on size. Upholstery cleaning is usually done per piece, with fees ranging from $50-$150.

Keys to Success

Working for another local company first may give you a good idea of what's needed to get started and how to proceed from there. As in most trades, experience is essential to success: knowing which contracts to take and which are just impossible, what are appropriate fees for your area, how billing works, and other general questions will make your start-up smoother. Sales skills are a plus since most people don't realize that they might need your service, or know how often they need it. Calling former customers to find out if the work was performed satisfactorily and offering to repeat it will keep you busy.

More Networking Tips

■ **The best time to make new contacts is when you don't need them.** It's best to call on others in happy times so that your business image is positive, and new contacts will respect you before you need help.

■ **Don't forget to follow up.** Most of all, never forget to say "thank you."

■ **Set up a good filing or business card management system.** Choose one that will actually work for you, not one that merely sounds good.

■ **Weed out nonproductive relationships every six months.** But don't throw away a card if you can help it. You never know when you'll need that person in the future.

■ **MOST IMPORTANT, ALWAYS BE YOURSELF.** We all have different styles of networking, and there are no real hard-and-fast rules when it comes to the joy of meeting new people—and making new friends.

Catalog Retailer

Start-up cost:	$15,000-$60,000 (depends on whether you're marketing your own or someone else's products)
Potential earnings:	25,000-$50,000+
Typical fees:	Products can sell from $5-$500 or more; you'll charge a third more than list
Advertising:	Direct mail; advertising co-ops with other catalog retailers in national publications
Qualifications:	Sales/marketing background
Equipment needed:	Postage meter, computer, printer, fax/modem, phone with 800 number for ease of ordering, credit card processing equipment
Staff required:	Not initially
Handicapped opportunity:	Yes
Hidden costs:	Insurance, purchase/lease of specialized mailing lists

What You Do

Catalogs have been around as long as there have been products to sell. But what seems to work best in the catalog/mail order business is to use niche marketing; that is, pick an area of specialization and only offer products related to that area. For instance, you might sell only products for golf lovers, or only baby items. Choose an area that is specific enough to catch instant attention, yet broad enough to include a wide variety of products. You'll build your customer base from lists you either rent or purchase; if you specialize, this will be an easy process for you (and cost less in the long run). Your days will be spent taking and filling orders in the most efficient way possible; you'll also be handling customer service and possibly returns. That's why, in addition to a terrific marketing background, you'll also need some accounting skills; it all gets to be quite complicated when you're dealing with hundreds of orders (which you'll need to break even). Make sure you have adequate storage space for at least some of the goods—your basement will run out of space quickly.

What You Need

Your earnings potential is unpredictable because you're dealing with various products at different prices and hoping they will all sell within a short period of time. Because you'll need to send out a thousand or so catalogs to make your sales efforts pay off, and because you'll need everything from a postage meter to credit card processing equipment and a computer system to maintain and run your business, expect to spend $15,000-$60,000. It'll be closer to the high end if you're actually selling your own product line; obviously, it's a little cheaper to work out agreements with other manufacturers and get a percentage of their take (usually 15 to 20 percent). Don't forget printing costs, either (these could run as high as $10,000-$15,000 per issue). You could potentially earn $25,000-$50,000 or more, depending on how interesting or different your product line is and how much of a price variance you offer.

Keys to Success

On the positive side, you'll be able to work in your pajamas if you want to, since you'll be in your office most of the day. The downside is, you *are* your work—and if you're having a bad day, orders won't get filled and you'll wind up losing money. Also, be sure that you're selling quality products—ask for samples; it's good customer service.

---

7 Keys to Building a Profitable Consulting Business

Experts agree that there are a few major steps to building a successful consulting business. Of course, you must first decide what field you're an expert in yourself before embarking on your roadmap to success.

Once you've identified your niche market, you can focus your energy on the following areas:

1. **Relationship-building.** It's the mantra of the '90s business professional: build relationships that last beyond the initial sale. Don't expend a lot of energy if it looks like you'll make only one sale; spending too much time with this kind of one-shot deal can blow a whole year of sales with another potential client.

2. **Clearly stating your objective and strategies.** As a consultant, you'll be expected to solve some problems of a fairly large nature. You need to be as clear as possible in your proposal as to what you'll be providing for the price you're asking. How else can a company determine whether you're worth it? (P.S. Always remind the client in your proposal of why they're needing you in the first place.)

3. **Present a polished, professional image.** You are in the image business, and your clients' perceptions of you are what ultimately bring in the sale. They need to see you as successful, in demand, and of the highest quality there is— so make sure all of your materials, from business cards to sample videos, convey the real you.

---

4. **Don't be afraid to offer free, introductory sessions when you need to.** So often, consultants get caught up in thinking that every hour should be a billable one. Keep in mind that you need to build awareness of your services before you can sell folks on them (particularly if you are just starting out); the best way to get them interested is to hold a free information seminar once every quarter or so.

5. **Charge by the hour, not by the job.** Too many consultants make the mistake of underestimating the number of hours a job will take. Make sure that although you have an hourly rate of $100 per hour, your estimate reflects additional hours that you project might occur. You can offer a 10 percent discount for timely payment—but never discount the value of your own time.

6. **Update your client list regularly.** At least once per year, weed out those folks who only generate a tiny portion of your annual income. To be profitable, you need to focus on the bigger accounts—and constantly fill your time with more of them.

7. **Remember to follow up with every client.** As a consultant, your job is never ending; once you sign on as an expert, you remain one for life (or until you make a mistake).

Caterer

Start-up cost:	$15,000-$23,000
Potential earnings:	30,000-$80,000
Typical fees:	$800-$15,000 per event
Advertising:	Brochures, press kits, direct mail, networking
Qualifications:	Cooking and menu planning experience, knowledge about sanitation and safe food handling, good people skills
Equipment needed:	Cooking equipment and supplies
Staff required:	Not initially; may be needed to grow
Handicapped opportunity:	No
Hidden costs:	In many states it is illegal to sell food prepared in a home kitchen; a commercial kitchen (which can be rented and/or shared) may be required

What You Do

If you have the right mixture of cooking know-how, business and good communication skills, catering can be a profitable and enjoyable enterprise. Though a commercial kitchen may be required, most catering services begin at home because start-up does not require years of training, expensive equipment, or capital investment. One fast-growing segment of this business is food delivery—especially lunches—to offices and corporations. Catering opportunities also abound in preparing private banquets at hotels, furnishing meals to airlines, cooking for parties, fund-raisers, and other events, or serving as an executive chef in a company dining room. Specializing in a particular item, such as gourmet wedding cakes or chocolate chip cookies, is another option. Caterers must observe health, safety, zoning, product liability, and other laws and regulations. Detailed record-keeping is also needed.

What You Need

Access to a commercial kitchen can range from about $8,000-$12,000; appropriate equipment (pots, pans, etc.) will be $500-$1,000. In addition, allow $3,000-$10,000 for insurance, legal and insurance fees, license, and advertising. You will also need a delivery vehicle. You will have to lay out the costs of your "raw materials," but you can charge them back to the customer.

Keys to Success

Successful catering requires a lot of hard work and careful planning. You have to devote time to meeting with—and cooking for—potential clients even though you may not be chosen to cater their event. Social catering involves weekend and evening work, and is also often seasonal in nature. Keep in mind you also will be responsible for serving and cleanup, as well as menu planning and cooking, unless you hire others to do these tasks. On the other hand, cooking is fun! It's a creative process, one that nourishes the cook as well as those who eat the food. You can control how much or how little you work. And you'll always be welcome in everyone's kitchen!

Child Care Referral Service

Start-up cost:	$500
Potential earnings:	10,000-$35,000
Typical fees:	$25 per client
Advertising:	Classified ads, bulletin boards
Qualifications:	Should be good at handling multiple tasks and somewhat detail-oriented
Equipment needed:	Answering machine, pager, or cellular phone
Staff required:	No
Handicapped opportunity:	Yes
Hidden costs:	None

What You Do

This is a perfect match for those who like to work alone and as a valued resource person. As a child care referral agent, you would provide names and phone numbers of reputable child care professionals in your area—at a cost of about $25 per caller. You would most likely get your start by placing a classified ad in your local newspaper, then scheduling a meeting time with the prospective client to discuss their needs and particulars with regard to the type of professional they're seeking. For instance, some career couples are in need of a caregiver to watch their kids all week long, while others just need part-time care for their children. Some will want individual care, others will want you to check out the local service.

What You Need

With a $500 minimal start-up covering mostly your advertising and telephone costs, you could begin to pull in a profit almost immediately. You will need to build a vast network of child care professionals, which you can easily accomplish by posting flyers in public places (such as Laundromats and grocery stores) and combing the ads in your local newspaper to find baby-sitters who are offering their services. If you have a little bit of extra money to play with at the beginning, you should also invest in professional-looking stationery and business cards to convey the best-possible image to your baby-sitters as well as your clients.

Keys to Success

What's not to like about setting your own hours and having essentially complete control over a low-overhead business? The only obstacle would be limitations with respect to the availability of child care providers or those in need of them. If you live in a small, rural area, this business could max out in a month—but if you are in suburbia, you could really make some decent cash.

Childbirth Instructor

Start-up cost:	$500-$1,000
Potential earnings:	15,000-$35,000
Typical fees:	$175 per couple
Advertising:	Bulletin boards, parents' newsletters, OB/GYN offices
Qualifications:	A nursing degree would be helpful—and respected by those needing your service
Equipment needed:	No
Staff required:	No
Handicapped opportunity:	Yes
Hidden costs:	None very serious (but you may want to invest in some educational materials such as models, books, and videos)

What You Do

Giving birth is a very natural experience that doesn't come naturally—that's why we need childbirth instructors to show us the way. First-time parents are especially uneasy (even frightened) about the pending event, and their fears are best calmed with detailed and expert information from a reliable source. If you've been in a delivery room, and have a nursing degree or related training, you would be a terrific candidate for this type of work. A childbirth instructor is essentially a teacher, so you must develop (and stick to) a teaching plan much the same as any other teacher. Most childbirth classes meet once a week for four to six weeks, so space your materials out accordingly. Begin with the basics and end with a strong visual, such as a childbirth film. Be sure to answer all questions, even the most common ones, courteously and compassionately—after all, many of your customers haven't a clue what they're in for, and it's your job to make their fears subside for a calm, secure birthing experience.

What You Need

You will be competing against hospitals (unless you contract with them), so you will need to spend some advertising dollars to get your name out there. In addition to advertising in parents' newsletters, you might also want to consider advertising at a children's consignment store—they often have bulletin boards for related services and you could provide some referrals for them in return. Speaking of referrals, you should also get to know a few obstetricians and midwives; they will comprise your strongest source of word-of-mouth business.

Keys to Success

The birth experience is a joyous occasion, and you will likely enjoy telling and retelling the story of this miracle of life. On the downside, the repetition can get on your nerves . . . after all, how many different ways can you tell people how babies are born?

Collectibles Broker

Start-up cost:	$5,000-$15,000
Potential earnings:	500-$20,000
Typical fees:	Varies on what you are selling and the going rate for it
Advertising:	Flea markets, swap meets, antique fairs, flyers, brochures
Qualifications:	Knowing how to spot money from junk
Equipment needed:	20-30 collectibles to start
Staff required:	No
Handicapped opportunity:	Yes
Hidden costs:	Table/space rental fees

What You Do

Everything old is new again! Remember the Morton Salt Girl or the Brady Bunch lunch boxes with radios in them? They are in popular demand right now and bringing in top dollars ($100 or more each). And so is anything retro: salt/pepper sets, board games, clothing, limited edition plates, Presidential items, cereal boxes, you name it—but that doesn't relieve you of the responsibility to heavily market your service. You can specialize in one era like the '50s and carry everything from that time period. Or, you can specialize in one item (like toasters through the century). Try to hit as many antique fairs, swap meets, and dealer conventions as possible; that's where you'll spend a little, but earn a lot.

What You Need

You will need equipment to show off your stuff, so that will be the biggest expense (about $1,000). The next will be your advertising and marketing. When you go to shows plan on paying $15-$100+ to rent a table or space to showcase your merchandise. Earning potential will be initially slow—$500-$20,000—until you've gotten established.

Keys to Success

People are crazy for the past. In some ways, it represents a simpler time in their lives, and that's something many people are willing to pay for. Collecting has become a $6-billion-dollar a year business, so if you have a collection you're willing to part with, you could make some serious money. Collecting interests tend to run in 20-year cycles, so this has a long-term possibility if you have an eye for what is collectible and what will sell. The danger is getting so caught up in acquiring certain pieces that you aren't willing to part with them yourself. Beware—collecting is intoxicating to those who enjoy it!

Gaining Credibility

Once you've opened your doors for business, how do you get the customers to learn your name and trust it as a reliable source in the community? Ultimately, the way to build credibility is to develop a strong business with a solid reputation for delivering what it promises the customer. But what can you do in the meantime (until you're a household name)? Here are some possibilities:

- **Volunteer at local charitable foundations and corporate events.** Simply being out there where other influential types are likely to be found (either as sponsors or as participants) will put you face-to-face with people who can help spread the word about your business. It's worth the donated hours on your part, and you'll get to widen your circle of acquaintances.

- **Offer yourself as an expert on your topic of interest.** Send regular press releases with tips for consumers to local and regional newspapers and magazines. Editors love such items and you stand a good chance of being interviewed the next time a story on your area of expertise rolls around. Be sure to keep in regular contact with the press, even if it's just a quick phone call to ask if they need any help with upcoming features.

- **Give free speeches at local association dinners.** Or lunches. Or breakfasts. Really, just about anywhere where potential clients gather to learn more about improving their professional (and possibly personal) lives. Association meetings work best because they are always in need for interesting new speakers; so are civic groups and universities.

- **Create and mail a regular newsletter with useful tips.** Giving some information for free can create positive awareness of your company and what it has to offer. People do tend to read newsletters, and even though they may not need your services today, such publications (if well-done) will keep you in their minds tomorrow.

- **Perform to your personal best.** Ultimately, it's going to be a reputation based on fair pricing, high quality, and exceptional service that will gain you the credibility you need to bring in new business. Set high standards and work every day toward achieving them, and you will have your credibility sooner than most.

Collection Agency

Start-up cost:	$3,000-$10,500
Potential earnings:	30,000-$60,000
Typical fees:	25 percent commission
Advertising:	Phone solicitation, networking, writing articles for local publications, public speaking
Qualifications:	Good communication skills, patience, high self-esteem, budgeting skills; clear understanding of the Federal Fair Debt Collection Practices Act, any relevant state laws and health insurance policies and billing practices if working with the medical field
Equipment needed:	Computer with modem, printer, fax, word-processing and spreadsheet software, specialized collection software and phone with optional headset
Staff required:	No
Handicapped opportunity:	Yes
Hidden costs:	Organizational dues for networking purposes; state, city, and/or county licenses are typically required; fees for on-line services

What You Do

Are you an addict of *Unsolved Mysteries*? Collectors are often put to the test as they track down elusive debtors. State laws typically require people who do collections to be bonded and licensed. Generally, it is not difficult to obtain the proper license provided your state does not prohibit home-based agencies. Using special collections software and a PC, a collection service becomes very efficient as it reduces the time and labor for handling mail and accounting. Additionally, on-line services cut the cost of tracking debtors considerably.

What You Need

It is essential that you take advantage of the many high-tech devices that will make the collection process easier. A computer and modem is essential, as is customized collection software. Costs ranging from $2,000-$7,000 for these basics are average. Don't forget to shop around for the best fee on phone line usage.

Keys to Success

The collection process is often frustrating. Keeping your self-esteem intact in the face of rejection is necessary. Although confrontation of unpaid bills can be emotionally draining, the work never ceases to be challenging and rewarding. In some cases, you are able to solve debtors' financial problems and keep them from bankruptcy. When all parties agree on a suitable payment plan, everyone wins.

Expert Advice

What sets your business apart from others like it?

"There are a lot of good agencies, and we all basically do the same things," says Deloris C. Lewis, President of Debt Credit Services & Associates in Akron, Ohio. "I cater to the needs of my clients and go out of my way to help them. I try to be fair to both the creditors and the debtors."

Things you couldn't do without:

Items such as an excellent, well-trained staff, speed dialers, computers, integrated skip tracing and bookkeeping software, a phone system, and mailing equipment, Lewis says.

Marketing tips/advice:

"Go after the large-dollar, small-account commercial business that's out there. Stay away from health care; if you're new, it will be too demanding and intense for you. Use networking and advertising to bring in new business, but depend heavily on referrals."

If you had to do it all over again . . .

"I'd have started with more capital . . . that means developing a sound business plan, which I didn't do in the beginning and which has held me back. I winged it—and now I'd be more organized so that I could get better funding."

College Application Consultant

Start-up cost:	$500-$1,000
Potential earnings:	15,000-$30,000
Typical fees:	Extremely varied; some consultants charge as high as $1,000 for this service
Advertising:	School and local papers, direct mail, Yellow Pages
Qualifications:	Familiarity with various colleges and programs
Equipment needed:	Computer, variety of available databases, reference materials
Staff required:	No
Handicapped opportunity:	Yes
Hidden costs:	Long distance phone calls and on-line time

What You Do

Nowadays the hardest part of getting into a college is choosing the right one; it's a vital decision for a young person's future, with far-reaching implications. Now more than ever, a bachelor's degree is almost a requirement to secure a decent, well-paying job. And although some high schools do have respectable advising departments, many do not invest the time and money into this important aspect of continuing education that they could and should. That's where you come in. As an independent college applica-tion consultant your services are in high demand in a low-competition field. What more could a business person ask for? If you are amenable to long hours of research and doc-umentation, this business could provide you with just the academic challenge you need. Your biggest hurdle is problem-solving for high school seniors and their families, dealing with emotional/sentimental issues (primarily of the parents), and helping anyone else interested in entering college who doesn't have access to the information they need. You would conduct a skills/needs assessment, match them to an appropriate choice of universities, assist the customer in obtaining and filling in financial aid and application forms properly (and mailing them on time). You will also relay necessary facts about: ACT/SATs, placement tests (such as math, English, and foreign languages), degrees, and extracurricular activities offered by the school that might be of interest to the student, program requirements, etc.

What You Need

A computer is the largest expense at about $1,500, if you choose to buy one. It isn't a necessity but it will tremendously speed the search process. College catalogs show list-ings of offered courses and a description of each, as well as some information about application procedures, fees, deadlines, and requirements and other general facts about the school. Buying many of these, as well as a few specialized publications that rate uni-versities or give little-known information about them, will cost several hundred dollars, but it's the basis for your business. Placing only small ads will help keep advertising costs down to $100 or so, but the price of calls to colleges may add up quickly, so remember to monitor your phone time. Charges for these tasks could be determined a number of ways: per task, per package of tasks, hourly, or however else seems reasonable for the area and best covers the particular request.

Keys to Success

Good listening skills and problem-solving ability are your biggest assets in this business. Customers are trusting you with a very important part of their lives: their futures. High self-motivation and research skills will also help keep you enthused and knowledgeable about colleges and what's new on campus. If you enjoy being the middleman, then college consulting is for you.

Marketing on a Shoestring

An effective marketing plan is essential. Work with it for a year, and reassess. Do not neglect some of the proven techniques for marketing that cost very little and serve to make your name known in your community.

■ **Cooperate with other businesses**—consider a joint promotion (for fitness classes and nutrition counseling, as an example).

■ **Be an expert**—give speeches before community groups, write articles on topics related to your service offerings, etc.

■ **Participate in trade shows**—with careful planning, you can gain follow-up opportunities, do many product demonstrations, and make contacts with prospects.

■ **Gain free media exposure**—get publicity at no cost, receive third-party presentation for your story.

■ **Consider direct mail**—guided by an expert, you can create an effective mailing list to reach your target market.

■ **Become involved in your community**—genuine public service on boards and committees enhances your reputation, makes friends for your business, and gets your name out.

■ **Publish a newsletter quarterly**—include information of interest to your target market, appealing graphics, and a focus on one of your products or services.

College Internship Placement

Start-up cost:	$1,500-$3,000
Potential earnings:	20,000-$50,000
Typical fees:	$75-$175 (paid by student/parents)
Advertising:	College newspapers, campus bulletin boards, direct mail to parents
Qualifications:	Background in placement services would be helpful
Equipment needed:	Computer with printer, fax/modem, e-mail address
Staff required:	No
Handicapped opportunity:	Yes
Hidden costs:	Insurance, on-line time

What You Do

It used to be that companies offering internships contacted colleges to find students for summer or short-term work. But, in the ever-competitive '90s, such companies are relying increasingly upon services such as yours to bring them talent in exchange for small pay and experience. It's challenging work to find a suitable internship for a student (and vice versa), and you'll have enough resources to choose from at your local library. There are plenty of books that detail such opportunities, and there should be plenty of postings for internships through on-line services or the Internet. You'd have to work pretty hard to exhaust all of the possibilities. You'd be wise to market to the parents of students, as they are typically the ones with the foresight to see the importance of an internship; they also are typically the ones with all the money, too!

What You Need

You'll need to have at least $1,500 for your computer system and another $1,000 or so for advertising in your first six months. Charging customers $75-$175 (depending on the size of the university or college market you're serving) will likely lead you to an annual salary of $20,000-$50,000 per year.

Keys to Success

Your work will be different every day, and the challenges will present themselves on a regular basis, too. Often, you'll work with folks you simply can't seem to please, or who don't come across as highly motivated. Remember that part of your job is to sell the student on the importance of internships—what they can mean later on to a job-seeking student is immeasurable.

Color Consultant

Start-up cost:	$2,000-$4,000
Potential earnings:	30,000-$50,000
Typical fees:	$35-$75 per hour analysis
Advertising:	Local newspapers, business publications, direct mail
Qualifications:	Possibly training through cosmetic firm, paint company, or similar business
Equipment needed:	Color swatches, color charts
Staff required:	No
Handicapped opportunity:	Yes
Hidden costs:	Travel expenses

What You Do

Have you ever wondered exactly how the major automobile manufacturers and appliance makers decide which colors to use on their products? Or where the world of fashion comes up with the latest hues? They use color consultants—experts who know the entire spectrum of the rainbow, including minute variations and redefining nuances that are invisible to the untrained eye. It is essential that a color consultant have a strong understanding of color dynamics (how color affects people) in addition to the natural ability to distinguish slight color variations. The former is a learned skill, while the latter is an inherent talent that must be present to ensure acceptance into training and success in the field. Once established in this business, your days will consist of working with anyone from cosmetic companies to corporate consultations to group workshops to appliance/furniture manufacturers to individual analyses. People will look to you for the trends of the future.

What You Need

Training with a company that is heavily dependent upon color and color dynamics is the biggest initial expense involved in becoming a consultant. Most often, the program is a week of intensive instruction on color theory and analysis, marketing techniques, and applications; expect to spend at least $1,200 on classes/certification (if available in your area). Other costs are directly related to visual materials to use in consultations and demonstrations (anywhere from $25-$1,000). Consultations often last an hour, with the average fee being $50-$75, depending upon the industry and geographic area of the country.

Keys to Success

Working with people is always a challenge, but more so when it involves personal issues such as what's aesthetically pleasing and what's not (which can be quite subjective). Staying on top of what's new in the ever-changing fashion world can be an exciting challenge, so if you like the idea of making other people look good and making money while doing it, this could be the career for you.

Commercial Photographer

Start-up cost:	$3,000-$5,000
Potential earnings:	35,000 and up
Typical fees:	$35-$50 per hour
Advertising:	Classifieds, trade publications, business groups, referrals, direct mail
Qualifications:	Photographic skills, excellent time management skills, ability to market and sell your services
Equipment needed:	Excellent camera equipment, office furniture, preferably a computer and printer, fax, business cards, letterhead, envelopes
Staff required:	No
Handicapped opportunity:	No
Hidden costs:	Equipment upgrades and repair, travel costs

What You Do

Commercial photography is an ideal business for the individual who can produce. If you can "see" the images needed by a business segment in your community, and produce them on time for a competitive cost, you can probably develop relationships with your customers that will bring you an ongoing stream of business. Photos always seem to be needed, but at the last minute. You will need to produce what is wanted under pressure, and have a reputation for getting it right the first time. Commercial photography requires an interesting combination of technical, artistic, sales, and business skills. If you have this mix, or can develop it, you can go far.

What You Need

The photographic equipment you use is, of course, the vital component of this business (should get started on $3,000). Having an effective home office is also necessary for supporting the "business" side of your business: receiving assignments, preparing invoices, and so on. You could earn upward of $35,000.

Keys to Success

Most successful commercial photographer specialize. And some have gone beyond providing the photographic image alone to offering related services—preparation of brochures, scanning and retouching images, or working in close association with graphic artists and copywriters to provide a completed piece. If you become known for excellence in photography of construction projects, retail store installations, or company board retreats, you will have a leg up on the competition. This is another crowded field with plenty of room at the top.

Expert Advice

What sets your business apart from others like it?

Tom Uhlman, owner of Tom Uhlman Photography in Cincinnati, Ohio, says that he stands apart from other commercial photographers by offering sound editorial judgment in addition to providing quality photographic work. "I'm dependable at finding interesting situations, giving publications the kinds of unusual photos they want and need without having to wait for assignment." Uhlman's photos have been picked up by the Associated Press and have appeared in *Newsweek*, the *New York Daily News*, and *USA Today*.

Things you couldn't do without:

Uhlman says he couldn't do without top-quality cameras with motor drives, flash equipment, better-than-average lenses, and dependable transportation. "I would also buy a police scanner, so you can shoot 'hard' news as it happens. It's the best way to break into newspapers, because they often don't have the staff or time to get these shots."

Marketing tips/advice:

"Look at the work of others and learn from it. But you'll probably learn the most from being out there and getting your own experience. Find photos that tell good news stories, and you should never have a problem selling."

If you had to do it all over again . . .

"I pretty much did everything in the right way and time, mainly because I didn't know any better. I learned early on that doing is what gets you there."

Commercial Plant Watering Service

Start-up cost:	$800-$1,000
Potential earnings:	30,000-$60,000
Typical fees:	$25-$50 per day; some work on monthly retainers of $500 and up
Advertising:	Referrals, Yellow Pages, affiliations with nursery businesses
Qualifications:	Knowledge of plants' requirements
Equipment needed:	Vehicle for traveling to client businesses
Staff required:	No
Handicapped opportunity:	No
Hidden costs:	None

What You Do

Interior plantings are more significant in some parts of the country than in others, but almost all large businesses maintain some kind of greenery to soften their offices. Once you show these organizations that you can care for their plants and make them stay healthy and attractive, you will have the opportunity to develop an ongoing business that brings you a steady income stream.

What You Need

Costs are minimal. You will need a car or truck to drive from client to client, and perhaps should consider business cards that you could leave near the plants to generate more business. Most larger plant maintenance services charge a flat monthly rate of $500 or more; if you're smaller, however, this will likely be a part-time job, earning you between $25-$50 per day.

Keys to Success

This is definitely a business for plant lovers. If you enjoy making things grow, you'll find plant watering to be a rewarding enterprise. However, there isn't much change from day to day, although you are in and out of different environments as you go from customer to customer. This is not a business for people who thrive on excitement—and not exactly a get-rich-quick enterprise, either.

Computer Consultant

Start-up cost:	$5,000-$13,000
Potential earnings:	40,000-$100,000
Typical fees:	$75-$150 per hour
Advertising:	Referrals, direct mail, publications, networking
Qualifications:	Technical knowledge, specialty knowledge, people and time-management skills
Equipment needed:	High-end computer, hardware and software, copier, fax, office furniture, business card, letterhead, envelopes
Staff required:	No; must be able to subcontract outside of specialty
Handicapped opportunity:	Yes
Hidden costs:	On-line service; time and expense of staying current in fast-changing field

What You Do

It's getting very hard to operate any business without a computer system, so almost anyone is a potential client if you know how to match up a computer system with their needs. Computer consulting is a big field today and will continue to grow rapidly in the near future. Many computer consultants become as essential to their clients as the systems themselves, earning a steady income in the process. This field is for individuals with wide expertise in hardware and software. Even more important is an ability to see issues from the client's point of view. What are his or her real problems, and what creative solutions to those problems will be best served using computer technology? You will probably need to focus on one area of specialization, such as networking computers, or on one type of business, such as retail outlets or physician offices.

What You Need

Your own business must have a computer system, including software, that is comparable to those of your clients. This will be your major expense, but if you have the expertise to operate this business, you probably have much of the equipment and software already. You'll also need a high-quality copier and a fax/modem. The essential organizational dues and on-line services can also add surprisingly to your operating expenses. But, if you charge the going rates of $75 and up per hour, you should be able to earn back your initial investment in as little as six months.

Keys to Success

Computer consulting is for big-picture people also skilled in keeping track of details. Each client and situation is different, making for a very stimulating work life. You will be able to function outside of normal time-space restrictions and you won't find competitors undercutting you with cookie-cutter services. But computer consulting is extremely demanding. You will often be working under a deadline or in a crisis situation; you must produce what you promise and be able to train your clients' employees to make the system work under real conditions. Bidding jobs is challenging, especially at first—keeping track of billing is essential.

Expert Advice

What sets your business apart from others like it?

Lee Hughes, Systems Engineer at Hughes Information Systems in Cloquet, Minnesota, says his business is successful because it streamlines and automates other businesses' operations. "We take an engineering approach to solving problems."

Things you couldn't do without:

"A personal computer, printer, modem, and phone."

Marketing tips/advice:

"It is virtually impossible to accurately estimate project costs. Try to build in a cushion when you provide an estimate."

If you had to do it all over again . . .

"I would educate myself much more in business management, sales/marketing and presentation/negotiation skills."

Computer Maintenance Service

Start-up cost:	$5,000-$10,000
Potential earnings:	50,000-$70,000
Typical fees:	$50 per hour on cleaning or repairs; $25-$40 per student (if teaching classes)
Advertising:	Word of mouth, Yellow Pages, flyers, business card, opportunities to teach classes
Qualifications:	Knowledge of computer hardware and interfaces, ability to deal with upset clients diplomatically and sympathetically
Equipment needed:	PC with modem, printer, and fax, tools, cleaning supplies, and diagnostic software, spare parts, office furniture, business card, reference books
Staff required:	No
Handicapped opportunity:	No
Hidden costs:	Staying abreast of new technology

What You Do

Computers and dust don't mix. That seems like a simple idea, but many people have little understanding of that concept. They don't understand why computers tend to crash without regular maintenance, and they need much reassurance before they will trust you to remove a cover and begin cleaning the drives. Once you gain trust and develop your clientele, though, you'll be able to negotiate ongoing service contracts that will give you a steady flow of work, and income. Twice a year you can service each client on your list, cleaning the vital components of the machines that keep their businesses running. You may also develop connections to possible add-on services you could offer, such as training, software installation, file backups, and other types of computer-related services.

What You Need

The computer for your own office is the largest expense because the actual computer cleaning tools are quite simple and not very costly. Fees are usually in the $50 per hour range. Your biggest challenge is to make potential clients aware of the benefit of maintaining their systems—all too often they'll wait until something catastrophic happens before they call you. Consequently, advertising and sending reminder cards will cost you at least $1,000-$2,000 per year.

Keys to Success

If you have the ability to clean computers and peripheral equipment, you can provide a service needed by almost all businesses and many individuals as well. Satisfied customers will probably provide you with plenty of referrals, but you will occasionally be working with distraught clients. You might need to work at your customers' sites, so careful planning is necessary to make best use of travel time.

Computer Trainer

Start-up cost:	$5,000-$16,000
Potential earnings:	40,000-$100,000
Typical fees:	$75+ per hour
Advertising:	Speaking at business meetings, referrals from software companies, networking, direct mail to specific companies, computer and trade publications
Qualifications:	Computer skills and/or certification by software company, writing and presentation skills, ability to handle group dynamics, background in teaching or education design
Equipment needed:	High-end computer, hardware and software, laser printer, comb binding machine for materials, office furniture, brochures and/or presentation folder, business card, letterhead, envelopes
Staff required:	No
Handicapped opportunity:	Yes
Hidden costs:	Certification training to teach specific programs

What You Do

As computers become even more important in the business world, so does computer training. New software is powerful, but added features mean that almost every employee needs training to use it productively. To be a successful computer trainer, you need a range of skills, beginning with expertise in each software package. Beyond the ability to use the software yourself, you need to understand how others use it. Computer trainers may work as tutors with one or two individuals at a time, but more often they teach classes to groups at a business location, so teaching and presentation skills are essential. Computer training can be a successful business for people who have computer skills, find teaching to be a creative enterprise, and like working with adults. You will need to focus on the areas where your expertise is easiest to keep updated: word processing, databases, or accounting programs, for example.

What You Need

Your computer, software and laser printer will be the largest start-up expenses, totaling as much as $10,000-$15,000. You will also need to produce your own training materials, and these will change as new versions of the software packages are installed by your clients. Most training is conducted on clients' premises, so your own office equipment can be added later. Charge at least $75 per hour to cover your expenses and make a tidy profit.

Keys to Success

If you are good at teaching, you can make a big difference in the work lives of the people you train. They must use computer equipment to complete their tasks, and knowing how the programs operate will greatly increase their efficiency. You will know that the services you provide are important to the employees you train and to the businesses that depend on them. You'll need to be good at defusing their computer anxiety, though. People who don't understand the intricacies of a program start pulling their hair out almost immediately. You will need to coax them gradually through each skill level until they gain confidence. Students who are new to an area often don't ask clear questions; anticipate that and listen carefully to give the right responses. Some adults find it very difficult to become students again. Also, there is a lot of competition in this field today. You will need to find a way to distinguish what you can offer from all the others. Finally, preparing training materials can be time-consuming and labor-intensive if you're not used to step-by-step approaches.

Businesses on the Success Track

What are the top opportunities for making money as an entrepreneur of the '90s? According to *Entrepreneur* magazine, they are actually quite varied, and some of them may be appealing to you:

- Internet consulting
- Home health care
- Executive temporary services/employee leasing
- Computer training services/consulting
- Exporting
- Environmental services
- Business and management consultants
- Adventure tourism

Concert Promoter

Start-up cost:	$15,000-$25,000
Potential earnings:	50,000-$100,000+
Typical fees:	25 to 30 percent of the concert gross
Advertising:	Promoters' magazine, industry trades, newspapers
Qualifications:	Should be well-connected in the music industry
Equipment needed:	Basic office setup, cellular phone
Staff required:	Yes
Handicapped opportunity:	Yes
Hidden costs:	Insurance, travel/entertainment costs

What You Do

Rock, opera, classical, folk . . . there are as many different acts to promote as there are types of music. If you are a real go-getter and have had an extensive background in the music industry, you stand a chance of making it as a concert promoter. You'll need to be supremely well-organized and detail-oriented, since your business hinges on every little detail. You will solicit the agent by telling him or her that, if a particular group or star is brought to your town, you will promote them aggressively every place there is a space. Network with local media to ensure good public relations, but don't promise agents the moon if you can't deliver. This business is full of hyped-up promoters who are really rip-off artists. You can't afford to be greedy until after you've established yourself; once you have a solid track record of successful promotions, you can go for the big bucks.

What You Need

Your start-up fee ($15,000-$25,000) will be wrapped up in getting your name out there and presenting a professional image. You have to be fairly well-known before someone will let you promote their act. Your fee will be 25 to 30 percent of the concert gross; if it's a big name, you could earn as much as $150,000 per show.

Keys to Success

There are long hours involved this occupation—and a lot of socializing, too. Not necessarily a good deal for a person with a family, but it's workable if you have a strong support staff. Expect a lot of trial and error in the beginning; learn from each experience and improve yourself with time.

Consulting Engineer

Start-up cost:	$20,000-$50,000
Potential earnings:	40,000-$85,000+
Typical fees:	Depends on length and extent of project; can be as little as $175 for a minor project and as high as several thousand for the larger ones
Advertising:	Trade journals, classified ads, federal publications, networking
Qualifications:	Degree and certification necessary (sometimes in each state you do business in)
Equipment needed:	Drafting equipment and reference materials, computer-aided design (CAD) software, perhaps surveying equipment
Staff required:	Not initially, although you may want to hire an administrative type early on
Handicapped opportunity:	Possibly
Hidden costs:	Liability insurance, mileage

What You Do

When a big project is launched at a corporation or even in a municipal environment, the expertise needed to actually create the "great idea" isn't exactly in-house. That's where you can really carve a nice niche for yourself—as a "hired gun" to pull together all the necessary finishing touches for construction, manufacturing, or technical situations. Consulting engineers offer their opinions or "hands-on" abilities to bring special projects to fruition. This could involve anything from CAD designs to developing a better means of production for wiring harnesses. If you don't mind the pressure of coming into a potentially volatile (and political) situation, and particularly if you are amenable to long hours for a short-term project, this could be a perfectly workable business for you. You would likely be called in as an expert; perhaps you'll be solving a snafu between the manufacturing and design departments of a major manufacturer.

What You Need

Your start-up costs (after, of course, your degrees and certifications are taken care of) will consist mainly of basic equipment. Expect to spend at least $20,000 (more if you're planning to have others working along with you). But if you're good at what you do, you'll be able to earn a considerable amount of money within the first year or two—perhaps as much as $100,000 or more.

Keys to Success

The key to success as a consulting engineer depends heavily on your ability to establish yourself as an industry expert of some kind. The more well-known you are for solving manufacturability problems, for instance, the more calls you're going to get—and the richer you'll become.

Cooking Class Instructor

Start-up cost:	$1,000-$5,000
Potential earnings:	10,000-$20,000
Typical fees:	$20-$45 per class
Advertising:	Newspaper ads, brochures, flyers
Qualifications:	Cooking experience, teaching ability, some marketing skills
Equipment needed:	Cooking equipment and supplies, a place to teach (if not teaching at home)
Staff required:	None
Handicapped opportunity:	Yes
Hidden costs:	Possible need to rent a facility to teach the classes; must have adequate stove(s), generous counter space

What You Do

Gourmet cooking and dining are both very popular right now. There are many television shows featuring chefs and cooks whose creativity pleases the palate, and gourmet restaurants and cooking supply stores abound. If you have (or can learn) the basics of cooking and have an interest in teaching others to do the same, this might be the business for you. You might check out the possibility of teaching in a home economics room at your local high school. This business can also be conducted easily from your home.

What You Need

Start-up costs can be minimal if you already have the cookware and utensils needed. In addition, factor in the purchase of a professional stove, if you don't have one, and the cost to rent a facility for the classes, if you don't want to teach at home. Teaching at home is only recommended if you have a large kitchen. The costs of your raw materials will need to be factored into your class fees.

Keys to Success

A cooking class business can be very rewarding. Everyone loves to eat, and learning to produce delightful meals will please your students. Marketing is probably the big hurdle for this type of business. You will need to advertise; you might be able to find related businesses to sponsor you or to spread the word about your classes. For instance, you could build a relationship with the owner of an upscale kitchen products company or offer your classes as "continuing education" through a high school's home economics department.

Counselor/Psychologist

Start-up cost:	$3,000-$5,000 (after college expenses)
Potential earnings:	35,000-$65,000
Typical fees:	$40-$75 per hour
Advertising:	Newspapers, referrals from physicians, Yellow Pages
Qualifications:	Degree and certification
Equipment needed:	Phone, fax, and answering service to field calls when you are not available
Staff required:	No (possibly an assistant for scheduling insurance claims)
Handicapped opportunity:	Yes
Hidden costs:	Keep scrupulous records of every meeting you have with a client—emergency meetings are frequent and could slip through the cracks if you aren't watching

What You Do

Do you have a knack for getting to the heart of a problem? Are you on top of all the self-help ideologies out there—their potential for both helping and worsening the problems of others? If so, you are well-suited to the profession of counselor/psychologist. You will not only listen to your clients' problems, but you'll also guide them to finding their own healthy solutions. You'll offer them resources to expand their own abilities in problem-solving—and provide creative exercises to get the clients to relax and open up their lives to you. But your job doesn't stop there. You must also keep accurate records of your meetings and what transpired, spending time reviewing these records before and after each meeting. Therefore, you must love detail and be able to budget your time appropriately in order to stay on top of your workload while helping your clients go on with their lives.

What You Need

Your initial costs are moderate and primarily cover advertising and promotion. You'll need business cards and stationery to invoice your clients with if you don't ask for cash up front (which most experts highly recommend). Add to that the cost of continuing your education via seminars and conferences (generally around $1,000 annually). Finally, you'll need someone who can process medical claims if you are not able to—and the insurance companies can be tricky to deal with if you're a novice.

Keys to Success

You may relish the opportunity to make sense out of someone else's life, but being a successful counselor or psychologist often means giving with a capital "G"—and not all of us are such martyrs. Your clients will be dependent upon you very heavily at first, then may possibly disappear altogether when they feel they are better. These up-and-down cycles can contribute to feelings of depression—and not even "couch" professionals are immune to that.

Coupon Distributor

Start-up cost:	$500-$1,500
Potential earnings:	10,000-$35,000
Typical fees:	$3-$5 per drop site or a bulk rate for mailings (usually $300 per thousand)
Advertising:	Word of mouth, cover letter with resume
Qualifications:	Postage meters and knowledge of postal regulations; a clean driving record
Equipment needed:	Solid, dependable vehicle
Staff required:	No
Handicapped opportunity:	Yes
Hidden costs:	Insurance, mileage

What You Do

Coupon books are a quick, positive means of getting a company's message across to consumers; what better incentive to buy than a discounted price for doing so? Producers of coupon books often don't have the time or resources to distribute the books themselves, so they hire out services such as yours to make sure that potential buyers receive their "golden" opportunities. You'll either drive around your community distributing such books by hand, or you'll use direct mail to ensure delivery by a specific date. Because coupons are of a time-sensitive nature, you'll always need to stay on track—invest in a good time-management system (a personal organizer or even a simple planner) to make sure that you never miss a deadline. Familiarize yourself early on with postal regulations; post offices regularly hold classes that teach you all the ins and outs of mass mailing. Networking with printers, advertising agencies, and coupon book producers will bring you the most business (rather than advertising your services in a publication).

What You Need

If you already have a dependable vehicle, you'll spend between $500-$1,500 getting this business off the ground. Mostly, you'll spend it on postage equipment and your own self-promotion. You'll charge about $300 per thousand, or $3-$5 per drop site if you're doing it via your own vehicle. You can expect your annual earnings to be between $10,000-$35,000 (depending on which method you choose to deliver the books).

Keys to Success

This is a good part-time profession, but it isn't exactly dependable, as many coupon book producers are disreputable or go out of business in a short period of time. Align yourself with the tried and true, and all will go smoothly. Otherwise, you might consider becoming a coupon book producer yourself.

Credit Consultant

Start-up cost:	$2,000-$3,000
Potential earnings:	25,000-$40,000
Typical fees:	Percentage of debt from client and from creditor (usually 10 to 15 percent from each)
Advertising:	Yellow Pages, seminars, speeches to community groups, classified ads, newspapers, radio spots
Qualifications:	A background in finance would be ideal
Equipment needed:	Business cards, letterhead, envelopes, computer, printer, fax, spreadsheet software
Staff required:	No
Handicapped opportunity:	Yes
Hidden costs:	Insurance, secretarial support if needed

What You Do

As a credit counselor you work with people who have overextended themselves financially. Your clients will come to you for help in dealing with an unmanageable credit burden. How big is this market? We've all heard the stories about the credit cards that pour into people's mailboxes, even cards with "Fido" printed on them in gold letters. Fido's credit rating has "already been preapproved." Credit card debt is at an historic high right now, and not everyone has budgeted for the payments. You will negotiate with the creditors to develop a manageable payment plan. Your client pays you a small percentage of what is owed, and the creditors also compensate you, as the plan you work out prevents the debt from most likely being a complete loss.

What You Need

Your office can be quite minimal at first; you should be able to get away with spending $3,000-$5,000 maximum. Since your business depends on how many clients you can secure (i.e., how many stay with the program, so to speak), you should be able to make a decent living ($25,000-$40,000).

Keys to Success

You're providing a valuable service to desperate, guilty, and frustrated people. This situation can be rewarding or draining, depending on the individuals involved. For most debtors, dealing with the pain feels much better than watching it spiral out of control. You will probably have the opportunity to add some education and psychological support into your services. This will allow you to gain the satisfaction of knowing that you have improved a person's or family's financial standing.

Damage Restoration Service

Start-up cost:	$15,000-$20,000
Potential earnings:	40,000-$65,000
Typical fees:	Varied according to damage; can be as little as $500 and as much as several thousand
Advertising:	Yellow Pages, coupon books, networking with Realtors and contractors
Qualifications:	Should have extensive knowledge about building structure and repair, codes and regulations regarding hazardous chemicals
Equipment needed:	A complete set of tools, painting/wallpapering equipment, varnishes and woodworking equipment, special solvents for cleaning up waste byproducts
Staff required:	Not initially
Handicapped opportunity:	Not typically
Hidden costs:	Insurance

What You Do

When a hurricane or other natural disaster strikes, any kind of professional who can fix homes or offices is called in to assess the damage, create an estimate, and work with insurance companies to get the job done. A damage restoration service is just one of the many services that can help fix the havoc that nature wreaked on a property. But it doesn't need to be a major natural disaster for your services to be called upon; more often than not, it is a fire or severe storm that warranted repair work to be done. Both fire and flood can cause structural damage to a building, but they can also ruin floors and walls. As a damage repair service professional, you'll spend the majority of your time fixing walls, ceilings, and floors, so you'll need to be familiar with every kind of chemical that cleans, repairs, or restores such surfaces. If peeling paint and waterlogged walls are up your alley, you'll enjoy each of the projects that comes your way. One thing is certain: this kind of work is never without its challenges.

What You Need

The smartest thing you can do is lease your equipment (and possibly even your tools) until you're sure of enough business to cover expenses. Leasing can cost you between $150-$300 per month, as opposed to a large initial outlay of cash ($10,000 or more) for repair equipment. Your charges will depend on the extent of damage done to the building; some repair jobs bill at a mere $500, while others are costlier ($1,500-$80,000).

Keys to Success

This business can be quite lucrative if you're in a hurricane-prone area, but sporadic if in other areas of the country. You might consider adding on related services, such as wallpaper installation or faux finishes, to keep the money rolling in.

Dance Instructor

Start-up cost:	$1,500-$3,000
Potential earnings:	25,500-$35,000
Typical fees:	$15 per lesson
Advertising:	Yellow Pages, entertainment sections of local papers, brochures, dance-wear retailers
Qualifications:	Experience, a degree to teach at the college/conservatory level
Equipment needed:	Studio, dance equipment
Staff required:	No
Handicapped opportunity:	No
Hidden costs:	Insurance, advertising

What You Do

Fred and Ginger made it look so good that everyone wanted to try it—and that's pretty much how the Fred Astaire School of Dance got its start so long ago. If you are an excellent dancer/choreographer yourself, and don't mind being patient with younger folks who aren't as focused as you are yet on the art of dance, you could dance your way into a respectable living. Physical strength, endurance, coordination, and creativity will help your business take off—but not more than referrals. Many dance instructors have years of training themselves or are retired from the profession. Some instructors will specialize in one area of dance such as tap or ballet in order to keep a cohesive following; others offer special packages where students can learn several different dances over a period of six to eight weeks.

What You Need

The cost includes the rental of studio space if you do not have a large room to hold classes in (start-up costs could be as little as $500). The other part of your expense will be advertising your services ($1,500-$3,000). Earnings, however, are pretty decent if you have a good reputation and get regular referrals. At the college level, a dance instructor could make $40,000+ and a private instructor $27,000.

Keys to Success

The long hours, especially evenings and weekends, may hinder some from pursuing this career. However, the grace, beauty, and strength of dancers are admired by many. Patience and the ability to critique without being hypercritical should come naturally if you want to be successful.

Dating Service

Start-up cost:	$5,000-$50,000 (depending on how high-tech you want to be)
Potential earnings:	50,000-$1.5 million
Typical fees:	$350 per client
Advertising:	Yellow Pages, classified ads, 900 numbers, television ads, singles magazines
Qualifications:	None
Equipment needed:	Extensive phone system for 900 numbers, computer (with many using computer video programs to showcase their clients)
Staff required:	Yes
Handicapped opportunity:	Yes
Hidden costs:	Computerized systems can run as high as $40,000

What You Do

Matchmaker, matchmaker, make me a living....Today's dating scene is vastly different from the old days, when a village woman made matches based on how her knee was feeling that day. Tired of meeting people in bars and the regular "sweat shops," many young professionals simply want a confidential, efficient way to meet the man or woman of their dreams. Because they don't have the time to screen a hundred or so applicants, you can provide this service for them—and at a competitive rate (just because they don't have time certainly doesn't mean they don't have money). You'll need to first decide what kind of dating service you'd most like to be: a well-respected, high-profile agency or an impersonal (yet profitable) 900 number. Either type requires you to manage profiles of your clients, so you'll need to have them answer questionnaires detailing their hobbies, interests, and desires in a potential mate. The next step is to make this information readily available to your client base—and keep track of your successes!

What You Need

Your start-up costs can be quite high, based on the fact that most of your competitors (both large and small) are investing in technology that does it all in a few steps: first conducting the interview, then recording the interviewee and, finally, selecting a potential match from the databank. All of this could run anywhere from $40,000-$150,000—so be sure to investigate those costs well enough to document them in your business plan, particularly if you are going to need investors.

Keys to Success

This is the love business, so what's not to love? For one thing, you'll be meeting quite an array of interesting people, and you'll be helping them to find long-lasting happiness. But what if it doesn't work out? Are you prepared to deal with broken hearts, all the while encouraging them to stay in the game? If the answer is yes, you'll be heartily rewarded for your efforts.

Day Care Service

Start-up cost:	$3,000
Potential earnings:	25,000-$40,000
Typical fees:	$40 per child per week or $50 per adult per week
Advertising:	Referral service, bulletin boards, classified ads
Qualifications:	Some states require a license and insurance
Equipment needed:	For children: cribs, toys, movies, and games; for adults:arts/crafts supplies and some form of entertainment
Staff required:	No (but many states impose a limit on the adult-to-child ratio; for example, in Ohio you may have no more than six children to one adult)
Handicapped opportunity:	No
Hidden costs:	Insurance

What You Do

The day care business has been growing in direct relation to the rising number of women choosing careers in addition to families—and never has it been more flexible. There is a need to care for both seniors and children—and a few innovative entrepreneurs have integrated both at their care centers, so that the two groups can enjoy and learn to appreciate one another. You can easily start a day care center in your home if you meet the necessary zoning requirements of your community. It works best if you have a large yard and extra room (perhaps a finished basement) so that there is plenty of room to play. You'll need to be clear in your rates/policies (especially about regular hours, vacations, and payment due dates), and be careful not to let the parents treat you like a baby-sitter who is at their beck and call. Be assertive about protecting your personal time with your own family.

What You Need

Your main start-up cost will be getting the word out about your service. Classified advertising, bulletin boards, and mothers' groups are a good way to build word of mouth. Your larger expenses will likely come from updating your home to meet zoning regulations; your home may have to pass inspection before licensing. If you decide not to license or not to carry insurance, be sure to let the parents/families know, because you will be held liable in the event of a disaster if you don't. Along those lines, be sure to familiarize yourself with safety procedures in case of an emergency.

Keys to Success

If you love to be around little people or seniors, you'll enjoy the opportunity to do so daily. Also, if you have children of your own, you can be paid for watching them play with others—not a bad position to be in. On the downside, although you are responsible for the children you watch, you are not their parent—a fact the parents themselves may constantly remind you of. Be sure to meet with the parents of children or the families of seniors on a regular basis to keep communications straight.

Designer/Retail Products

Start-up cost:	$10,000-$20,000
Potential earnings:	50,000-$150,000+
Typical fees:	Varied according to project; can be as low as $500 for a simple design sketch to several thousand for a complete design/technical layout with product specifications
Advertising:	Referral and direct mail
Qualifications:	Degree in product design
Equipment needed:	Computerized product design software (CAD)
Staff required:	No
Handicapped opportunity:	Yes
Hidden costs:	Insurance, excessive changes in product specifications (make sure you're clear on what's expected—and get it in writing)

What You Do

Behind every good product that is made is a strong design team, and you could offer your services to such a team on a contract basis—if you have a reputation for quality product design done on a quick-turnaround basis and within budget. If you can accomplish all of that, you stand a very good chance of building lasting relationships with product manufacturers; they'll depend on your flair and expertise to pull off products that at first seem challenging to make. Your experience in design for manufacturability (i.e., designing products with the manufacturing team's constraints in mind) will be a valuable commodity among your clients; they appreciate working with professionals who understand that good design isn't just artistic; it's practical, too.

What You Need

You'll need to invest between $10,000-$20,000 in a high-end computer with a large monitor and a computer-aided design (CAD) software package. Your advertising budget will be virtually nonexistent, because your area of expertise depends heavily on word of mouth. If you are successful in building the kinds of contacts you'll need to survive on your own, you'll be making anywhere from $50,000-$150,000 or more; obviously, if you're working for large, well-known manufacturers, your earnings will be on the high end because these companies are more apt to pay big bucks for quality design.

Keys to Success

Your work will not always be your own; since you'll be working on a contract basis most of the time, you will often be brought in to solve design problems or pick up where another designer left off—not the biggest boost to your creativity. Still, the work is solid, it's demanding, and it's profitable for the talented.

Desktop Publisher

Start-up cost:	$15,000-$25,000
Potential earnings:	20,00-$100,000
Typical fees:	$500 (newsletter) to $20,000 (for a large-run book or magazine)
Advertising:	Direct solicitation, Yellow Pages, local publications, word of mouth, networking, advertising in writers' magazines
Qualifications:	Computer skills, knowledge of typefaces, design, and layout, writing and editing skills, communication skills
Equipment needed:	Computer with scanner, laser printer, and CD-ROM, publishing, word-processing, and drawing software, fax, office furniture, business card, letterhead, envelopes
Staff required:	No
Handicapped opportunity:	Yes
Hidden costs:	Marketing; keeping up with changes in software

What You Do

Desktop publishing (DTP) enables people who understand graphic design and typography to offer a range of services to clients. Skills with computer software will allow you to produce books, flyers, and almost every kind of printed material in between. Many small DTP businesses succeed by specializing; for example, they might create newsletters for a specific type of business. Others produce entire books or focus on annual reports. Most will provide only the camera-ready master and subcontract the larger printing jobs to a commercial printer. The DTP field includes many small and large businesses, but there is room for people who do excellent work, produce it on time, and focus on their clients' needs and expectations.

What You Need

The computer equipment required can be very expensive, depending largely on the graphics capability you need. And you must have a work space that supports the complex nature of some DTP tasks. Figure marketing costs, too, of $1,000-$2,000 in the financial section of your business plan. Your income will be dependent upon how many clients you can win in a short period of time, so you'll need to advertise your services (unless your former employer has become a major client). Billing can be done hourly ($50-$75 per) or, more typically, on a per-job basis. Smaller jobs can net $50-$300; larger ones can bring in $5,000 or more.

Keys to Success

Although working on several different creative projects at one time can be interesting and challenging, the pressure can be unbelievable. In the days of instant information and 24-hour turnaround, everybody expects their work done today. That can be a problem when you have 10 or more clients you're juggling—try to express realistic deadlines with your clients to avoid all-nighters and stress-filled days, and be sure to schedule time for yourself to complete the work.

Expert Advice

What sets your business apart from others like it?

"We produce healthy recipes and a common-sense approach to healthy living," says JoAnna M. Lund, President and CEO of Healthy Exchange, Inc., in DeWitt, Louisiana. "We appeal to the average person and offer quick, healthy recipes that taste good using easy-to-find ingredients."

Things you couldn't do without:

A computer and laser printer, plus a fax machine.

Marketing tips/advice:

It's challenging to stay on top of changes in your field, but it can pay you well to do so, says Lund. Make sure you're an expert on that which you're reporting about.

If you had to do it all over again . . .

"Nothing. I'm quite happy where I am."

Desktop Publisher:
Community-Based Coupon Books

Start-up cost:	$1,000-$5,000
Potential earnings:	15,000-$30,000
Typical fees:	Ad rates vary (but generally start at $300-$500 per ad); plus, you can sell the books to the public for an average cover price of $29.95
Advertising:	Yellow Pages, community newspapers, local radio
Qualifications:	Ability to relate to both businesses and the public, one-on-one
Equipment needed:	Computer, software, printer
Staff required:	Yes
Handicapped opportunity:	Yes
Hidden costs:	Phone and mileage for ad sales reps

What You Do

You'll be providing a useful service for both the businesses and the public. Businesses offer discounts to attract customers; you are aiding them in their marketing strategies by publicizing these discounts. You will sell advertising space in your coupon books, produce them with a printer, and then sell them to consumers through the mail. If you enjoy people and are good at presenting your "product," you will find that many customers in your community are receptive to receiving discounts from businesses they know and respect. The best part is, your revenue is collected from both sides (the advertiser and the buyer)—so you have a double stream of income.

What You Need

It requires a lot of legwork to get a business like this started, but the end-product—an inexpensively printed booklet—is your major cost. Perhaps you can strike a deal with a local printer, offering a percentage of the take. Or, shell out the $1,000-$5,000 in your first six months of start-up—if you sell enough ads and begin to generate simultaneous interest from the public, you'll make enough to cover printing (and still have quite a bit left over).

Keys to Success

You're creating a business enterprise out of almost nothing as you develop and sell your coupon book. This is truly a business that depends on hard work. Many individuals find a deep sense of satisfaction in knowing that they have provided a useful community service while making a profit at the same time. However, gathering enough coupon commitments from businesses is difficult: selling has its discouraging days. This is an enterprise for people with a lot of determination and a great deal of free time to successfully promote the book to the public.

Digital Imaging Service

Start-up cost:	$20,000-$40,000
Potential earnings:	25,000-$45,000
Typical fees:	$15-$45 per scanned-image product
Advertising:	Yellow Pages, mall kiosks and other high people-volume locations
Qualifications:	Training in equipment
Equipment needed:	Computer with scanner and video imaging capability
Staff required:	No
Handicapped opportunity:	Possibly
Hidden costs:	Insurance, equipment maintenance and upgrades

What You Do

The digital craze is on—and it's not limited to musical instruments or compact disks. You can cash in on the trend by starting your own digital imaging service. You've probably seen such businesses in your local shopping mall or at a community flea market: the proprietor simply takes a video image of a person and places it onto a computer screen for printing on a color printer; the image is then transferred to a product (such as a felt banner, T-shirt, or coffee mug) and a personalized gift has been created. It's that simple, and the product generally sells itself if positioned in a high-traveled area. You can buy a franchise or start your own version if you are familiar enough with the equipment and can work with product vendors. Expect to market your service aggressively; you'll need to talk to people and have excellent sales ability to make enough money to cover your expenses (particularly mall rent). Still, it's a fun method of gift-giving for many consumers—and they will buy if you are visible enough.

What You Need

You'll need $20,000-$40,000 for your equipment and space rental, slightly more if you buy a franchise. Your equipment will include a computer with color printer, video camera, and software that permits image transfer from video to computer screen to printer. Thermal transfer equipment will also be necessary to produce those personalized coffee mugs and T-shirts. On the plus side, you might see as much as $45,000 for little effort on your part.

Keys to Success

Your business will fluctuate according to season; expect low times in the fall and spring, and a Christmas high (complete with long hours and heavy volume).

Direct Marketing/Sales

Start-up cost:	$1,000-$3,000
Potential earnings:	20,000-$50,000
Typical fees:	Percentage basis
Advertising:	Word of mouth, direct mail, cold calling
Qualifications:	Energy, persistence, ability to manage time well
Equipment needed:	None
Staff required:	None at first
Handicapped opportunity:	No
Hidden costs:	Some organizations charge for catalogs and other sales materials, attendance at meetings, inventory replacement

What You Do

Many, many people try their hand at direct sales, yet only a few of them make it big. What is the difference? Consider your goals. Do you want to make a few bucks and sell a line of products you like to family, friends, and acquaintances? Is your main goal to make your own purchases at a discount? Or are you planning to put the effort and commitment into direct sales that you would into establishing any other type of small business? Many products are best sold person-to-person because they benefit from demonstration. Finding an excellent product line to work with is vital, and you should feel confident in the company as well. The rest is up to your selling skills and personal drive. Many direct sales-oriented companies encourage their salespeople to create networks, additional salespeople whose sales bring a percentage to the person who recruited them. This practice acts as an incentive to everyone in the sales force. It is the way to large earnings, if you can achieve it.

What You Need

Costs to start are very low (around $1,000), but watch out for hidden charges and fees from the manufacturers. These should warn you off the companies that might exploit you. An income of $20,000 in the beginning is realistic.

Keys to Success

How many opportunities are left in this country in which your own hard work will define your success? Direct sales is one of them. Are you comfortable with cold-calling? Are you committed enough to keep yourself going with no one to answer to but yourself? Do you genuinely like people and enjoy helping them find products that will add something to their lives? Or, on the other hand, would you be satisfied with direct sales as an add-on to some other activity? Be sure you're clear on what you want, and what you will need to do to achieve it. If you have big ambitions, you'll need a very big commitment to achieve them in direct marketing and sales.

Disability Consultant

Start-up cost:	$2,000-$4,000
Potential earnings:	50,000-$75,000
Typical fees:	$60-$80 per hour
Advertising:	Direct mail, referrals, membership in business organizations
Qualifications:	Extensive experience in field, college degree in related area, ability to communicate well with employers and employees, good writing skills
Equipment needed:	Computer, printer, office furniture, business cards, letterhead, envelopes
Staff required:	No
Handicapped opportunity:	Yes
Hidden costs:	Insurance, dues for organizations, conferences and seminars

What You Do

As a disability consultant you will advise corporations on disability claims and assist them in meeting the requirements of all government and regulatory bodies. Nothing is cut and dried about the disability field, and rapid changes have left even the best-intentioned employers confused about what they must do to be in compliance. Disability claims made by employees are a major cost in some industries, and your recommendations for alterations in the setup of the workplace or refinements in work processes could be seen as extremely valuable.

Managing medical claims is another important function. The conflicts arising from the most common worker problem—back pain—need expert management, both for medical treatment and for the maintenance of good relations with the employee. The third aspect of this field is the requirement to make reasonable accommodations for disabled workers. Creative consultants can often find ways to make small alterations, for example, in the height of a counter, that can enable a wheelchair-bound person to fill a position at the company.

What You Need

Most of your work will be carried out at the companies you are assessing and handling claims for, but you will need your own office for production of reports and possibly for client meetings. Expect to spend $2,000-$4,000 for your computer system and first few months of rent. Charge $60-$80 per hour for this service that can save a company thousands of dollars per year.

Keys to Success

If you have experience in this complex field and can communicate with both sides, the disabled and the employer, you can build a business as a disability consultant. In fact, many disabled people do just this, using their own perspectives to enrich the services they can offer to other organizations. Enabling challenged people to hold a job is an important service, and it keeps employers on the right side of the law as well.

Dog Trainer

Start-up cost:	$1,000-2,000
Potential earnings:	35,000-$45,000
Typical fees:	$300 for a three-week session is fairly common
Advertising:	Flyers, direct mail, Yellow Pages, classifieds, referrals from vets, free clinics
Qualifications:	Experience with different breeds, track record of success, patience, and credibility
Equipment needed:	Space for pets to roam, be fed, etc., kennel area for sleeping
Staff required:	No
Handicapped opportunity:	No
Hidden costs:	Advertising, travel

What You Do

Working dogs need considerable training, depending on the jobs they have to perform. Drug-sniffing dogs, guard dogs, guide dogs, movie dogs, and herding dogs all have their specialized training systems. Often these dogs receive much of their training from their breeders or owners, although some trainers of working dogs have national reputations for their skill and effectiveness.

A much bigger market is training services for pets. Most pet owners wake up a bit late to the need for training (usually after half of the carpet has been eaten), but you can present your service as the solution to those nagging problems that make pet dogs so frustrating at times. Some trainers give classes for owner and dog together while others go to a pet's home and provide individual sessions. Network with veterinarians; they are usually the first to hear about animal problems.

What You Need

Your main start-up cost is for whatever marketing and advertising approaches seem best for your community. Somewhere between $500-$1,000 would be an average amount to spend on launching this business. Remember, though, that you'll be charging as much as $300 per dog for a three-week session—that can add up to a tidy profit early in the game.

Keys to Success

This job is immensely enjoyable if you love dogs and can tolerate their owners (remember, you'll be training them, too). Gaining the trust of an animal is an essential part of any training process, but some trainers find that getting the human side of the equation to cooperate is even harder. Once the pets in your class begin to give up eating the curtains and jumping all over Grandma, however, you will seem like a genius. Then the class can proceed to the really hard stuff such as coming when called (the pet) and being patient (the owner). For most trainers this is not a route to wealth, but a decent living can be made if you keep up your marketing.

Doll Repair Service

Start-up cost:	$500-$1,000
Potential earnings:	20,000-$40,000
Typical fees:	Depends on what needs to be replaced and whether the doll is an antique (could be $50-$300 or more)
Advertising:	Yellow Pages, antique shows, specialty shops, hobby magazines
Qualifications:	Enjoying the art of doll-making and repair; special knowledge of antique dolls
Equipment needed:	Spare parts, precision tools
Staff required:	No
Handicapped opportunity:	Yes
Hidden costs:	Liability insurance, shipping

What You Do

This is a thriving business. As dolls get older, they become more popular to collect—and if they're going to be worth anything later on, they need to be in the best possible shape to command the highest dollars. One early Barbie doll can be worth as much as $500, but only if she's in mint condition. That's where you come in: you repair and restore dolls to their original state—and sometimes that means purchasing used dolls for spare parts. Keep all types of doll parts on hand and network with other repair services to locate spare parts. Pay attention to detail and have the hands of a surgeon. Dolls aren't just plastic—there are many different types, such as bisque, china, wax, and mechanical. Know what is special about each doll and what precautions to take when repairing them. Market your service especially hard at antique fairs and specialty shops. Have them keep your business cards by their cash register. You may want to offer related services such as collectibles connections (matching buyers and sellers) and a retail doll shop as well.

What You Need

Advertising will be key to generating most of your business (about $1,000); the rest of your cost will go to spare parts (about $500 to start). Some may be expensive, so you may want to hold off ordering until there is a need. You will be repairing high-end and antique dolls, so gauge your earnings between $20,000-$40,000.

Keys to Success

Some doll repair services have given the business a bad name. You'll have to overcome this by knowing the ins and outs of doll-making. It is much easier to repair something if you know how it is put together. Take your time and know what you are doing; if you ruin a doll you may have to buy it. Be sure your packaging is secure when you deliver or ship to avoid any damage.

Draftsman/Blueprinting Service

Start-up cost:	$5,000-$10,000
Potential earnings:	35,000-$65,000
Typical fees:	$150-$500 per blueprint
Advertising:	Yellow Pages, referral, ads in trade publications
Qualifications:	Degree in drafting
Equipment needed:	Blueprint photocopier, drafting table, related small tools
Staff required:	No
Handicapped opportunity:	Not typically
Hidden costs:	Insurance, equipment maintenance/upgrade

What You Do

You're detail-oriented, with a flair for putting the finishing touches on someone else's work. You've also likely studied drafting in college before embarking on this entrepreneurial endeavor; you have the experience that your customers will eventually come to rely on. As a draftsman/blueprinting service, you will ultimately produce the blueprints that architects and builders need to complete their dynamic new projects. You will make any requested number of copies of each blueprint as well. Although individuals may hire you for smaller projects, most of your customers will be architects and building professionals, so you'll need to be well-connected to get any share of the work that's out there. Set yourself apart by adding additional services or special treatment (such as free delivery to work sites).

What You Need

You'll need between $5,000-$10,000 to get started in drafting and blueprinting, primarily to cover your equipment costs for such items as a blueprint photocopier ($4,000 or so) and drafting table with drafting pencils, etc. You'll likely earn $35,000-$65,000 for your efforts.

Keys to Success

It's very precise work you're doing, and often it's a thankless job (seeing as how the architects and builders take all the glory). Oh, well . . . you should always remember that without you, the project might not have gotten done. Stick close to the builders and architects, since they'll ultimately make up your referral system.

Efficiency Expert

Start-up cost:	$5,000-$10,000
Potential earnings:	35,000-$75,000+ (depending on your market)
Typical fees:	$75-$100 per hour or a monthly retainer of $3,000-$5,000
Advertising:	Trade publications, Yellow Pages, direct mail, business newspapers
Qualifications:	Ability to spot potential problems and time-wasters before and as they occur
Equipment needed:	Computer, fax/modem, printer, resource materials
Staff required:	No
Handicapped opportunity:	Yes
Hidden costs:	Insurance, underbilling for amount of time spent (watch your own clock)

What You Do

Corporations often have CEOs who want the company run like clockwork, particularly if there are production goals to be met regularly. As an efficiency expert, you will come into a company for a period of about two to four weeks and carefully monitor exactly how things are being done. You will ask workers questions such as, "Why are you repeatedly moving across the room to accomplish one simple task?" and "Is there any other way to minimize the steps involved in your particular process?" You are, in a sense, a detective searching for answers to the big question (which is, of course: "How can this company achieve more in a better and more economical way?"). Next, you'll print up a report or make a formal presentation, telling the CEO where he or she can improve operations. You should have a rather broad background in business operations, management experience, and a strong eye for detail. After all, your client companies will be paying you big bucks to figure out what needs to be improved upon at their facilities; you have to convey the idea that you're worth it, so watch your own image and always give it 110 percent.

What You Need

Start-up will be relatively low (in the $5,000-$10,000 range), but you should do quite well when you consider what you might be able to earn if you're good at what you do ($35,000-$75,000 or more). You'll need a basic office setup and lots of good resource materials to help workers achieve greater effectiveness.

Keys to Success

While some corporate moguls will hire you to tell them what's wrong with their organization, they may not be willing to actually listen. You'll need to be clear from the beginning that you are merely offering your professional opinions and advice—that way, your personal liability will be kept in check.

Electrical Contractor

Start-up cost:	$10,000-$15,000
Potential earnings:	40,000-$60,000
Typical fees:	$40 per service call; more for parts and labor
Advertising:	Yellow Pages, classifieds, neighborhood flyers, community bulletin boards, word of mouth, radio spots
Qualifications:	Skill and experience as an electrician, ability to manage time and expenses, good people skills. Most states require certification and regular credit hours toward career development
Equipment needed:	Tools, parts, and equipment related to the nature of the work, van, marketing materials.
Staff required:	No
Handicapped opportunity:	No
Hidden costs:	Inventory of parts, vehicle maintenance, insurance

What You Do

Skilled electricians are always in demand, especially ones who can work with undecided homeowners and impatient small business people. As the general population becomes less handy with tools and wires, your electrical knowledge and expertise will become more and more valuable. This is a classic one-person business, and you may find considerable competition. You will need good estimating skills to assess the cost and complexity of the work you are asked to do. Sometimes it seems as if electricians have to be part detective to interpret the hidden wiring in an old house or to trace the cause of a short "somewhere in the wall." Of course, you'll be familiar with code standards in all the communities in your service area.

What You Need

Costs are relatively high as you must equip yourself to do whatever electrical job is offered. You'll also need to secure certification, and your educational requirements to stay certified may also demand that you take regular refresher courses. Set aside at least $5,000 for all of this—then add your equipment, liability insurance, and related costs.

Keys to Success

Many electricians have made an excellent living by focusing on upgrading the wiring in old houses. If your area has a charming neighborhood of old Victorians, twenties bungalows, or quaint cottages that are being restored, you have a golden opportunity to build a client base. Other electricians work closely with an independent builder to install wiring in new structures. For these jobs, getting the work done according to the overall construction schedule will have a big influence on profits for the builder. Your planning and time-management skills can help build you a steady stream of referrals and repeat projects from builders.

Employee Benefits Consultant

Start-up cost:	$5,000-$8,000
Potential earnings:	30,000-$70,000
Typical fees:	$25 and up
Advertising:	Direct mail, networking, memberships in business and community organizations
Qualifications:	Extensive experience in insurance sales, ability to reach business owners, detail orientation, communications skills
Equipment needed:	Office furniture, computer, modem, fax, laser printer, cellular phone, business card, letterhead, envelopes
Staff required:	No
Handicapped opportunity:	Yes
Hidden costs:	Preparation of presentation materials, on-line fees, errors and omissions insurance

What You Do

An effective employee benefits program is an important factor in building a loyal workforce. The challenge is to create a combination of benefits that meets the needs of the organization and also fits its budget. As an employee benefits consultant, you will help growing businesses survey their employees to learn their needs and wants regarding employer-paid insurance. You will work with the business owner to design the best combination of benefits for the dollars available. The likeliest market is businesses with 20 to 200 employees, which are too small to have a large human resources department.

What You Need

Most of your client contact will take place at their locations, so your office can be functional rather than impressive ($4,000 should get you started). You'll need to be easy for potential and current clients to reach, and you'll need to produce professional-looking presentations to client companies. You should plan to earn about $30,000 in the beginning.

Keys to Success

Many insurance agents have terrible sales approaches. They seem very eager for their commissions and do not give ongoing service throughout the year. As annual review time rolls around, these agents show up again with a plan to change to new providers for a few dollars less. But implementation and employee education are lacking. You will be able to set yourself apart if your focus is on customer service, not your own profit (at least outwardly). Experience in assisting with claims and with any conflicts that may arise is also an important selling point for your enterprise.

Employee Leasing

Start-up cost:	$15,000-$35,000
Potential earnings:	60,000-$80,000
Typical fees:	Mark up the going rates by 40 to 50 percent
Advertising:	Direct mail, networking in business and trade associations, publishing a newsletter
Qualifications:	Knowledge of and contacts in a specific field, excellent organizational skills
Equipment needed:	Office furniture, computer, printer, fax, telephone headset, business card, letterhead, envelopes, brochure
Staff required:	No
Handicapped opportunity:	Yes
Hidden costs:	Liability insurance against employee misconduct

What You Do

While you may not be able to compete with the big general help agencies, a small employee leasing agency can provide workers with specialized skills who cannot be reached through the traditional temp services. This business produces good earnings relative to time and materials: you're not doing the actual work—just the organization. Build your database of specialists in a field you have experience with, then begin direct mail to your prospective clients.

What You Need

Although the cost of building your initial database and center of operations is not high, you will need a sizable initial investment ($20,000) to cover the delays in cash flow between your clients and your employees. You could see at least $60,000 at the end of your first year.

Keys to Success

You may need to consult an attorney to stay abreast of the laws regarding taxes, workers' compensation, and employment. Some types of temps will need to be bonded, and you will need to measure the advantages of incorporation over the extra costs and red tape involved.

Etiquette Adviser

Start-up cost:	Under $1,000
Potential earnings:	20,000-$50,000
Typical fees:	$15-$35 per class
Advertising:	Newspapers, business publications, networking with community organizations
Qualifications:	Extremely good taste and a sense of moral superiority
Equipment needed:	Good resource materials
Staff required:	No
Handicapped opportunity:	Yes
Hidden costs:	Networking in high places could set you out some considerable cash in your entertainment budget—be careful not to live too well until you're making enough money to cover it

What You Do

You've always known the answer to seemingly eternal questions: which fork do I start with, and what is that spoon across the top of my plate really for? People rely on your expertise for such sticky situations as who to invite to a wedding, where to place divorced parents in a room together, when not to send a thank-you card, and how long is too long to respond to an RSVP. That's why your talents are needed, but how do you charge for them and still maintain your dignity? Easy—you offer your services in six simple courses. It's too difficult for an etiquette advisor to make serious money handling each question piecemeal, so develop a curriculum and offer your classes to the public or (better yet) the Corporate Confused seeking to become the Corporate Elite. You could offer tips on everything from proper conversation to handling potentially embarrassing situations; for instance, what should you do if your crouton shoots out from your plate to your bosses' during lunch?

What You Need

Your start-up costs are so minimal, you needn't worry about whether it is proper to launch this business. Just make sure you have good reference materials for the questions that stump you—and leave a little extra for entertaining (which could be your main course to bringing in business).

Keys to Success

You'll love the authority and power of being a moral authority—but try not to let it get to your head. The last thing any one of your clients wants is a know-it-all. Be matter-of-fact, and try to inject some humor into your profession. Believe it or not, humor is the best teacher in a delicate, personal subject such as etiquette.

Executive Search Firm

Start-up cost:	$5,500-$9,000
Potential earnings:	From $40,000 to as much as $150,000 (gross)
Typical fees:	Varies, but often equals 25 percent of first-year earnings of person placed with client
Advertising:	Cold calls, attending trade shows, newsletter to potential clients, direct mail, ads in publications
Qualifications:	Excellent people skills, patience, self-confidence, knowledge of specialized fields to be able to select appropriate candidates for jobs
Equipment needed:	Computer and office equipment, telephone, business cards, letterhead, brochures
Staff required:	None
Handicapped opportunity:	Yes
Hidden costs:	Phone expenses and advertising costs could exceed budget early

What You Do

Executive recruiters (also known as "headhunters") are paid by companies to fill man-agement, professional, and technical slots within their firms. Most of a recruiter's work is done via phone and E-mail, so you can do this job anywhere, although networking face-to-face is also important. You will collect as many qualified applicants as you can (gleaned mostly from your vast resume collection and a few friends in high places). Many consultants choose niches in which to specialize; others serve all areas. A sales personality is helpful in this business, as is the ability to be self-motivated. Often, finding good people for the positions is easier than finding clients who will hire you to conduct the job search. You will need self-confidence, tenacity, and good networking skills to make it as a recruiter. This career choice gives you a great deal of flexibility and personal freedom, since you can work from any location that has a phone.

What You Need

A computer and printer are essential, as is database, word processing, and communications software. These items will cost from $2,500 to $5,000. You will need a telephone, a headset, and fax, along with office furniture and business cards, letterhead, and brochures to promote your business. These pieces will cost $1,500-$4,500. You'll earn an average 25 percent of the new hire's salary—so it behooves you to search for the high-end, top-level managers.

Keys to Success

Competition for the best companies and top-notch candidates is stiff, and you get paid only when you successfully match a company with a candidate, but the financial rewards can be considerable, and the satisfaction of helping a good candidate to find a job and your client to fill a key position, make your efforts worthwhile.

Fan Club Management

Start-up cost:	Minimal, if artist pays for expenses; $3,000-$5,000 if you're totally self-sufficient
Potential earnings:	10,000-$30,000
Typical fees:	$10-$25 each for memberships; you can also derive a percentage from merchandising products
Advertising:	Direct mail and word of mouth
Qualifications:	Membership in the National Association of Fan Clubs
Equipment needed:	Computer, printer, fax/modem, copier, database/label and desktop publishing software, phone system with voice mail capabilities
Staff required:	Not initially
Handicapped opportunity:	Possibly
Hidden costs:	Postage and printing costs

What You Do

When a celebrity becomes a celebrity, the last thing they want to do is sit around answering fan mail. Still, many celebrities do realize that their fans are who put them where they are, and they don't necessarily want to ignore them. That's why it makes sense for popular artists to hire fan club managers to keep in touch with their many admirers: they recognize the importance of staying where they are by staying in touch with those whose opinions ultimately matter the most. If you have the right credentials (such as having been a professional writer or prior experience in radio or television), then you might be able to convince a celebrity to let you take charge of his or her mail. In addition to opening and answering huge bags of mail, you'll offer services such as quarterly or semiannual newsletter and merchandising (offering promotional products like T-shirts, posters, and autographed photos for sale and taking a small percentage for yourself). Like the celebrity, if you're in the right place at the right time, this could be the right opportunity for you.

What You Need

You won't need very much at all to get started if you can convince a celebrity to foot the bill for his or her fan club; some celebrities actually do see the worth of paying someone else to handle the mail and requests for signed photos. However, most fan clubs operate on their own (with or without celebrity endorsement, but obviously it's easier with), leaving you with a start-up cost of $3,000-$5,000 if you operate on a shoestring. You could sell memberships for $10-$25 each, and offer incentives for joining (such as a free T-shirt or baseball cap). At any rate, you'll be producing newsletters (at $500-$1,000 each) a few times per year, so you'll need to be sure you've sold enough memberships to cover printing and postage rates. If all goes well, you could make $10,000-$30,000 per year doing something enjoyable and high-profile; not enough to make you rich, but certainly enough to make you smile.

Keys to Success

This seems on the surface to be a glamorous job, and it is—until you get barraged with unreasonable requests, tight deadlines on newsletters, and ego-maniacal celebrities who think treating "underlings" accordingly is the path to greater success. It might help if you continually remind the celebrity just how much more money the fan club is ultimately making them in boosting record or ticket sales.

Expert Advice

What sets your business apart from others like it?

"We are an authorized fan club management company and I have a highly specialized background in radio," says Joyce Logan, President of Fan Emporium, Inc., a Branford, Connecticut-based firm representing entertainers such as Michael Bolton, Carly Simon, John Mellencamp, and Mariah Carey. "I put myself in the fan's shoes and give every fan the personal touch . . . we produce newsletters, answer fan mail, sell authorized merchandise, and even have a 900-number service for fans to get concert updates and messages from their favorite superstars."

Things you couldn't do without:

Computer with a good database management program, printer and labeling program, fax, and modem.

Marketing tips/advice:

"Start with just one celebrity, and know that you can't just run a fan club for a little while. This is a serious commitment to the celebrity and the fans. You're dealing with people's emotional links to their favorite celebrity . . . you are a 'merchant of emotions.'"

If you had to do it all over again . . .

"I would have made contracts with the artists a little bit differently, so that they would assume all the costs of printing and mailing. We are a public relations firm just like any other, and we need to be recognized as such to stay profitable."

Fax-on-Demand Service

Start-up cost:	$12,000-$15,000
Potential earnings:	20,000-$50,000
Typical fees:	$150-$300/month to cover incoming calls, with unlimited responses, or lower monthly fees with charge for each response
Advertising:	Advertising in trade journals, direct mail, direct solicitations, seminars
Qualifications:	Knowledge of technology and software, marketing ability
Equipment needed:	Modified computer with special fax board, customized software, scanner, office furniture
Staff required:	No
Handicapped opportunity:	Yes
Hidden costs:	Additional phone lines

What You Do

You will provide the technology that allows smaller companies and professionals to match the fax-on-demand systems being set up in-house by large organizations. Your clients will make information available to their customers or employees around the clock. These people call to ask for information, and your automated faxing system sends them the newsletter, data sheet, or restaurant menu they have requested instantly. Automatic broadcasting can reach sales reps or members of an interest group. Once businesses understand how their marketing efforts can be supported by fax-on-demand, they will form an ongoing clientele and a source of steady income for you. But your first task will be to help them see the possibilities inherent in this new technology. You're going to be creating the market for this service.

What You Need

This is an expensive business to get into, with start-up costs averaging $15,000. Getting the funding to set it up may present quite a challenge, since it is a relatively new type of business with little track record to fall back on. Still, if you're creative, you'll find ways to purchase the equipment you need economically; and you'll be billing $150-$300 per client per month, so you will have decent income once you're customer base is well-established.

Keys to Success

You're going to need a silver tongue and a genius for marketing to get a fax-on-demand service off the ground. Finding organizations that need to send out up-to-date printed materials in high volume will be the first step. Creating possibilities that click in with your prospects' needs and assumptions will allow you to get your message through to the people who can see advantages to cutting-edge approaches.

Financial Aid Consultant

Start-up cost:	$2,000-$4,000
Potential earnings:	15,000-$40,000
Typical fees:	Flat rates of $150-$500
Advertising:	Yellow Pages, classified ads, direct mail, membership and participation in community organizations related to education, seminars and speeches for community groups, networking, referrals from high schools
Qualifications:	Experience as a school guidance counselor or college admissions officer, extensive knowledge of the field, ability to relate well to college applicants and their parents
Equipment needed:	Office with conference table for meeting clients, computer, suite software, modem, fax, printer, business cards, letterhead, envelopes
Staff required:	No
Handicapped opportunity:	Yes
Hidden costs:	Subscriptions, on-line time, dues

What You Do

The cost of higher education continues to escalate. And while it is always said that many types of financial aid are available, finding them is quite another matter. Families need guidance and assistance in preparing the paperwork and in finding the sources to which they can apply. Your services as a financial aid consultant will be in great demand once your name gets known to the community at large. Word of mouth from students you have helped, and their parents, will bring you new business regularly. You will need a lot of familiarity with financial aid options to make a success of this type of consulting, and you will need excellent people skills as well. Some financial aid consultants research options on the Internet, while other specialize in aid for secondary, or even elementary school tuition. The bulk of the market, though, is for students entering college.

What You Need

Keeping your own knowledge up to date and providing a suitable place for interviewing clients are your two main expenses ($2,000 to start). Part-time could earn you $15,000; rates could range anywhere from $150-$500 per job.

Keys to Success

Many parents experience major sticker shock when they first realize how much having one or more children enrolled in the ivied halls is going to set them back. And even the "simple" financial aid forms for determining basic financial need are far from easy to cope with. Beyond that, you can give vital help in finding the multitude of special scholarships for students with a certain heritage, a special academic interest, or some other unusual characteristic.

Financial Planner

Start-up cost:	$5,000-$8,000
Potential earnings:	40,000-$60,000
Typical fees:	Set fee depending on investments, typically $250-$500 or more
Advertising:	Referrals, networking, memberships in community and business groups, local magazines and newspapers, programs of fund-raisers
Qualifications:	Certification is becoming essential; familiarity with financial issues. Excellent people skills for marketing, and for creating a plan suitable to the client's needs; ability to inspire trust
Equipment needed:	Computer, printer, suite software, fax, modem, on-line account, furniture, business card, letterhead, envelopes
Staff required:	No
Handicapped opportunity:	Yes
Hidden costs:	Subscriptions to newspapers and financial periodicals, errors and omissions insurance

What You Do

The market for financial planning services is becoming very large, especially as the baby boom generation draws close to retirement. Your difficulty in establishing your business will be that so many others are competing with you. You'll probably need to be part of a close network of family, friends, and acquaintances who will work with you and refer you to their friends. This is a very personal business, and your ability to inspire confidence will be vital. Creativity in helping your clients plan their financial future and skill at helping them achieve those goals will set you apart. Is there an underserved group you can target? Can you design plans for self-employed people, the elderly, or investment clubs? Can you work in association with related businesses such as accountant firms to add your service onto their offerings?

What You Need

Your office needs to give you the up-to-the-moment information you need for proper service to your clients (around $3,000 to start); however, you could earn upward of $40,000.

Keys to Success

Most people manage their money very poorly, if at all. They don't plan well or budget, and they haven't faced up to the question of providing for retirement. All these are difficult topics, and can make dealing with these sensitive issues uncomfortable. You can smooth things over with a reassuring attitude, and by paying attention to the details of your client's finances that they obviously overlook.

Expert Advice

What sets your business apart from others like it?

Dianne Winnen, a Certified Financial Planner in Akron, Ohio, says she is different because her business caters to middle-income people rather than focusing on seniors with retirement funds. "I'm one of 31,000 CFPs in the country, and I'm proud to be a part of a select group."

Things you couldn't do without:

"I couldn't do without my computer, telephone, and copier."

Marketing tips/advice:

"You really have to want to be in this field to make it successful for you. Read and educate yourself about business matters."

If you had to do it all over again . . .

"I would've gone in with more realistic expectations about what it would take to survive the first couple of years."

First Aid/CPR Instructor

Start-up cost:	$300-$500
Potential earnings:	15,000-$20,000
Typical fees:	$10-$20 per participant
Advertising:	YMCA, hospitals, churches, associations, schools, swim clubs
Qualifications:	American Red Cross or American Heart Association certification required
Equipment needed:	"Annie-are-you-okay" dummy for practice
Staff required:	No
Handicapped opportunity:	Possibly
Hidden costs:	Some educational materials could cost you more than expected; you'll find out what you really need and what you don't from your training instructor

What You Do

The blond woman is stretched out on the floor, with a small crowd of people around her. "Annie, Annie—are you okay?" someone asks. She is not breathing, and one person gives mouth-to-mouth resuscitation while another provides heart massage to bring her back to life. Does this scene ring a bell? Many of us have been given CPR training at schools, churches, or swim clubs, and if you've always been interested in teaching people to save lives, this could be your calling. It is not particularly profitable (as volunteers from many associations offer similar courses), but you could set yourself apart by adding on a related service, such as a speakers bureau that offers tips on CPR in the Age of AIDS or some other topic of current concern.

What You Need

It really doesn't cost much to instruct others on the benefits of life-saving techniques; your biggest up-front cost will be for the practice dummy and related resource materials such as models and diagrams. One innovative place you could offer your services is to restaurants; their staffs always have diagrams of what to do in an emergency, but do they really read them and have they actually practiced on anyone? Not likely. Offer them a group discount!

Keys to Success

The challenge of setting yourself apart from competing services offered free of charge can seem overwhelming at first—but get creative and you can make a small, yet profitable, business for yourself. Be positive and look for the big guys who can help provide a steady flow of business (i.e., health clubs, restaurant associations, and human resource managers at large corporations).

Food Delivery Service

Start-up cost:	$1,000 or more
Potential earnings:	25,000 and up
Typical fees:	$5-$10 per "run"
Advertising:	Brochures in office buildings, newspaper ads
Qualifications:	Ability to create attractive, healthy, portable meals
Equipment needed:	Kitchen, cooking supplies and equipment, food packaging
Staff required:	Part-time delivery person, if needed
Handicapped opportunity:	Yes
Hidden costs:	May need delivery vehicle; check out legal and health requirements

What You Do

Food delivery to the home or office is an idea whose time has come. Delivering lunches to office workers is especially lucrative. Harried people will love seeing your delicious dinner brought to their door as they arrive home after a long day at work. The menus need not be extensive, which simplifies the operation. You can "pick up" from a variety of local restaurants, or prepare your own meals. Challenges include safe food handling practices "on the road," keeping foods hot or cold, as appropriate, and maintaining on-time deliveries.

What You Need

This business isn't costly to start up, especially if you opt to offer a lunch-only service. If you offer sandwiches and soups, salads and rolls, beverages and dessert, for instance, you need very little equipment to prepare the meals. You will need to invest in packaging for the foods (disposable plastic bowls, cellophane or foil wrapping, for instance); the cost will vary depending on the foods you're selling. Create a flier that can be posted in heavily populated office complexes to get started; always deliver the next day's menu with each meal as you drop them off. Make sure your insurance policy will cover your vehicle while it is being used for deliveries and, if you are hiring a delivery helper, make sure your insurance covers that employee in your car.

Keys to Success

Most people in the food delivery business get up early in the morning to bake and/or cook; night owls may not survive! Expect a long day of work, especially if you deliver at dinnertime in the evening. You'll need an ability to deal successfully with vendors and suppliers to keep your costs down and the food quality consistent. On the upside, the future is bright for food delivery businesses. More and more people have less and less time to cook; everyone is tired of the typical "fast food." Start-up costs in most cases are modest, and you can net $70-$100 a day right from the start (the sky is the limit after that, as you add more routes).

Food Item Manufacturer

Start-up cost:	$500-$5,000 (depending on the food product)
Potential earnings:	30,000-$75,000
Typical fees:	As high as $50 for some items, but most range $2-$25 each
Advertising:	Mail-order catalogs, brochures, direct mail, groceries, farmers' markets
Qualifications:	Knowledge of how to manufacture and market the item
Equipment needed:	Depends on the item
Staff required:	None
Handicapped opportunity:	Yes
Hidden costs:	Legal advice

What You Do

The sky is the limit in food production—anything from eggs and bottled water to candy and organically grown tomatoes can be manufactured by a home-based entrepreneur. What's involved in such a business varies greatly, depending upon which product you choose, but either offering a unique food item or marketing a tried-and-true favorite in a new way spells success. A package of pasta, for example, can be produced for as little as 46 cents and sold for $3.50 or more. How about pizza? Everyone loves pizza, it's easy to make and, with your own marketing or recipe twists, you can make a tremendous amount of money. Want more ideas? How about food by mail order, a food-preserving business, specialty breads, sassafras tea, holiday cookies, or maple syrup? If you are willing to learn the ins and outs of producing and marketing a particular food product, you can establish a profitable business.

What You Need

Start-up costs depend on the food product you choose. If you need ovens or an assembly line to manufacture your products, it may be relatively expensive to begin. On the other hand, a product such as soup can be started on a shoestring. Packaging and marketing costs for any product must be carefully considered; explore your market area, examine packaging of similar products, and research the costs.

Keys to Success

Your livelihood is greatly affected by weather and the seasons, if it requires growing a crop. You may need considerable knowledge about fertilizers, plant diseases, etc. You must have a consistent supply of ingredients and a consistent manufacturing method to ensure that your products always taste the same. Any food product is subject to safety and health regulations. The good news is that many food manufacturing operations are quite simple, requiring few ingredients and no great technical skills. Everyone loves to eat, so food products are always in vogue.

Framing Service

Start-up cost:	$40,000-$60,000
Potential earnings:	40,000-$50,000
Typical fees:	$15 per hour for custom work plus materials; materials only for frame-it-yourself
Advertising:	Yellow Pages, local newspapers
Qualifications:	Understanding of operating a retail business plus skill in framing and training a staff, ability to teach customers to frame
Equipment needed:	Framing supplies, special cutters for glass, wood, mats, cash register, retail space
Staff required:	Yes
Handicapped opportunity:	No
Hidden costs:	Insurance and materials costs

What You Do

This business is lucrative because many people buy prints and other artwork or want to frame their own pieces. Some people don't have the time or patience to frame, so the custom aspect should not be ignored. Take into consideration, however, that about 60 percent frame their own, while 40 percent request custom framing. Material costs fall somewhere around 26 to 32 percent, and gross profits about 68 to 74 percent.

What You Need

You'll spend at least $30,000 launching a frame shop, primarily because you'll need lots of storage space and work area with sufficient lighting. More than likely, you'll rent space somewhere close to an art gallery. Charges will vary according to size and make of frame.

Keys to Success

Be mindful that this is a retail establishment, so take into consideration the size of the shop, location, rent. You might want to sell some ready-made frames and prints to supplement the framing business.

Freelance Writer/Editor/Illustrator

Start-up cost:	$2,000-$5,000
Potential earnings:	22,500-$50,000
Typical fees:	$50-$150 per hour, depending on area and experience level
Advertising:	Personal contacts, trade publications
Qualifications:	Writing and communication skills; attention to detail and organizational ability, sense for graphics and design
Equipment needed:	High-end computer with light pen or graphics tablet and a high resolution graphics video card, scanner, laser printer, word processing, design, and contact management software, fax, office furniture, reference books, business cards
Staff required:	No
Handicapped opportunity:	Yes
Hidden costs:	Maintaining personal contacts (business lunches, etc.), memberships in trade organizations, software upgrades

What You Do

Many people have made careers out of freelance writing, editing, and illustrating—and many more are trying. Success will come for you when you can distinguish your services from those of others who will work for peanuts. Excellent communication skills are required to discover exactly what your clients want and need. You then turn those skills around to produce the corrected materials, written texts, or illustrations that will support your clients' marketing plans. This is a personal business that requires building up trust slowly and carefully before you can obtain the big projects that bring in enough income to make you successful. Creativity and goal-directedness are both essential. No detail can slip by your eye. But successful projects will bring you referrals, and each small step can lead to a bigger one.

As a writer, you will work on special editorial projects for clients ranging from small business owners to universities to newspapers—and you may even be lucky enough to snag a corporate client or two in the meantime. Your projects might be as specialized as an article for a trade journal or a corporate history; then again, you could be a generalist who writes articles on a wide variety of topics for various magazines and newspapers. Your best bet, at least in the beginning, is to produce brochures for small businesses.

As an editor, you will focus your energies on making sure everything that you see goes back out to a publisher totally free of mistakes—including grammatical errors, spelling and punctuation mistakes, and even poor sentence flow. Your job is to ensure that all the words on the page make sense and have a certain rhythm to them, so that the reader is carried along through the book logically and concisely, You may end up editing thousands of projects, from annual reports to menus to book-length manuscripts.

As a freelance illustrator, you will market your work to various publishing houses, ultimately in search of a regular contract with at least one. If you do secure a contract, you may design and produce book covers as well as any artwork to go into the book itself. This area of expertise is particularly lucrative for those who can produce lively, entertaining illustrations for children's books. If you should decide to stay unaffiliated with a large publishing house, your projects will always be varied and you'll have the challenge of getting to know what each of your client companies wants—over and over again. Many illustrators adore that challenge.

What You Need

You'll be spending a lot of time in your office, so whether you plan to meet clients there or not, you'll need to make it an effective work space. The high-end computer equipment needed to produce professional results is costly, averaging $2,000-$5,000. Your hourly rates should cover all of your overhead, so price yourself competitively in the $75-$150 per hour range.

Keys to Success

You can indulge your love of words and graphics to the max in this field. You will be learning something new with each project, and you will have the satisfaction of seeing everything you produce be published (unlike poets and novelists). Working to support your client businesses can result in a satisfying partnership. However, pricing your services can be very difficult. Nonwriters often do not appreciate the time and effort that goes into producing an effective piece of writing, and there are many writers out there in the marketplace who are likely to undercut you. You'll have to spend long hours staring at your blank computer monitor and then actually completing the projects you have fought so hard to get. Deadlines are always too short, and sometimes it can be difficult to obtain the background information needed from a client. Freelance writers have earned the circles under their eyes the hard way.

Expert Advice

What sets your business apart from others like it?

Ruth Dean, owner of The Writing Toolbox in Akron, Ohio, says her business is unique because she listens well and helps clients clarify their ideas and plans. She specializes in technical marketing communications and gets her best results by writing to appeal to the client's intended audience, not just to the client.

Things you couldn't do without:

"The fax is essential. Clients want instant communication." A computer and laser printer would also be necessities.

Marketing tips/advice:

Dean markets by networking. "I just ask clients about their business and listen. That's all it takes. It's important to have writing samples available in simple 'packages' so that clients who are not accustomed to working with writers can figure out how to hire you."

If you had to do it all over again . . .

"I wouldn't have waited so long to go out on my own."

Garage Sale Coordinator

Start-up cost:	$500-$700
Potential earnings:	15,000-$25,000
Typical fees:	Often a flat fee of $25-$50 per garage sale; sometimes an additional percentage (5 to 10 percent)
Advertising:	Classified ads, bulletin boards, community newspapers, condo associations
Qualifications:	Organizational skills, strong marketing ability
Equipment needed:	Phone, computer with letter-quality printer, fax, hammer and nails for posting signs
Staff required:	No
Handicapped opportunity:	Yes
Hidden costs:	Gas and mileage may get out of hand; try to cover these costs in your fee

What You Do

Are you a garage sale goddess? Do you spend your entire weekend cavorting around town in search of great bargains? This could be a business made in heaven expressly for you. As a garage sale coordinator/marketer, you would first advertise your services stressing your skill at saving folks time and energy so that they can relax and make money from their old stuff. Then you would organize all of the details involved in putting together a successful garage sale, including marketing (posting signs and placing publicity in newspapers, etc.), and running the sale itself (tagging, bartering, and keeping a record of what's been sold). Don't wait for the individual, single-home customers to build your business; try to work with condo associations, churches, and apartment complexes to organize large-group garage sales—these will bring in your best dollars and provide you with the greatest marketing opportunity, since many bargain hunters like the idea of one-stop shopping.

What You Need

This business could be a real bargain for you, because it involves minimal start-up cost and the ability to be paid for something you truly enjoy. Advertising in the newspaper classifieds will be your biggest cost, averaging $500-$700. You can earn a pretty good penny for yourself in all of this, especially when you work with large groups. Charge between $25-$50 per individual garage sale, and add on a percentage of the profits if you'd like (5 to 10 percent is typical).

Keys to Success

Many large newspapers offer free garage sale kits, complete with signs, records, and tips for making a garage sale a success. Call or write to request one of these kits—they could become a standard for your business and make your job even easier.

Gardening Consultant

Start-up cost:	$5,000-$10,000 (more if you need to purchase a vehicle)
Potential earnings:	40,000-$60,000
Typical fees:	Varied; can be as low as $125 or as high as several thousand per project (depending on whether you're working for an individual or a corporation)
Advertising:	Yellow Pages, community newspapers, city magazines, direct mail, bulletin boards, networking, speaking to community organizations
Qualifications:	Extensive knowledge of plants, growing seasons, and regional climates
Equipment needed:	Gardening tools, hoses, seeds, perhaps a van
Staff required:	Yes (1-5 people to work on several projects simultaneously)
Handicapped opportunity:	Not likely
Hidden costs:	Liability insurance and workers' compensation

What You Do

There's nothing lovelier in the springtime than a perfectly planned garden in bloom. If you've always been the type who can effectively plan such perennial pleasures, you would likely be well-suited to this line of business. Especially if you don't mind working outside in the dirt for long periods of time during the warmest times of the year. As a gardening consultant, you will meet with either homeowners or business owners to work out the details of what will bloom where. Develop a portfolio of your best work, then reel in more business through speaking engagements or presentations to community organizations that are always looking for gardening experts because they appeal to large groups of people. Be sure to always be clear on what your services entail— many well-meaning folks will confuse your services with those of professional landscapers. If you don't cut grass, say so.

What You Need

If you've already been involved in gardening, you likely have many of the tools you'll need to start. However, keep in mind that you'll probably be adding a staff once the phone starts ringing, so you'll need to double or possibly triple the number of tools you have on hand. Also, if you need a vehicle, such as a van, consider leasing and applying a magnetic sign to the door advertising your services. All said and done, you'll shell out about $5,000-$10,000—more if you add staff. But your fees, which will vary from $125 to several thousand dollars, should help offset any costs.

Keys to Success

Plan your speaking engagements and other forms of promotion during the off-season; chances are, you'll be too busy during the spring and summer months.

Genealogical Service

Start-up cost:	$500-$1,500 (depending on whether you have a computer)
Potential earnings:	15,000-$25,000
Typical fees:	$25-$125 per search; $200-$500 per written family history
Advertising:	Magazines with a historic slant, newspapers, Yellow Pages
Qualifications:	None
Equipment needed:	Computer with family tree software program
Staff required:	No
Handicapped opportunity:	Yes
Hidden costs:	If you're billing on a per-job basis, don't spend too much time on each project

What You Do

Everyone would like to know their roots, and what better way to find out than through a genealogical service? By hiring such a service, you could learn about everyone from the first generation of your family to the black sheep that every family seems to have. As a family history writer, you would meet with family members to obtain every known detail about a family—and then compile the information into a family tree diagram or a written report. Mind you, not all is known about every member of every family, but the Mormon church has an extensive genealogical service that you could use to find seemingly obscure bits and pieces. And this service is provided for everyone, not just for Mormons. There are also census reports at major metropolitan libraries to assist you with your search. If you aren't afraid of a lot of research and detail-oriented writing work, this could be a great business for you. Every family has a different, yet fascinating, story to tell.

What You Need

You'll need to have a good computer system and genealogical software to produce the kinds of detail-oriented reports necessary in the family history writing business. Expect to spend anywhere from $500-$1,500 on those items alone, then factor in your advertising costs at around another $350-$500 and up (depending on the size of the publication you advertise in).

Keys to Success

Your work is much in demand in these nostalgic times, and while there is not a high upfront investment, your time is worth money—and you could spend more of that than you are paid for. Make sure you budget your time accordingly or you could easily (and quickly) come up short.

Gerontology Consultant

Start-up cost:	$500
Potential earnings:	25,000-$40,000
Typical fees:	$20-$40 per hour
Advertising:	Direct mail, networking with psychologists and medical professionals, speaking engagements
Qualifications:	Background in psychology or sociology
Equipment needed:	No
Staff required:	No
Handicapped opportunity:	Yes
Hidden costs:	None (but watch your mileage)

What You Do

Into the next century, the population over the age of 60 is expected to rise to as high as 65 percent of the total population. That's because many of us have chosen healthier lifestyles—but also because life expectancy itself is on the rise. With more and more folks still in control of their lives after age 80, the need for skilled professionals to help others understand the process and effects of aging will become more apparent. As a gerontology expert, you will work in conjunction with hospitals and psychologists to help patients and their families adjust to the many changes and challenges of their loved ones growing older. You will counsel them on issues ranging from health care to assisted living programs, and may be called on frequently as a resource person for hospitals and the community at large.

What You Need

Assuming that you have the necessary credentials (i.e., a college education in psychology or a related field), your start-up costs should be minimal. The first thing you'll need is professional-looking stationery and business cards, so allow about $500 for that and some preliminary advertising. A gerontology consultant works primarily on-site; that is, at the place where your services have been contracted. Because of this, you can easily use your home as an office, but do make sure you have dependable transportation.

Keys to Success

You will probably enjoy the favorable attention you'll receive from people in need of your services, but you should also keep in mind that many of your clients are under unbelievable stress because they are balancing their careers with the need to care for aging relatives. They simply can't be in two places at once, and they may be difficult to deal with at times as a result.

Gift Basket Business

Start-up cost:	$5,000-$15,000
Potential earnings:	25,000-$45,000
Typical fees:	Baskets are individually priced anywhere from $25-$350
Advertising:	Local newspapers, flyers, bulletin boards, direct mail to busy executives, Yellow Pages
Qualifications:	Natural creativity mixed with a strong business sense
Equipment needed:	Baskets and gift materials, glue gun, shrink wrap machine, delivery vehicle
Staff required:	No
Handicapped opportunity:	Yes
Hidden costs:	Shipping costs

What You Do

There's nothing nicer to receive than a basket full of goodies meant especially for you . . . that's why gift basket businesses have been cropping up everywhere. Some are even offered as franchise opportunities. On the surface, this business seems so simple anyone could do it: you just round up a bunch of neat items, place them in a basket, put ribbons and shrink wrap around all and voila! But there is much more to it than that; you must also be a gifted buyer (to get the best bargains on gift items and materials) and a real go-getter of a salesperson to bring in the constant flow of business needed to stay afloat. In other words, you should have all the marketing skills of a seasoned retailer in addition to a dynamic and creative mind. If you can handle all of that, you will likely succeed if your market area isn't already saturated. Be sure to set yourself apart from the others as much as possible: since there are so many in this emerging and trendy business, the competition is fierce and you'll lose out if you don't carve an interesting niche for yourself. Perhaps you could fill your gift baskets with only a particular type of product, such as products manufactured only in your state, or special theme packages.

What You Need

Your start-up costs hinge on whether you're renting a storefront and whether you're investing in a delivery vehicle or merely using your own car or van. As far as the store-front goes, it could generate some walk-in business, but rent is awful steep for straggler-type businesses. You really should try to keep this one lean and mean for as long as you can, having your clients shop from a catalog rather than in person. You'll need to advertise heavily in places your customers are most likely to think of needing your services, and that will run you in the neighborhood of $500-$3,000. Your money will come from the gift baskets you sell (minus production and commission costs); most gift basket businesses offer a wide range of prices for an array of baskets, anywhere from $25-$300.

Keys to Success

Since the national recognition of one woman's company, everyone is trying to get into this seemingly easy business. If you feel you can create a gift basket business that truly stands apart in some way, you stand a good chance of earning a living. If you're unsure about this critical piece of advice, think it over or (better yet) rewrite your business plan. It's so competitive that you have to have a niche to survive unless you're in a remote part of the country (but, then, your customer base will also be limited). Still, if you're creative about gift baskets, you'll be creative in coming up with a way to sell them.

Becoming a Networking Giant

Want to move to the networking fast-track? Here are some great tips on becoming a top networking professional:

- **Develop as many contacts as you can.** Add one new person each day, and you'll have met at least twenty new people
  per month.
- **Tell people the one thing you feel you do best.** Don't give them a rundown of all that you can do. It confuses, and even annoys, some people when the conversation seems one-sided; be concise about what you do so that the other person may reciprocate.
- **Become a host/leader, not a wallflower.** Show initiative; introduce yourself. Don't throw your card at anybody until after you've established a verbal introduction.
- **Cultivate your contacts.** Don't try to use the situation to get immediate business; instead, ask to meet privately later on. Nobody likes to feel pressure in social situations.
- **Extend your own expertise first whenever possible.** Be available to those who call on you for help when they need it.
- **Keep in touch.** Mail or fax articles that might be of interest to your contacts—it shows you were listening when you met them, and that you remembered what they said.

Government Contract Consulting

Start-up cost:	$3,000-$6,000
Potential earnings:	40,000-$65,000
Typical fees:	$50-$150 per hour or a flat rate of $175+
Advertising:	Trade journals, association memberships, direct mail, networking, referrals
Qualifications:	Experience in obtaining government contracts, contacts in Washington, writing skills
Equipment needed:	Computer, suite software, fax/modem, copier, printer, mobile phone, office furniture, business cards, letterhead, envelopes
Staff required:	No
Handicapped opportunity:	Yes
Hidden costs:	On-line time, telephone bills

What You Do

As companies downsize, they no longer employ people who can thread their way through the complex world of government contracts. Yet these contracts can be a source of business growth to many companies. Your clients should not be ignored on the basis that the requirements seem too difficult. Instead, you will guide these organizations into the land of business opportunity that government contracts represent. Your experience with the special language that government agencies use (and the number of pieces of red tape involved in each transaction) plus your contacts in different departments and agencies will help you help your clients in doing business with the government. This is a specialized field, but it can be a very rewarding one. Often success in gaining one contract will smooth the path for future work. If you can produce the contracts, you have a very large potential market of companies that would love to have your services.

What You Need

Equipping your office is the main expense; expect to spend at least $3,000-$6,000. But, considering that some government contract consultants charge as much as $150 per hour for their valued service, your expenses will be minimal in relation to your earnings.

Keys to Success

This is an insider business, so you'll need to sell yourself as an insider if you aren't one already. Don't worry—as you begin to achieve success, you will become more of a real insider. The other factor here is a good business sense. What approach to obtaining a government contract would be most appropriate for each of your clients? How can you guide a specific business organization through the process? You are doing a lot of good for your clients each time you are successful, and that should make up for the frequent need to work under time pressure.

Grants/Proposal Writer

Start-up cost:	$1,000-$2,000
Potential earnings:	45,000-$100,000
Typical fees:	$500+ per project or an hourly rate of $25 or more
Advertising:	Networking, direct mail, word of mouth
Qualifications:	Knowledge of the regulations governing formal proposals, knowledge of technology and industry, ability to write clearly and logically
Equipment needed:	Computer, office suite software, laser printer, fax, modem, office furniture, business cards, letterhead, envelopes
Staff required:	No
Handicapped opportunity:	Yes
Hidden costs:	Printing and publishing documents

What You Do

Organizations that want to do business with the federal or state government, cities, counties, and special districts often must respond in writing to a request for proposal (RFP). Writing an effective proposal is a highly skilled activity, and often businesses must contract out the work. A related activity is grant writing, which helps a charitable organization establish its relationship to a foundation. In either case, the piece of writing must conform to the specifications in the RFP, outlining the methods to be used, the needs to be met, and the financial background and expected outcomes of the project.

Some proposal writers are generalists, while others focus on one field, such as education or health care administration. The emphasis, though, is on good writing skills applicable to any field—clear organization, logical exposition, and excellent grammar. Aptitude with numerical data in graphs and spreadsheets is required; business communication savvy is necessary to work with the client's group of employees who are planning the bid or funding request.

What You Need

You will need to be able to produce professional-looking documents that may include graphs, charts, and tabular data. Buy a computer system with high-resolution and graphics capabilities (around $2,000-$3,000). Your physical office needs to function well as this is a desk-intensive job (buy a comfortable chair, around $200). You can bill hourly ($25-$50 per hour) or on a per-job basis ($500 and up).

Keys to Success

A skilled grant and proposal writer provides the essential link between the client and the funding, whether it is a grant for a nonprofit organization or a contract for a business. It's challenging work that involves constant learning and creative solutions. It can take a long time to gain enough experience and contacts to be effective. Pricing is always a challenge unless you can negotiate an unlimited hourly rate.

Graphic Designer

Start-up cost:	$6,000-$10,000
Potential earnings:	30,000-$75,000
Typical fees:	$75-$100 per hour or average retainer fees of $1,000 per month
Advertising:	Business publications, promotional mailings to people in the gift business; referrals
Qualifications:	Background in graphics, type design and color, communication and marketing skills, artistic inclination
Equipment needed:	High-end computer with quality graphics design software, color scanner, large-screen monitor, laser printer; fax/modem, office furniture that includes a light table, business card, letterhead, envelopes
Staff required:	No
Handicapped opportunity:	Yes
Hidden costs:	Training in new software programs

What You Do

In most communities there is a lot of competition in this field, but skilled, creative graphic designers stand out above the rest. Experienced graphic designers who want to work independently can make an excellent living producing work for a range of clients in a home-based setting. Freelance graphic designers work for a variety of different businesses, including book publishers, newspapers, consumer product manufacturers, and even other small start-ups, designing letterhead and logos. Eventually you may decide to set up a studio and employ others to work with you. An ability to communicate well with clients is essential. It is not enough to create designs that appeal to your own aesthetic sense. You need to be part marketer and part psychologist to produce the designs your clients want and need.

What You Need

The computer equipment required is very expensive. You will need the latest software as well, in addition to an efficient and comfortable work space. Figure your charges to be in the $75-$100 per hour range. Be careful of bidding on a per-job basis; many companies will demand that you do only to take advantage of your time later.

Keys to Success

You can make an excellent living as a graphic designer once you distinguish yourself from the competition and build up a reputation for excellence and on-time work. Good working relationships will lead to a satisfied group of clients that return to you again and again. It can be difficult to bid jobs accurately and sometimes a few clients will be very slow to pay. Working under rush conditions seems to be the norm, and occasionally you will encounter a customer that is impossible to please.

Expert Advice

What sets your business apart from others like it?

Kelvin Oden, owner of Oh Snap! Design in Brooklyn, New York, says he's had to pay his dues to get where he is. "On the positive side, I'm a young company and can work without limitation or restriction. I can go against the norm."

Things you couldn't do without:

A computer, laser printer with at least 600 dpi, and clients are all Oden says he needs to survive.

Marketing tips/advice:

"The most important thing is to build really good relationships with your clients. If they're comfortable with you as a person, they'll come back to you."

If you had to do it all over again . . .

"I wouldn't change anything . . . I'm extremely happy doing what I'm doing."

Handbill Distribution

Start-up cost:	$200-$500
Potential earnings:	15,000-$20,000
Typical fees:	$5-$10 per drop-off
Advertising:	Flyers or classified ads
Qualifications:	Marketing sense, time-management skills
Equipment needed:	None
Staff required:	Yes
Handicapped opportunity:	Yes
Hidden costs:	Spot-checking the distribution crew

What You Do

Businesses are moving beyond the traditional marketing avenues (magazine and news-paper advertising, radio spots, etc.) to develop less expensive, more effective alterna-tives. In many areas there is a return to a very old advertising method, handbill distrib-ution. If you live in an area with a high concentration of people on foot, near a mall or in a large city, you can develop a handbill distribution service that forms a significant part of your clients' marketing strategies. You will need a crew of people to do the actual dis-tribution, and you should carry out spot checks to see that they are actually handing each bill out and not dumping them. If all goes well, handbill distribution can be a very effective and direct marketing approach.

What You Need

The flyers with which you advertise your own business are about the only cost for a handbill distribution business, aside from what you pay to your crews. You may need to carry insurance for work-related mishaps; check with your agent. Expect to bill between $5-$10 per drop-off or location; add extra for those jobs involving more time and effort.

Keys to Success

The simplicity of this business has great appeal. It's person-to-person, face-to-face. Creating a business that is an almost pure service can be very satisfying to those who love to make something out of nothing. A lot of your energy will be consumed in marketing your operation, however, and more will be needed to hire and manage your crew.

Handyman Network

Start-up cost:	$500-$1,000
Potential earnings:	20,000-$45,000
Typical fees:	10 to 20 percent of the repair cost
Advertising:	Yellow Pages, community newspapers, coupon books
Qualifications:	Good communications skills
Equipment needed:	Phone, well-stocked van(s) with tools
Staff required:	Yes (stable of handymen willing to work on-call)
Handicapped opportunity:	Possibly
Hidden costs:	Workers' compensation, tool maintenance costs

What You Do

A handyman network is the perfect way to find employment for the retired tinkerer; here, you'll run a business similar to a referral service, where you get the call and then match a fixer-upper to a customer in distress. You will dispatch one of your dozen or so handymen to a caller, then sit back and let the work happen. When it's done, the handyman will bring you a completed work order and a check for the service rendered. At regular intervals (typically twice per month), you'll cut a check to each handyman for his percentage of each completed job. You'll be handling everything from dripping faucets to deck-building or possibly even roofing—the possibilities are limited only by your staff's capabilities. Make sure to hire a wide variety of specialists, so that you have enough workers to cover any anticipated project.

What You Need

If you've already got a van for carrying your tools and equipment to house calls you make, you'll need only $500-$1,000 to get started in this business. With some hard work and heavy promotion, you can turn a profit of $20,000-$45,000. One tip: make sure you advertise on your van; it's surprising how many handyman networks get referrals that way.

Keys to Success

It's a win-win . . . you're helping out retired and possibly displaced workers who need to do something to make ends meet, but you're also helping a customer solve a problem in his or her home. The income is not fantastic, but it's respectable.

Home Entertainment
System Service

Start-up cost:	$10,000-$15,000
Potential earnings:	35,000-$50,000
Typical fees:	$20-$45 per hour (more for parts)
Advertising:	Classified ads, entertainment magazines and newspaper sections, referrals, neighborhood flyers, direct mail
Qualifications:	Electronics skill, interest in music, knowledge of entertainment systems operation, hookups
Equipment needed:	Tools, cellular phone
Staff required:	No
Handicapped opportunity:	Not typically
Hidden costs:	Vehicle maintenance, phone bills

What You Do

Home entertainment systems can do wonderful things—but only if they are operating properly. Simply getting them installed is beyond the skills of many people, and taking one component out of all the wiring so that it can be delivered to a store for repair seems impossible. All those jokes about not knowing how to operate a VCR really aren't funny. What they do is highlight your market: the owners of home entertainment systems that need help getting them together and keeping them running right. Becoming a home entertainment system service person means that you have a large but very focused market. Each successful job ought to lead to referrals.

What You Need

You'll need tools and possibly an inventory of parts.

Keys to Success

Referrals from individual customers will take you far, and a relationship with a dealer for service and repairs would also be an excellent marketing tactic. Many homes have the makings of entertainment centers. If the components were purchased at a mass market outlet, or even by mail, the owner may well have no one but you to do the setup and repairs. Your electronics know-how ought to find a ready market.

Home Inspector

Start-up cost:	$30,000-$40,000
Potential earnings:	50,000-$75,000
Typical fees:	$200-$400, depending on size of home
Advertising:	Yellow Pages, real estate publications, local newspapers, networking with real estate agents
Qualifications:	Thorough knowledge of home construction and building codes or experience in contracting and building; depending on the area of the country, license or permits might be required
Equipment needed:	Electrical tracer, circuit tester, gas detector, basic tools like screwdrivers, flashlights, and ladders, computer, fax, printer
Staff required:	No
Handicapped opportunity:	Not typically
Hidden costs:	Insurance, telephone bills, association dues

What You Do

In this litigious society, home buyers, sellers, and realtors are all looking for the best protection they can get. Learning the condition of a home up front from a third party ensures that buyers will know just what kind of home they are purchasing before the sale is complete. Unfortunately, home inspectors are often targets for litigation, too, so look into certification and licensing requirements in your area and protect yourself by either incorporating or affiliating yourself with a franchise organization. Whichever you choose, your work will change on a daily basis, as you'll be moving from one home to another to inspect everything from the condition of the wiring to shingles on the roof. You'll be checking off items in a large binder as you proceed, and this is what you will leave as a permanent record for the potential home owner. It's a necessary service in this buyer beware kind of market.

What You Need

Mostly, you'll need the funds to either develop or secure rights to the information contained in each binder you provide your customers. This business will be much easier to get up and running effectively (and in a shorter period of time) if you pay a franchise fee (anywhere from $30,000-$50,000) to an already established company in this field. That way, you're also protected legally.

Keys to Success

Don't underestimate the value of contact with real estate agents. Many of your best referrals will come from them. Likewise, thorough and honest inspections will result in satisfied home buyers, a valuable source of word-of-mouth advertising. You'll have lots of face-to-face contact with them, so excellent communication and people skills are a must.

Home Office Consultant

Start-up cost:	$5,000-$10,000
Potential earnings:	30,000-$45,000
Typical fees:	$40-$50 per hour
Advertising:	Direct mail to entrepreneurs, networking with entrepreneurial assistance organizations such as (Service Corps of Retired Executives), Yellow Pages, newspapers
Qualifications:	Business degree or previous entrepreneurial experience
Equipment needed:	Computer, printer, fax/modem, copier, pager or cellular phone
Staff required:	No
Handicapped opportunity:	Yes
Hidden costs:	Slow payment for your services as many beginning entrepreneurs have cash-flow problems

What You Do

Home offices are a large part of the burgeoning entrepreneurial marketplace—and you can cash in on the ground floor if you have the expertise needed to help a home office get off on the right foot. Your biggest problem will likely be in locating those thinking about working from home—although there are a few directions that may prove helpful. One excellent way to find clients is through on-line services and work-at-home forums, where you can offer your expert advice free of charge in an effort to get your name and company information out there. You can also comb the business, professional, and entrepreneurial groups that meet in your community for potential clients. Once you get a client base going, you will work with each client on projects that range from advice on computer systems to office ergonomics to marketing strategy. You really need to be well-rounded in your realm of experience, as you'll be giving the best advice you can on a wide variety of topics. Make sure that you focus heavily on the types of equipment a home office might need, as well as tips on balancing home and family (since both are closely entwined in this venture). The trouble is, your likelihood of having repeat customers is low, since most home offices only launch once; stay on top of things and be constantly on the lookout for new prospects (many will come via referral).

What You Need

Your launch fees ($5,000-$10,000) will mostly cover your basic office setup and some preliminary list rentals so that you can send some direct mail pieces to folks who work from home. Expect to earn $30,000-$45,000 once you get established; charge $40-$50 per hour for your services.

Keys to Success

While it may be interesting and even exciting to be part of an innovative young company's beginning, it may take a while to secure payment for your services. If you can charge up front, and particularly if you accept credit cards, you'll have a much better chance of collecting what your services are worth.

Creative Idea-Generating

You have a business problem (or opportunity) staring you in the face; now, how do you come up with a suitable solution or answer in a short period of time?

Try one or more of these tactics:

- **Mind-mapping.** You draw a circle with the ultimate goal in the center, and lines extending outward like a sunburst. On each line, you write down one possible way to achieve your goal. Often, you map out all the smaller details of each method—leading to clearer goal-setting.

- **Brainstorming.** Invite a few business friends (or, better yet, fellow business owners) over for an evening of pizza and brainstorming. Listen to what others have to say, even if you like your own initial ideas more. Their feedback might influence you later.

- **Learn from others' mistakes.** Read trade journals and business publications—or e-mail other business owners in entrepreneurial or specialty business forums on on-line services.

- **Go where your customers are (if they're not with you).** If you have a resume service, you might hang out in the resume book section of your local bookstore to listen in to what your potential customers are needing and wanting.

The important thing to remember is that there isn't just one possible solution; the value of thinking creatively is that you can explore many different possibilities—and if one doesn't work, you still have others left to choose from.

Home Schooling Consultant

Start-up cost:	$300-$1,000
Potential earnings:	15,000-$45,000
Typical fees:	$25-$45 per hour
Advertising:	School boards, Yellow Pages, local newspapers
Qualifications:	Degree in education plus a teaching certificate
Equipment needed:	Books, teachers' guides, monthly planners
Staff required:	No
Handicapped opportunity:	Yes
Hidden costs:	Mileage

What You Do

Communication, organization, and the ability to juggle several things at once are need-ed in this field. Your job will be to set up the school curriculum and schedule classes for parents who seek to teach their children at home instead of in public (or even private) schools. You could possibly consult for a parent who doesn't want the child in the school system for religious or intellectual reasons, or whose child has to be out of school for a long period of time due to illness or injury. If you are establishing a new curriculum, you will need the ability to evaluate the child's skill level. If you are helping the student who is out for a long period, you will have to communicate with their orig-inal school on a regular basis.

What You Need

Start-up is low (after you have obtained your degree). Be prepared to buy books up front and be reimbursed for them later. Charging $45 per hour on a regular basis could earn you up to $45,000 per year.

Keys to Success

You may need to join a national, state, or local education association program in order to get a job. This business allows for excellent, high-standard teaching without all the hassles of dealing with a classroom. You don't have to answer to a boss and if you find you don't care for the environment, you can quit. Networking is a definite necessity, but with enough contacts, you could find yourself with year-round work.

Image Consultant

Start-up cost:	$1,500-$5,000 (depending on equipment choices)
Potential earnings:	20,000-$50,000
Typical fees:	$50-$200 per session
Advertising:	Classified advertising or ads in women's or business newspapers, bulletin boards, coupon books, direct mail
Qualifications:	None except to be a good example yourself
Equipment needed:	You may wish to use a computerized video system to demonstrate what your suggestions will look like on your client
Staff required:	No
Handicapped opportunity:	Yes
Hidden costs:	Mileage costs

What You Do

How many times have you seen a misguided soul wearing colors that should only be on a flag—or makeup that dates back to Cleopatra? Did you have the guts to pull that person aside and offer suggestions on self-improvement? Probably not. Yet that is exactly what image consultants are paid to do. Particularly in the business world, people are concerned about the way they come across—and your most frequent clients are likely to be those embarking on career changes or job searches, recent college graduates, and brides. Your mission: to help them make a more positive impact on others through look and attitude. In some respects, you will be like the mother who tells it like it is: "You should wear cool blues instead of muddy browns, which make your face appear yellowish." If you are fashion-minded and have an impeccable sense of balance and color, you are likely to find clients nearly anywhere.

What You Need

If you're just starting out, you really needn't invest in much more than mirrors, color swatches, and makeup samples. Once you become a little more established, however, you might add on innovative pieces of equipment such as a computerized video system that "morphs" changes on a picture of your client. A good place to set up shop in a heavy-traffic area would be a mall kiosk (carts can be rented for $300-$500 per week, but the attention might be worth it). Also, wouldn't it be interesting to form a cooperative marketing venture with a related (but noncompeting) business, such as a hairstylist or resume service? You could each offer discounts for the other's service as an incentive for clients to buy your own.

Keys to Success

It is fun to play "dress-up" with people who are in the mood for a change, but keep in mind that these people are probably going through some emotional changes that prompted them into action. Be careful, then, of hurting their feelings . . . criticism is easier to take if it sounds encouraging rather than critical.

Expert Advice

What sets your business apart from others like it?

Janet Neyrinck, Image Consultant and Certified Color Analyst in Akron, Ohio, says her business is set apart by the fact that it offers many services. "We're not just trying to sell makeup; our goal is to create a total harmonious image, including everything from dress and makeup to hair color. We believe in 'personality' dressing."

Things you couldn't do without:

"I need to have my makeup kit and, most important, my fabrics (for color draping). These are the basis of everything I do."

Marketing tips/advice:

"Be out there, be everywhere you can and introduce yourself. Also, be prepared to do a lot of research before buying your equipment."

If you had to do it all over again . . .

"I think that before I'd commit to one method or company's approach to image consulting, I would investigate all of the options out there. I would check the Directory of Image Consultants and ask others what's worked for them."

Incorporation Service for Businesses

Start-up cost:	$500-$1,000
Potential earnings:	25,000-$45,000
Typical fees:	$175-$300 (depending on area)
Advertising:	Yellow Pages, business publications, direct mail to entrepreneur groups, classified postings on on-line services or Internet
Qualifications:	A good working knowledge of incorporation law
Equipment needed:	Computer, fax, legal forms, business cards
Staff required:	No
Handicapped opportunity:	Yes
Hidden costs:	None

What You Do

With more business start-ups than ever before, the need for quick, inexpensive help in forming a corporation is greater than ever. Many people who consider starting a business simply have no idea which form of business is more advantageous for them. A nice benefit to incorporating is that you are personally protected from any lawsuits filed against the company (in other words, you probably won't lose your house or car). As an incorporator, you'll be networking with entrepreneurial groups to find clients in need of your services (or fielding calls from your advertisements), then meeting with the client(s) to fill out the necessary, and often straightforward, forms required by the government. You may also have to set up the client's Employer Identification Number, and you'll present them with their corporate package, which will include easy-to-fill-out forms such as the Articles of Incorporation, any minutes from board of director meetings, stock certificates, etc. Essentially, you'll be getting a company started on the road to greater growth or expansion potential.

What You Need

Advertising will be your largest out-of-pocket expense (between $500-$1,000). It would also help you to have business cards for networking (add another $100-$200). But you could charge as little as $175 and as much as $300 for your services, depending on your area or the size and complexity of the client company.

Keys to Success

If you like working day in and day out filling out the same forms, this job could be just what you're looking for. If, on the other hand, you thrive on excitement and variety, perhaps you should look into starting a business that specializes in putting together business plans.

In-Home Mail Service

Start-up cost:	Under $500
Potential earnings:	10,000-$15,000
Typical fees:	25 to 50 cents per envelope
Advertising:	Flyers and mailings to companies without in-house mailing services
Qualifications:	Knowledge of postal regulations
Equipment needed:	None (except for an envelope folder/sealer)
Staff required:	No
Handicapped opportunity:	Yes
Hidden costs:	Watch out for clients who seek to pay one flat fee and then dump extra work on you

What You Do

Companies who use direct mail in their advertising or promotional campaigns need help stuffing the envelopes and getting them properly prepared for the post office. If you're skillful at the manual end of this business (folding/stuffing/sealing envelopes), you'll be amazed at how much you can earn with only a few hours' worth of work. You'll need to market your services well—and if you find that you have too much business, it's a perfect opportunity to hire handicapped and retired folks who might be on the lookout for such straightforward, low-pressure work. Make sure you schedule your jobs realistically to allow for quick turnaround, because that is what will likely be expected of you from most of your clients.

What You Need

You may spend a few hundred dollars or so on items such as letter folders and envelope sealers, but this business still shouldn't cost more than $500 to launch. Get the word out by networking with small- to medium-size companies; they usually have the need for others to help them on projects of this kind. Charge between 25 and 50 cents per envelope, and try not to quote a flat rate if you can help it; you may be taken advantage of after the ink is dry on your agreement.

Keys to Success

Let's face it—stuffing envelopes is pretty boring work. If you don't mind the tedium— if you can manage to do your work and still catch *Oprah* when you want to—this could be a perfect way to either supplement an existing income or build a modest single income. However, remember that your success depends largely on your own marketing ability.

Insurance Agent

Start-up cost:	$10,000-$15,000
Potential earnings:	45,000-$60,000
Typical fees:	Commissions range from 20 to 35 percent
Advertising:	Cold-calling, membership in community groups, radio, newspapers, community publications, billboards and (of course) your outdoor sign
Qualifications:	License, experience, outstanding selling ability, affiliation with a particular company
Equipment needed:	Office furniture, computer, suite software, printer, business card, letterhead, envelopes
Staff required:	No
Handicapped opportunity:	Yes
Hidden costs:	Membership dues, errors and omissions insurance

What You Do

As a single agent, you will need to develop a focus or specialty to set yourself apart in the crowded field of insurance sales. One possibility is business insurance, with a special focus on insuring home businesses. Dedicated service to your customers is essential in distinguishing your business from the competition. You will be working closely with individuals and small organizations, and you will depend on your financial expertise and your ability to listen to the wants and needs of the buyer. If you can find a way to help people and companies manage their risk appropriately (which is what insurance is all about) without making them feel pushed or confused, you will be performing a useful service. You will be earning your agent's commission many times over.

What You Need

Knowledge and experience are far more important than equipment, although you will need a computer system that can be networked to your corporate headquarters if you're affiliated or own a franchise. In that case, your start-up costs will be considerably higher (potentially $50,000-$75,000 for training, licensing the company name, and heavy advertising), but you'll get the support you need instead of having to go it alone. However, should you decide to go alone, you can expect to spend between $10,000-$15,000 for your basic office setup, some advertising, and the fees you'll use to take your exam. Either way, your commissions should net between 20 to 35 percent and ultimately lead to an income potential of $45,000-$60,000 or more.

Keys to Success

Being an insurance agent can be tough—but people make fun of lawyers and accountants, too. Once you become established, you will have an excellent business that can support your family and possibly make you rich. Being successful in this type of enterprise requires excellent selling skills, up-to-date information on financial issues, and long hours of hard work. You're using people skills and numerical facility intensively. Most of all, you're unwilling to be discouraged if the first hundred sales calls are no's.

Hiring Smart

Even though there are, generally speaking, more workers available than ever before, you need to be choosy when sifting through the resumes of potential employees. Here are three things you should look for in an outstanding candidate.

- **A willingness to learn new things.** So often, as you embark on your entrepreneurial venture, you'll develop job descriptions that are subject to change. Hiring someone who is flexible and willing to try a new assignment could be the smartest move you could make.

- **Experience in the areas you need to cover most.** If you're looking for an accounting or bookkeeping professional, you'll need to be certain that the candidate's primary area of expertise is in those fields. Even though you may be looking for flexibility, you need to be sure you can adequately cover the necessary areas first and foremost.

- **Demonstrated results.** It's one thing for a candidate to say that their responsibilities included X, Y, and Z; it's quite another to see what kind of impact that employee had on the rest of the organization. Look for key phrases that document some kind of end result, such as "increased profit share by 110 percent" or "boosted credibility and public awareness of product."

Interior Designer

Start-up cost:	$3,000-$5,000
Potential earnings:	30,000-$50,000
Typical fees:	$50 per hour or a flat, per-job rate
Advertising:	Yellow Pages, newspapers, networking with builders/contractors
Qualifications:	Some states require certification; you should be a member of at least one professional association related to this field
Equipment needed:	Swatches, sample books, catalogs, computer, cellular phone or pager
Staff required:	No
Handicapped opportunity:	Possibly
Hidden costs:	Getting set up with distributors and manufacturer's reps can run your phone bills up at first; budget accordingly

What You Do

As more people buy older homes with fix-up potential, there is more work for interior designers who are skilled at filling spaces with dynamic statements about the presence of a room. Do you read *Metropolitan Home* regularly? Are you addicted to the latest home fashions and accessories? If so, you may make a fine interior designer. But the work is more than plaster-deep; you'll need the ability to work with builders and contractors if a room is being redesigned with a specific aesthetic effect in mind. If you apprentice with an interior designer first, you'll gain much more detailed knowledge about the intricacies and nuances of this incredibly subjective business. Personalities are the most difficult aspect of the job—getting others to cooperate and work as a team with a unified vision is probably your biggest challenge. Keeping up with fast-changing trends is another. Still, if you like meeting with people and helping to create the (interior) home of their dreams, you'll enjoy the challenges and learn to overlook the difficulties.

What You Need

Your start-up costs with an interior design service will be in the $3,000-$5,000 range, primarily to cover your first six months of advertising. You'll need classy business cards and brochures about your service, so set aside $500-$1,000 for these items alone. Set your fees at $50 per hour (or a per-job basis for larger work), and re-evaluate your prices after your first year of business. The more clients with prestige, the higher your prices.

Keys to Success

If you truly like working with people in their most intimate surrounding, this is the job for you. However, expect there to be difficulties such as timing (what if you get too many clients at once?), and clients who request too many changes and wind up costing you money. Learn to set some policies in writing ahead of time to avoid these annoyances; add a surcharge for any work that goes above and beyond your initial agreement.

Expert Advice

What sets your business apart from others like it?

"I seem to be the remedy person," says Linda Chiera, President of Studio Space Design in Akron, Ohio. "People usually come to me after they've experienced a problem elsewhere . . . I'm working on getting them to think of me first!" Chiera feels that her business is unique in that it provides expert service and assistance with complex projects. "We learn a person's work style and incorporate that into whatever we do for them, whether it be redecorating a home or redesigning their office space."

Things you couldn't do without:

Chiera couldn't do without a computer and CAD system, fax, phone, sample books/resources, tape measure, scale, and business cards.

Marketing tips/advice:

"Get sales training and get out there . . . join networking organizations such as the Chamber of Commerce, and if there's a mentoring program available in your area, enlist in it. Offer yourself as a speaker, advertise wisely (knowing your exact market), and hire seasoned professionals to do the things you can't." Finally, says Chiera, don't be afraid to make mistakes.

If you had to do it all over again . . .

"I would have been wiser about target marketing and advertising. I should have been more careful about selecting the right niche and also should have tried to become more comfortable earlier on about the selling aspect of my job. I'm trained as a designer, and sales and self-promotion have been a bit of a challenge for me until recently."

Internet Marketing Specialist

Start-up cost:	$2,000-$4,000
Potential earnings:	20,000-$40,000
Typical fees:	Hourly rate of $45+
Advertising:	Bulletin Board Services, direct mail, trade journals, business publications
Qualifications:	Knowledge of marketing, business savvy, awareness of the unwritten rules and limitless possibilities out there on the Internet
Equipment needed:	Computer, modem, printer, fax, office furniture
Staff required:	No
Handicapped opportunity:	Yes
Hidden costs:	On-line time, time spent educating client

What You Do

Marketing is always creative; Internet marketing is even more so. You'll be creating the actual marketing approaches for a variety of different businesses to get the word out on the Internet. So if newness is your bag, then this is your game. Even more than with conventional marketing, you will need to deliver more than you promise, to tell more than you sell, and attract the attention of potential customers rather than push products at them. The Internet is the perfect way to inform people about some products and services, but it is still useless for others. You'll spend enough time developing your own markets, but once you do, expect to earn more of a cutting-edge salary for your toils.

What You Need

The ability to create effective Internet messages will require increasing levels of computing power (equipment costs $2,000-$4,000). Expect to spend a pretty penny initially for on-line services, because you'll likely end up subscribing to all of them in addition to the Internet. Subscriptions to newsletters and magazines on the computer industry are also essential as resource guides—estimate spending at least $2000 per year to keep up-to-date. You can charge $45 per hour until you feel you're experienced enough to command (and get) $75 per hour; you may decide to accept MC/Visa over the 'Net, so be sure to include in your price the surcharge for such capabilities.

Keys to Success

Experience, good sense, and highly refined marketing skills will make you successful at this new game. You'll need to be persistent in creating your own market before you can begin creating customers for your clients. You'll need a high tolerance for monitor-staring, and you'll need to watch out for the uncharted pitfalls that accompany any cutting-edge activity (such as time spent educating and rewriting).

Expert Advice

What sets your business apart from others like it?

Tim DiScipio, President of Easton Media Group in Greenwich, Connecticut, says he has a unique niche in the electronic marketplace. "I've got valuable years of experience in this field; something others can't claim in an emerging industry. It's attractive to companies that want someone who's been in the industry for a while and knows their way around."

Things you couldn't do without:

Obviously, DiScipio couldn't do without a 586 computer (he has two), but he also needs a high-speed modem, a two-line telephone, and a fax machine.

Marketing tips/advice:

"If you're going to thrive in this business, you really need to network and expand your contacts regularly. Everyone in this industry has a different, unique niche . . . align yourself with the real players who can help you expand to where you need to be. Stay within your own niche; don't try to be everything to everyone."

If you had to do it all over again . . .

"I would have relinquished the time-consuming business operations duties and focused on my areas of specialty. It would have simplified my problems and allowed me to remain focused."

Jewelry Designer

Start-up cost:	$500-$1,000
Potential earnings:	25,000-$75,000
Typical fees:	Some pieces sell for $50-$75; others for thousands
Advertising:	Jewelry trade shows, newspapers, jewelry retailers, craft shows
Qualifications:	Geological Institute of America (GIA) certificate may be helpful but not required; some formal art training and knowledge of jewelry
Equipment needed:	Vices, pliers, jeweler's loop, magnifying glass, molds, melting equipment
Staff required:	No
Handicapped opportunity:	Yes
Hidden costs:	Travel expenses

What You Do

For those who like to create intricate detail with their hands and have an artistic flair, this business could be ideal for you. Some people just jump into this with their natural ability; others who really make it big have some form of formal art training and have also been picked up by a major distributor. In the meantime, hit the jewelry trade shows, craft shows, and antique shows with a vengeance and take a lot of business cards with you. A GIA certificate will be helpful with the respect that you'll have studied different types of precious and semiprecious stones and you'll be able to better price your pieces. This certificate also allows an additional income potential as a licensed jewelry appraiser; you could also buy back old jewelry and reset the stones in your own designs.

What You Need

Jewelry has one of the highest markups going (100 percent minimum). So with little investment (around $500), a lot of imagination, and some smart marketing, you could be well on your way to a first-year income of $25,000. Try to get noticed by the press, and you'll nab more business than you can handle because people really appreciate having one-of-a-kind jewelry.

Keys to Success

Ever hear of the expression the "small but mighty"? Jewelry has been known to bring in thousands of dollars for a single piece. Here's your opportunity to cash in on your one-of-a-kind creation. Since not everyone's tastes are the same, you can create until you're out of ideas (which, hopefully, will never happen). The only problem with the GIA certificate is that it's a six-month program and offered only in New York and California.

Knitting/Crocheting Lessons

Start-up cost:	$100-$300
Potential earnings:	3,000-$15,000
Typical fees:	$5-$10 per class
Advertising:	Craft shows, local library, flyers
Qualifications:	Knowledge of knitting and crocheting
Equipment needed:	Needles, thread, yarn, material, scissors
Staff required:	No
Handicapped opportunity:	Yes
Hidden costs:	Fluctuating materials costs

What You Do

Beautiful baby blankets, sweaters, and booties have an heirloom quality in addition to their warmth factor. After all, you don't buy or make a special, handmade blanket merely for its practicality. You choose such items for their sentimental value—and what better way to make a living if that's what you already enjoy doing? You could teach others your craft if you have patience and an eye for detail. You already know how much time is involved with each project and you can read intricate patterns, but can you teach others without winding up doing it all yourself? Marketing yourself at craft shops and networking with related fields will be some of your best advertising. Sell some of your work at art and craft shows to showcase your abilities. Always have plenty of business cards on hand.

What You Need

If you are giving lessons, you most likely have all the equipment you need. Keep some extra supplies on hand. Have your students purchase their supplies before they come to class, which relieves you from making an up-front purchase. Plan on grossing around $5,000 per year; this would be a great sideline business.

Keys to Success

This can be a very relaxing venture to do in your home. You get to be creative and pass down these centuries-old techniques to others. Be prepared to hold class at hours convenient for your students, including weekends and evenings. On the downside, there is always the possibility that a student may drop out without notice. Try to fill your classes with more students than you think you need.

Lactation Consultant

Start-up cost:	Under $1,000
Potential earnings:	$25,000-$40,000
Typical fees:	$40+ per hour
Advertising:	Doctor's offices, Yellow Pages, visiting nurse centers
Qualifications:	Nursing or related degree; some states merely require certification
Equipment needed:	None
Staff required:	No
Handicapped opportunity:	Possibly
Hidden costs:	Mileage

What You Do

The womanly art of breast-feeding is not always an easy one to master for new mothers. For one thing, many of them are frightened by the prospect of having to be completely responsible for another human being; for another, many hospital professionals are simply not well-trained in teaching new moms how to breast-feed properly. As a result, there are many young women out there who are breast-feeding incorrectly—and quite painfully so. Your prospects look good for this consulting business if you are patient and caring enough to show them the way, and with hospitals increasingly being forced to release mothers and their newborns in a short period of time after the birth, there will be plenty of room (and need) for outside professionals. Your word-of-mouth advertising could bring in quite a few referrals, since many new moms like to share their positive experiences.

What You Need

Your start-up costs are minimal; mostly, you'll need to make sure you have an adequate amount of resource materials and dependable transportation. For marketing materials, invest in professionally designed business cards—something that gives off a warm, caring feeling. Your fees should start at $40 per hour, collected at time of service.

Keys to Success

It can be stressful dealing with frightened new mothers and helpless fathers; you'll need a cool head to deliver this service. On the bright side, once you've accomplished teaching the mother how to feed her baby properly, the stress level will sharply subside and you'll have at least three happy customers.

Expert Advice

What sets your business apart from others like it?

Service is what sets apart International Board Certified Lactation Consultant Barbara Taylor's Breast-feeding Specialties in Lake Jackson, Texas. "I offer the added bonus of breast pump rental services as well as one-on-one work with new moms. Also, I have an extremely high referral rate."

Things you couldn't do without:

"My own business line with an answering machine; also, my own office space in my home for professionalism and confidentiality."

Marketing tips/advice:

"Network with other professionals . . . being in a small town, I often feel cut off. Most of my networking involves a long-distance call! Also, you need to find out what mistakes others have made and share ideas about how to promote your businesses as an industry."

If you had to do it all over again . . .

"It would be much easier to succeed in this business if I had been a Registered Nurse."

Laundry Service

Start-up cost:	$100-$1,000
Potential earnings:	20,000-$30,000
Typical fees:	$10 per pound of clothes (this includes "The Works": wash/dry/iron)
Advertising:	Local papers, bulletin boards, flyers, Yellow Pages
Qualifications:	Knowledge of fabric do's and don'ts
Equipment needed:	Extra-large capacity industrial washer/dryer; iron/board or a professional press
Staff required:	No
Handicapped opportunity:	Yes
Hidden costs:	Insurance or "mistake money"

What You Do

Have some business cards handy for this profession and lots of happy customers to refer additional business to you. You should especially seek out professional women who simply don't have the time for laundry detail. There is no other business where word of mouth can make or break you as much as this one. You'll need to be a perfectionist and pay attention to every detail: people tend to think that the clothes make the person and if you make a mistake on their clothing, they take it personally. You should have a room especially devoted to this venture. Have clotheslines available for drip-dry, special laundry soap on hand, softeners, and starches. If you don't invest in a professional steam press, have more than one iron available, just in case. Be sure to keep all of your warranties up to date on your machines, since they are the lifeline to your business.

What You Need

Overhead has the possibility to be low (under $1,000) if you already have the machines. Any washer or dryer in good working condition will do, but the extra-large capacity will cut your time in half allowing you to do more laundry in a shorter period of time. The large capacity also allows you to do big-ticket items such as comforters. Since your start-up cost may be low, you could easily make $20,000 in 40-hour work weeks.

Keys to Success

You either love or hate to do laundry. Since this is a home-based business, you still have time to catch a soap opera or talk show and feed your baby. Be prepared to correct any mistakes, even if they are not your fault (i.e., replace missing buttons, fix a shoulder pad, or totally replace the garment). For this reason, keep some extra "mistake money" on hand. If you make small repairs at no charge, it tends to be good for business, and the word will spread.

Lawn Care Service

Start-up cost:	$500-$1,500
Potential earnings:	15,000-$25,000
Typical fees:	$12-15 per hour or a flat rate of $50-$75 per job
Advertising:	Flyers left in front doors, ads in local or community newspapers
Qualifications:	Love for working outdoors and some knowledge about lawn care
Equipment needed:	Power mower, rakes, power trimmer and spreader, pickup truck or station wagon
Staff required:	No
Handicapped opportunity:	No
Hidden costs:	Insurance, transportation, some equipment rental

What You Do

Most people can squeeze in time to mow their own lawns, but it's the weeding and trimming, fertilizing, aerating, and leaf removal that takes up the extra time. By providing these services, you can rake in profits for yourself. Don't try to compete with neighborhood youth who mow lawns or with professional lawn services that include landscaping and related services. Plant your seeds, develop your niche, and cultivate the business.

What You Need

You'll shell out at least $300 for basic equipment; more for a power lawn mower. Double or triple those costs if you decide to have a team of workers mowing a lawn simultaneously (as is often done). You'll make roughly $50-$75 per job in a residential lawn care business; more if handling corporate accounts in addition. However, your income isn't limited to flat fees, because many happy customers also include a tip for your trouble.

Keys to Success

By scheduling some or all of these services with the same customers in the same neighborhoods, you will save on transportation and rental costs. One day you might be mowing lawns and another you'll be aerating. You might have to rent an aeration roller for $25 a day. But if you schedule aerations in one neighborhood for the same day, you'll easily recoup the investment.

"Must-Have" Checklist for New Businesses

Here are some of the more critical items you'll need for your new business:

- Computer system with a printer, fax/modem, and special software packages pertaining to your business and its needs (accounting, desktop publishing, etc.)

- Phone system with voice mail capability or answering machine

- File cabinets with a filing system

- Comfortable, ergonomically designed chair (often a last thought, but incredibly important to your productivity)

- Desk with plenty of arm space (for working on projects without bumping into your computer)

- Bookshelf to hold your numerous resources

- Office supplies: stapler/staples, paper clips, pens/pencils, tape, corrective fluid, date stamp

- Storage shelves or cabinet (usually to house supplies)

- Garbage bins (don't forget one for recyclable paper)

- Background music (if that's important to you or your customers)

- Most important: good lighting. One tiny desk lamp just won't do, and your staff will work as productively as you do if you invest in proper, clear lighting.

Lawyer

Start-up cost:	$15,000-$30,000 (less if sharing space and resources)
Potential earnings:	50,000-$80,000
Typical fees:	$125/hour outside the major cities
Advertising:	Yellow Pages, networking, referrals (many legal restrictions on lawyer advertising apply), organization memberships
Qualifications:	Law degree, persistence, people skills
Equipment needed:	Office space decorated in a professional (not necessarily ostentatious) manner, access to law library, computer, modem, fax, software, laser printer, business card, letterhead, envelopes
Staff required:	Not initially (if you can type)
Handicapped opportunity:	Yes
Hidden costs:	Drain on your billable time from people wanting free advice, insurance, on-line time

What You Do

Abraham Lincoln did it, so why can't you? It has been fashionable to mock the "single shingle" lawyer, but opportunities to join huge firms right out of law school—and make huge bucks—have just about vanished today. One way to use the degree you have just suffered through is to start your own business. You create the clientele, you develop the specialty, you do the billing, you reap the rewards. Can you find a way to show total commitment to the success of small businesses in your area? Are you able to disentangle the affairs of wealthy individuals and keep them in control of their lives? Can you deal with the anguish of divorcing people and help them manage the separation process through mediation and negotiation? If you answered yes to any of these questions, you can make a go of your single-shingle operation and give up the frustrating struggle to be hired by someone else.

What You Need

Many solo practitioners share office space, support staff, and other necessary costs of setting up in business. You'll need an appropriate and professional-looking space in which to meet your clients, and you must produce and store the paperwork. Spend at least $5,000 on your office and its contents (include an extra $3,000 for a high-power computer to make on-line searches less time-consuming and, hence, less costly). Bill out at around $125 to start; after your reputation is as good as old Abe's, you can start charging like the big boys ($200-$300 per hour).

Keys to Success

Probably the most important factor in your success will be your connections to the community you hope to serve. The average Joe tends to have a negative view of all lawyers, and you're going to need to keep struggling against this stereotype. Building trust is so challenging that you will have little chance for success unless you start with a network of people who know and like you. Eventually you will become known as the helpful, skilled lawyer to go to when a need for work in your specialty arises. Another difficulty is that you will be constantly asked to work for free. Everyone needs a lawyer from time to time, but many people are reluctant to pay for a lawyer's experience, expertise, and legal skills. It will be your job to track hours, send bills, and make sure the funds are collected. This is a tedious, time-consuming process. One tip: Consider offering prepaid legal services, which works much like insurance.

Expert Advice

What sets your business apart from others like it?

Stanford M. Altschul, sole practitioner based in Long Island, New York, says he picked a niche and set about servicing it with free information (in the form of marketing materials such as brochures and newsletters). "I market myself regularly to my clients, keeping my name in front of them via newsletters, brochures, and other direct mail pieces I produce myself."

Things you couldn't do without:

Altschul could not do without a computer and laser printer, telephone, copier, and fax machine.

Marketing tips/advice:

"You should definitely be networking with certain industries that will bring you referral business, such as accounting, real estate, and banking. All of these professionals are in regular contact with those who need your services."

If you had to do it all over again . . .

"I made a mistake in being in a partnership that wasn't a good partnership . . . It took me over twenty years to figure out that I prefer working alone."

Lead Exchange/
Business Networking Service

Start-up cost:	$5,000-$10,000
Potential earnings:	20,000-$80,000
Typical fees:	$200-$300 per year per member
Advertising:	Business publications, newspapers, Yellow Pages, direct mail, networking
Qualifications:	The ability to organize and lead groups
Equipment needed:	You'll need to rent meeting space on a monthly basis (negotiate a special rate based on frequency)
Staff required:	None initially
Handicapped opportunity:	Yes
Hidden costs:	Phone costs can grow as business owners run on about their business; keep it short and sweet

What You Do

There are at least 5,000 new businesses launched every day of the week, and all of them need to connect with other businesses to exchange leads and helpful ideas. Your business brings these entrepreneurial minds to the table, encouraging interaction and support. That's what your members essentially get from joining a business networking service. What you get from this service is a steady income and the rewards of facilitating the success of others. You'll round up as many new business owners as you can, invite them to an introductory session, and hook them up with seasoned professionals. Then, secure a financial commitment of anywhere from $200-$300 per year from each member organization, and you've got a business networking service. What sets you apart from other associations (like the Chamber of Commerce, for example) is that you provide expert ability to mix exactly the right combination of professionals, allowing only one company to join in a given category so that there is not direct competition. You can also provide monthly speakers to inspire and motivate the entire group to continued success.

What You Need

You'll need to advertise your service extensively at first; set aside at least $1,500 for this necessity (until your own networking members bring you additional business). You will also need to rent a monthly meeting place; check hotels, churches, and universities for the best rates. Charges are typically $200-$300 per business member.

Keys to Success

If bringing people and businesses together to work for the group's common good pleases you, you will be pleasing others and making a great deal of money doing it. However, be sure not to invite any unethical businesses into the group; check each out with the Better Business Bureau before accepting their application. It will go miles toward preserving your credibility.

Licensing Agent

Start-up cost:	$3,000-$6,000
Potential earnings:	50,000-$100,000
Typical fees:	Percentage of the deal (typically around 15 percent)
Advertising:	Referrals, association memberships, networking
Qualifications:	Salesmanship, outgoing personality, confidence, ability to communicate with the technical people, the business types, and the manufacturing specialists
Equipment needed:	Computer, fax/modem, copier, laser printer, office furniture, business cards, letterhead, envelopes
Staff required:	No
Handicapped opportunity:	Yes
Hidden costs:	Insurance, attorney's fees to draw up contracts

What You Do

The licensing agent acts as a go-between, helping a technology-driven company find a manufacturer for its invention. In addition, you help manufacturers or service companies find organizations that offer the technology they need. The service provided by a licensing agent is often transnational. Possibly you will be finding technology for Chinese companies that cannot develop it locally. Licensing agents usually specialize in one industry—shoe products, electronic products—in which they have developed extensive experience and contacts. This way they already know many people on both sides of the street before they start. Some technical competence in the field is required, but this can be gained through experience. The other important quality for a licensing agent is patience. You may work for a long time on several deals, only one of which pays off.

What You Need

Equipping your office to produce professional-looking reports and keep in touch with the world is the main start-up cost; expect to spend at least $3,000 on that alone. However, considering that your 15 percent is spread across a wide range of potential projects, your earnings could be as high as $100,000.

Keys to Success

Becoming a licensing agent is an excellent way for a newly laid-off person to use his/her contacts. It can be a welcome alternative to simply struggling to get the same job with a competitor. If you've got the sales skills, the contacts, and the ability to communicate with the "techie" dreamers as easily as the hard-nosed business types, you can build a successful enterprise. Keep in mind that you will be paid a percentage of the final deal. This can take a long time to bear fruit, and it is essential to have the agreement in writing from the start. There tend to be a lot of disputes if that percentage turns into big money.

Literary Agent

Start-up cost:	$500-$1,500
Potential earnings:	20,000-$60,000+
Typical fees:	15 percent commission on domestic sales, 25 percent on foreign rights, 20 percent on film rights
Advertising:	Listing in the Guide to Literary Agents and Art/Photo Reps; ads in Writer's Digest and The Writer magazines, networking at writer's conferences
Qualifications:	Should know a good book a mile away
Equipment needed:	Computer, printer, fax/modem, copier, phone system
Staff required:	No
Handicapped opportunity:	Yes
Hidden costs:	Insurance, copying, postage, phone expenses

What You Do

The literary life is indeed a glamorous one, especially if you're a literary agent. Imagine entire days filled with power meetings at large publishing houses, where you're negotiating for the best deal for one of the many writers you represent. You'll be offering everything from the right to publish to film and foreign rights (for publication overseas). Your business may also extend to book promotion, as you could negotiate book tours and publicity for your client in addition to the sale of the book project itself. Of course, you would hope to represent that one unknown client who could really score big in the publishing industry, such as Robert James Waller did with his *Bridges of Madison County*; look everywhere for talent—even in remote cities or small rural towns. No matter how hard you try, realize that not all literary agents can represent a Stephen King—and you should go in with an open mind whenever you look through the piles of manuscripts and queries on your desk. The successes could really surprise you.

What You Need

Your start-up is relatively low ($500-$1,500) and mostly covers your initial advertising costs and basic office equipment setup. With your commission, you stand a good chance of earning a respectable income of at least $20,000—but look forward to making as much as $60,000 or more (depending on whether you get that "big break").

Keys to Success

On the one hand, you'll be making a good piece of change hanging around the best media minds in the business. On the other hand, you'll have to know when to give up on a particular project, even if it seems totally worthwhile. Often in the publishing world, trends take over and dominate what's likely to be published (remember, for instance, the Mafia book craze a few years back?). You'll need to constantly stay on top of what's hot.

Litigation Management Services

Start-up cost:	$5,000-$10,000
Potential earnings:	40,000-$75,000
Typical fees:	Equivalent to the prevailing fee level for lawyers in the community; about $125/hour for small firms outside major U.S. cities.
Advertising:	Local business associations, advertising in trade journals and business publications, referrals
Qualifications:	Law or accounting background, experience in case management and billing assessment, litigation experience
Equipment needed:	Business office, computer, modem, fax, software, printer, business card, letterhead, envelopes
Staff required:	No
Handicapped opportunity:	Yes
Hidden costs:	Insurance

What You Do

The movement is under way to rein in legal costs. Above all, the astronomical costs of litigation are being managed as closely as possible. For business organizations with a small in-house legal staff or none at all, you can provide this important cost-management service. Assessing ongoing billing can spotlight waste, duplication of services, over-billing, and incorrect entries. This is painstaking work, and often busy in-house lawyers do not have time to comb through the bills their organization receives from outside counsel. The economic benefit of having an outside service perform this function should far outweigh its cost to the organization.

What You Need

Equipping your office to be functional and present a professional image will be expensive ($4,000-$10,000). This business is not a candidate for running from a corner of your dining-room table. Still, you'll be able to charge around $125 an hour for your services, so you should be able to afford a decent office.

Keys to Success

This service is a creative way to utilize a background that combines legal training with financial and accounting skills. More and more lawyers are competing for the shrinking number of jobs, but few have the combination of expertise and experience that will make you a success in this tightly focused service niche. Marketing your services will be challenging as the concept is new. One success will lead to referrals, though. You will need to allow yourself considerable time to build the business. A thick skin is necessary to face up to possible negative reactions from the lawyers whose accounts you are checking.

Expert Advice

What sets your business apart from others like it?

Marie Dutton Brown, President of Marie Brown Associates literary agency in New York City, says her business is unique because her agency primarily represents African-American authors. "We connect clients to the publishing industry and provide counsel for writers . . . we focus on black life and culture as well as books of general interest."

Things you couldn't do without:

Phone, fax, copier, computer, and typewriter.

Marketing tips/advice:

"Start small, think big, and follow your niche," says Brown. She enjoys the process of bringing an interesting creative project to fruition, and thrives on positive publicity. She has been profiled by the Associated Press, and that has certainly been a profitable marketing tool.

If you had to do it all over again . . .

"I would have started with more capital. As it was, I started at home with only $1,000. It takes more than that to get things rolling."

Magician

Start-up cost:	$500-$1,000
Potential earnings:	6,500-$20,000 or more
Typical fees:	Not necessarily carved in stone, but generally $50 per two-hour children's party, $300 per two-hour adult event
Advertising:	Yellow Pages, entertainment section of newspapers, bulletin boards, networking with civic organizations
Qualifications:	Ability to perform magic tricks convincingly, outgoing personality
Equipment needed:	Magic trick equipment, business cards
Staff required:	No
Handicapped opportunity:	Possibly
Hidden costs:	Advertising

What You Do

To be a good magician, you must have the ability to learn magic tricks and perform them quite convincingly (despite the audience's willing suspension of disbelief). You can buy kits from party centers/entertainment retailers or possibly take a continuing education course from your local university/college. Working as an assistant for an established magician is also a good way to learn the business. Having a good personality and the ability to work well with people is a strong selling point.

What You Need

Start-up should be minimal depending on what you invest in. Visit the local library to find books on magic for an inexpensive way to learn the art. Investing in magic kits from retailers will cost you a little more. The most expensive start-up cost would be to take a class.

Keys to Success

Perform for free at your friends' parties or children's school functions to get exposure. Once your name gets on the streets, start charging for your services. Attempt to work with your city's parks/recreation department for leads or a convention center to get jobs at conferences. Working with an events planner or advertising agency is another good way to get your own name pulled out of the hat.

Mailing List Service

Start-up cost:	$5,000-$9,000
Potential earnings:	40,000-$100,000 per year
Typical fees:	15 to 25 cents per entry (name, address, city, state, zip); about $1 per entry per year to maintain the list. Mailing out 10,000 pieces of mail could cost $800-$1,200
Advertising:	Contacting local stores, associations, churches, clubs, etc. to offer to maintain their lists for them, networking in business organizations, Yellow Pages, direct mail
Qualifications:	Detailed knowledge of postal regulations for bulk mailings, computer expertise, fast, accurate typing skills, ability to meet deadlines
Equipment needed:	Computer, printer, specialized software, database, post office permits, office furniture, business card, letterhead, postage machine
Staff required:	None
Handicapped opportunity:	Yes
Hidden costs:	Be sure to invest in backup tapes for your computer system in the event of disaster

What You Do

Although we all deplore the amount of "junk mail" that is dumped in our mailboxes each day, the amazing growth of direct mail is going to continue—and the opportunity to succeed in running a mailing list service for the companies sending those materials is tremendous. Start-up costs are low, skills needed are easy to acquire, and money is there to be made. Your service can include list maintenance, mailings, creation of lists, list brokering, and even teaching others about mailing lists. Understanding and meeting the changing regulations of the U.S. Postal Service is perhaps the most challenging part of the job. However, software, pamphlets, and seminars abound to bring you up to speed.

What You Need

You will spend from $5,000 to $9,000 on the equipment and supplies needed for this business. Depending on your specialty, you may be able to begin for even less, especially if you lease a postage meter machine and some of the other equipment. Charges will vary for your services, but you'll need to set two rates from the get-go: a per-entry fee (usually 15 to 25 cents per name) and an annual list maintenance fee of $1 per entry.

Keys to Success

Mailing list businesses are relatively easy to start and to promote. You can have as large a customer base as you wish, rather than relying on just a few key clients. The actual work of creating and maintaining the lists is pretty routine, although it does require attention to detail and great accuracy. A thorough understanding of postal regulations is vitally important—and the regulations are constantly changing. You have to be sure you know what you're doing to gain and keep your customers' business.

Makeup Artist

Start-up cost:	$500-$1,500
Potential earnings:	20,000-$40,000
Typical fees:	$20-$30 per session
Advertising:	Newspapers, beauty salons, bridal consultants, funeral homes, department stores
Qualifications:	Eye for color and contour
Equipment needed:	Makeup samples/kits, brushes, cotton swabs, a director's chair
Staff required:	No
Handicapped opportunity:	Possibly
Hidden costs:	Insurance

What You Do

If you enjoy making eyes for people, or just plain giving them lip, you will revel in the opportunity to be a professional makeup artist. Your services are needed in extremely diverse areas, from the life and action of the stage to the stately composure of the funeral home. You could offer makeovers for brides-to-be, new moms, college graduates, and those simply in the mood for a new look. Or, you could specialize in helping those who are disfigured due to accident or illness. Whomever you choose as your clientele, you will need to be familiar with all skin types and problems, matching your products carefully with each client's basic needs. With an astounding array of cosmetic products currently available (even at wholesale prices), you could produce professional and fabulous-looking results for just about any client in no time. Study facial structure to know where to shade and what to hide, and you're on your way to a beautiful new beginning!

What You Need

Your costs are relatively nominal. Start out with some makeup kits and samples, supplies, and a sturdy chair for your clients to sit on—then add your brochures, business cards, or flyers. All of this should cost you no more than $1,000—but add a little more if you decide to sell the products you're using, because you'll need to secure a vendor's license.

Keys to Success

While you may enjoy the freedom and creativity of being a professional makeup artist, you may also find the lack of predictable income unnerving. Try to offer your services to groups to maximize your marketing moments, because the one-customer-at-a-time philosophy doesn't cut it with this business.

Management Consultant

Start-up cost:	$5,000-$15,000
Potential earnings:	30,000-$60,000 (average); some make as much as $300,000/year
Typical fees:	Varies by market and client needs: average of $500-$1,500 per day (can charge by hour, day, or job)
Advertising:	Networking, referrals, creating audio- or videotapes showing your skills, ads in professional organizations' magazines and newsletters, brochures, direct mail
Qualifications:	Technical knowledge, expertise, and experience, good problem-solving skills, good people skills, excellent communication skills (written and oral)
Equipment needed:	Computer, printer, appropriate software, fax, phone, office furniture, reference books
Staff required:	No
Handicapped opportunity:	Yes
Hidden costs:	Special insurance, such as errors and omissions coverage, may be needed. Budget the time and money for continuing education to keep your skills up-to-date (techniques, technology, etc.)

What You Do

The Institute of Management Consulting has members handling more than 250 specialties. Professional consulting is a fast-growing field that is expected to increase by 25 percent by the end of the '90s, and management consulting is the biggest segment of that field. U.S. companies rely heavily on management consultants, especially in the areas of compliance (with many government agencies) and the introduction of new technologies, and to take the place of permanent staff as companies become leaner. Consultants provide many services, from strategy-planning and implementation to analysis and problem-solving. Many who choose to become consultants are those with top-level skills and experience. They want the freedom and greater variety of working for themselves and recognize the world of opportunity that exists in assisting smaller, entrepreneurial companies get their businesses off the ground.

What You Need

Start-up costs will vary according to the requirements of the specialty you choose. No matter what you decide, however, you will require the basic office and computer equipment (costing as little as $2,500); depending on the quality and extent of computer equipment needed, this figure could reach $12,000. You will also need to budget $800-$1,800 for continuing education, organizational dues, and reference books.

Keys to Success

To succeed in this business, you must first analyze yourself: decide what sorts of problems you can solve for a client, based on your experience and expertise. Research the companies (or types of companies) for which you want to offer your services to help you discover needs you can fill. Network with every contact you have in your target areas. Remember, though, that not everyone with good technical skills can be a successful consultant. You need excellent listening and counseling abilities—and patience. Not only does it take time to "grow" your business, but often it takes considerable time to determine if your efforts have paid off for the client. Meeting the challenges of working as a consultant can be financially rewarding. You will have the opportunity to work on a wide variety of projects and enjoy helping clients find creative, successful solutions to their problems.

Expert Advice

What sets your business apart from others like it?

Norma J. Rist, owner of The Boardroom Group based in Akron, Ohio, says her business assists women business owners to become clear about their goals and to achieve them in a shorter period of time and in an easier way by providing resources and business information in a group setting.

Things you couldn't do without:

A business phone line, fax, copier, and personal computer. Also, a meeting/conference room is useful for generating group discussion and participation.

Marketing tips/advice:

"Segment your niche even more . . . I started 'Spirit Groups' for home-based business owners at the same time so that I could serve a broader population of women owners and generate more income potential simultaneously."

If you had to do it all over again . . .

"I would have segmented much earlier."

Manicurist

Start-up cost:	$5,000-$10,000
Potential earnings:	15,000-$35,000
Typical fees:	$50 per set of nails (for length additions) and $15 for a simple manicure or pedicure
Advertising:	Newspapers, coupon books, bulletin boards, Yellow Pages
Qualifications:	Certification in cosmetology or as a nail technician often required
Equipment needed:	Manicuring table with a strong light, credit card processing equipment (if you decide to accept plastic), and nail enhancement or beautification products
Staff required:	No
Handicapped opportunity:	Possibly
Hidden costs:	Liability insurance and materials

What You Do

Luxurious nails are no longer for the rich and famous only—brides want them, society mavens want them, young women want them. You'll only stand to make money from this business if you are a licensed professional, mainly because there are simply not enough skilled nail technicians to go around. Often, the wait to have fiberglass or acrylic nails is two to three weeks (for reputable places) and you could potentially make enough money off of your competitors' overflow. At any rate, you'll be providing a timeless personal service for those who appreciate the finer things in life (translation: don't be afraid to charge a little more than you're worth). You'll create beautiful long nails that would make Cher green with envy, or you'll simply clean and shape nails for folks who are in the limelight often (even if it's only before a board of directors). Yes, men and women alike use the services of a manicurist, so try not to forget that in your marketing pieces.

What You Need

Essentially, you'll need a good, strong table and a bright enough light to work with, in addition to your nail polishes and assorted nail maintenance equipment. All of this could cost $1,000-$3,000—but add on more if you're planning to rent space somewhere. Charge at least $40-$60 for acrylic, fiberglass, or gel nails; $15 for a simple manicure.

Keys to Success

If you like working with people from several different walks of life, this could be your kind of business—hands down. However, the community gossip might leave you with information you'd rather not know.

Manufacturer's Representative

Start-up cost:	$2,500-$9,000
Potential earnings:	Up to $150,000 (gross) in first three years
Typical fees:	Commission basis, usually 5 to 15 percent of product sale (depends on product, level of difficulty in selling it, size of territory, and other factors)
Advertising:	Cold-calling, networking, presentations, reference publications
Qualifications:	Sales experience or expertise in a particular field, good people skills, an ability to negotiate
Equipment needed:	Computer, fax, phone, cellular phone, office furniture, business cards, letterhead
Staff required:	No
Handicapped opportunity:	Yes
Hidden costs:	Mileage

What You Do

Companies are operating with slimmer sales forces these days, creating a need for other alternatives in marketing and selling their products. Independent reps can take on an interesting variety of products to sell—everything from gifts and sporting goods to chemicals, adhesives, and heavy machinery. Many experts recommend that manufacturing agents handle eight to ten lines of goods in order to make a nice profit. In addition to a thorough understanding of your product's features and benefits, you also need a solid customer base for each line and enough money to carry you while you get established, which can take up to a year. Having a background in the product(s) you rep is the easiest way to succeed. Look for opportunities with emerging companies, such as those profiled in entrepreneurial publications and business newspapers. Be sure to include a client list or background sheet on yourself when approaching new companies—they appreciate and often require that level of professionalism.

What You Need

As mentioned, costs start at approximately $2,500 for computer and office equipment. You may also need a laptop, cellular phone, and modem to use while "on the road;" if so, tack on another $5,000-$6,000. At 5 to 25 percent commission, it could take a while to develop cash flow—but one good sale is all you need to turn into more business.

Keys to Success

Sales can be one of the most lucrative home businesses of all. Meeting and working with people can be very rewarding, as can the freedom of choosing the companies you will represent and setting your own hours. On the downside, repping for a living can mean long periods of travel and, sometimes, a long wait to be paid for your services. Also, sales in some fields will require you to be aggressive and highly competitive to succeed. Can you swim with the sharks—or will you be eaten alive?

Marketing Consultant

Start-up cost:	$5,000-$10,000
Potential earnings:	60,000-$150,000
Typical fees:	Hourly fees range from $50 to $200, while the fee for leading a workshop might be $2,000-$4,000.
Advertising:	Referrals, word of mouth
Qualifications:	Broad expertise in marketing or specialization in one area, business savvy, high energy level, excellent written/oral communications skills, creativity, persistence
Equipment needed:	Computer, laptop, laser printer, fax/modem, copier, office furniture, business card, letterhead, envelopes
Staff required:	No
Handicapped opportunity:	No
Hidden costs:	Membership dues, phone bills, on-line time

What You Do

Customers are the lifeblood of all businesses—and marketing is how companies attract them. Sales are the end result of the entire marketing process, which can take almost as many forms as there are enterprises. Developing ads, writing printed materials and letters, creating promotions, gaining publicity, and designing sales strategies are all facets of marketing. Just developing a focused marketing plan is a demanding activity, and most executives need the services of a marketing professional to produce effective results. Marketing consultants are filling in the gaps left by downsizing at big organizations, as well as supplying these services to small companies. Even though this is the second largest category of consulting after management consulting, opportunities abound if you can produce results.

What You Need

Marketing materials require a sophisticated and flexible computer setup ($4,000-$6,000). You'll need to be able to produce drafts even if the client's art department or an ad agency creates the final versions. You'll spend an equal amount on marketing efforts of your own (including joining associations in which you can build a strong network). If you're persistent and have the kind of marketing personality that draws customers in, you can earn as much as $150,000 a year.

Keys to Success

Above all, effective marketing takes imagination. What do potential customers want, and what kind of message will enable them to see that your client's product is that very thing? Knowing how to create these interactions will make you a success as a marketing consultant, if you combine that expertise with an ability to scope out your client company. To prove your worth, try to highlight strengths that they may not have realized they had. You may need to structure the goals for the marketing plan and get buy-in from the executives before the ads, promos, or sales letters are developed. Be sure to get a contract with payment milestones in writing as these projects can take many months to come to fruition.

Dynamic Goal-Setting

If you want to succeed in business, you need to start with a good goal-setting program. Seek out professional help in this area if you are not sure how to identify and set your own goals.

Here are just a few tips to get you started:

1. **Remember to make your goals specific.** The only goals that stand a chance of being achieved are the ones that are clear enough to become part of a mind-set and visualization process. The clearer the goal, the easier to accomplish.

2. **Have a deadline for achievement.** You can have a terrific goal, but wander around aimlessly without a drop-dead date for its achievement. Someone once said that a goal is a dream with a deadline.

3. **Consider and anticipate your obstacles.** Know where the pitfalls might occur, and devise a plan to work around such impediments.

Above all else, make sure there is a personal benefit to achieving the goal, or it will not serve to motivate you. You need to reward yourself with a vacation if you sell one million dollars' worth of product, or you might not be able to see the benefit of working so hard to achieve that goal.

Massage Therapist

Start-up cost:	$1,000-$5,000
Potential earnings:	15,000-$35,000
Typical fees:	$45-$60 per hour session
Advertising:	Newspapers, Yellow Pages, bulletin boards, direct mail to corporations
Qualifications:	Must be state-certified (in most states)
Equipment needed:	Massage table, products such as oils and relaxing music
Staff required:	None
Handicapped opportunity:	Not likely
Hidden costs:	You may have to carry liability insurance

What You Do

If you can't keep your hands off of anyone, being a massage therapist could bring you immediate (financial) satisfaction. Seriously, massage therapists are finally entering their own as certified professionals rather than as euphemisms for other, less desirable types of professionals. They must study human anatomy as clinically and carefully as a para-medical professional would, and must have the ability to make people relax enough to enjoy the service itself. With many of us leading increasingly stressful lives, such professionals should be welcome almost anywhere—from health clubs to wellness centers and even metaphysical bookstores. Many massage therapists offer their services to harried executives, and visit them on-site to work out the kinks in their backs and necks. Still others work out of their homes or in small, quiet offices.

What You Need

If you decide to lease a small office, you can expect to spend at least $350 and up per month on rent alone. Add to that your massage table (about $500) and some relaxing music, soothing oils, and clean towels (allow another $250 or so for these). Finally, you must get the word out via advertising and/or direct mail to individuals or corporate clients, so expect to spend about $500-$1,000 on marketing, too.

Keys to Success

Working in a relaxing atmosphere while helping others relieve stress can be positively exhilarating for you—but it can also be tiring. Are you sure you can stand up to the physical demands of this business—which usually leaves you on your feet most of the day. If the answer is yes to that question, the rest will, like tense muscles, fall back into place.

Advertising Effectively— and Economically

You've started a business and you need to get the word out. The problem is, you simply don't have the kind of budget that General Motors does to advertise your products or services. What can you do? You could try one or more of these economical methods:

- **Press releases.** Free press is the best, when you are lucky enough to get it. Try to offer tips to a particular group of people, and you'll have a better chance of catching the interest of an editor.

- **Flyers.** Post them everywhere your potential customers go. If you've got a moving or packing service, a flyer strategically located at a laundromat or apartment complex bulletin board might yield some quick results for you. Be where they are, and you'll go far.

- **Get an Internet address, or design a Web Page.** The advertising wave of the future is on the 'Net. Why? Because it is so inexpensive compared to print media. Will it help you get all the business you need? That remains to be seen, but all indications are good. One pie baker sold a thousand pies the first few months after she posted her Web Site. If she can do that, imagine what you could do.

- **Offer coupon deals regularly.** Coupons are ads that come with souvenirs for your customers; you get the sale, they walk away with a prize for doing business with you: a lower price or a better deal. Who can beat that?

- **Trades for advertising space.** Often, you might have a service that a local newspaper or TV/radio station needs. You can sometimes trade your services for free space or airtime.

- **Direct mail.** You can spend a small amount of money and reach a large number of potentials through direct mail pieces. Be sure to design something that's interesting and captivating. Your clients are deluged with such pieces (sometimes referred to as "junk mail") so yours needs to be fairly innovative and attention-getting. Work with a professional (you can trade services here, too) to write and design your direct mail pieces.

Mediator

Start-up cost:	$5,000-$10,000
Potential earnings:	40,000-$65,000
Typical fees:	$75-$300 (usually split between the disputing parties)
Advertising:	Yellow Pages, newspapers, bulletin boards, networking with legal groups
Qualifications:	Some states require license
Equipment needed:	Office with comfortable furniture, phones, computer
Staff required:	No
Handicapped opportunity:	Yes
Hidden costs:	Some cases are more complicated than others; try to see the writing on the wall when it comes to the bigger jobs

What You Do

The wave of the legal future is the mediator, especially with the rising cost of attorneys. While attorneys are paid to reach an eventual settlement, a mediator looks for ways to settle any disputes with compromise and without going to court. Because many marriages end in bitter divorce, mediators have their ripest ground in the domestic sector, where they can save the parties literally thousands of dollars in litigation and get to the heart of the matter through mutual conciliation. Identifying what each party truly wants out of the deal is the most critical part of successful mediation. Keeping the parties from killing each other is the next. Are you skilled at bringing people back to the issues at hand instead of hurling pointless accusations at each other? Can you help them to see the big picture in this situation? If so, you would make a fine mediator. You're essentially being paid to help fighting folks stay out of court. It's an admirable profession—and getting to be more and more profitable for those involved.

What You Need

You'll need a nice, comfortable office for these transitional customers of yours, so expect to lay out at least $3,000 for your "digs." Next, spend some money advertising in places potential clients typically look for help (namely, the Yellow Pages). You'll charge $75-$300 per job; more if the work gets complicated.

Keys to Success

While this is an admirable profession and is much more respected than others in the legal profession, it's still a personally challenging one. Can you listen all day to folks fighting over trivial and petty things (like who gets the washing machine)? If you're able to keep them focused on the goal of an amicable settlement, you'll do well. But do take time for yourself—you'll need it.

Expert Advice

What sets your business apart from others like it?

Albert H. Couch, a Family, Divorce and Community Mediator for Akron Family Mediation in Akron, Ohio, says three things set his business apart from others like it. "We have a full-time commitment to mediation, and a lot of mediators don't have that. Second, we cap our fees so that our customers know there's a limit to what they'll spend with us. Finally, we have experience in our field and are aggressive in promoting mediation in general. When I'm not mediating, I'm talking about mediating somewhere."

Things you couldn't do without:

Couch says he couldn't do without a computer, phone and, most important, the training he's had in his field.

Marketing tips/advice:

"Learn mediation inside and out, that's first and foremost." But the second most important thing you can do, according to Couch, is to talk mediation with just about anyone who'll listen. "This is primarily a word-of-mouth business."

If you had to do it all over again . . .

"I'd spend less money up front on advertising, since so much of my business comes from referrals. I advise others to get involved in their community and give as many speeches as you can to promote your business."

Medical Claims Processing

Start-up cost:	$5,000-$12,500
Potential earnings:	12,000-$48,000
Typical fees:	Monthly rates of $800-$1,500 per client
Advertising:	Direct mail, networking, telemarketing
Qualifications:	Knowledge of insurance billing including CPT coding, Medicare and Medicaid regulations, capitation, changes in legislation and subsequent forms
Equipment needed:	Desk, computer with hard drive and modem, printer, medical billing software, fax, typewriter, CPT coding manual
Staff required:	Not initially; may be needed to grow
Handicapped opportunity:	Yes
Hidden costs:	If you are new to the insurance claims arena, it is strongly suggested that you attend various seminars and training sessions

What You Do

As regulation of the medical field continues, the number of businesses that simplify the claims process will also grow. Due to an aging population and the 1990 federal law requiring physicians to submit claims for all their Medicare patients, many medical offices are inundated with paperwork. This has created the need to hire outside billing services to process the claim and provide various other services such as invoicing, collecting any copayments required from the patient, tracking past due and uncollectible accounts, and answering all patient questions regarding their claim. A minimum of four to six doctors or practices is required to remain reasonably profitable. If you are looking for a challenging opportunity that utilizes computer technology and sharp interpersonal skills this is a very promising field.

What You Need

Access to a computer, modem, and updated medical billing software is a must to really compete in this market (costs range from $3,000-$5,000). In addition, allow for hourly wages of additional staff as your business begins to grow. Be sure to shop around for the best rate on phone line service since the modem will be used extensively.

Keys to Success

Medical claims processing requires patience and attention to detail. The work is often challenging and interesting due to the ever-changing nature of health insurance and Medicare. Although selling your services may be difficult at first, good communication skills and persistence will result in lasting relationships with those doctors or offices that you service. Once your business is established, processing claims electronically takes little time and can be done at your convenience. Most importantly, a successful medical billing service can be quite profitable.

Medical Transcriptionist

Start-up cost:	$5,000-$9,000
Potential earnings:	30,000-$60,000 (billing 2,000 hours a year)
Typical fees:	$30-$40 per hour
Advertising:	Advertise in publications of local medical societies, direct mail, telemarketing, networking
Qualifications:	Excellent listening skills and good eye, hand, and auditory coordination, knowledge of word processing, dictation and transcription equipment, understanding of medical diagnostic procedures and terminology, good typing skills, impeccable spelling
Equipment needed:	Computer, printer if not using modem, transcriber, word-processing software, reference books
Staff required:	Not initially; may be needed to grow
Handicapped opportunity:	Yes
Hidden costs:	As many as one to two years of education may be required if you have little or no experience. Business cards, letterhead, envelopes are necessary to promote a professional image

What You Do

According to the American Association of Medical Transcription (AAMT), there is a shortage of qualified transcriptionists. This job is in demand for two reasons: many insurance companies are requiring transcribed reports before they will pay doctors or hospitals and transcribed copy provides health care professionals with the necessary documentation for review of patients' history, legal evidence of patient care, data for research, or to render continuing patient care. Since turnaround time of transcription is a primary concern for health care providers, increase your competitiveness by offering pickup and delivery, seven-day-a-week service, same-day service, and phone-in dictation service.

What You Need

Computer hardware and software will run you anywhere from $1,900-$5,000 with a transcriber unit ranging from $200-$800. Do not forget that this job requires hours sitting in front of a computer; a good chair and desk at the proper height is a smart investment.

Keys to Success

Medical transcribing can become somewhat monotonous. You must possess high levels of self-discipline and focus as you work. In addition, the demand for faster turnaround times occasionally necessitates working nights and weekends. On the other hand, medical transcription work is steady and resistant to recession! This field is rapidly expanding with more work than there are trained transcriptionists.

Meeting Planner

Start-up cost:	$2,500-$6,500
Potential earnings:	25,000 to start per year; possibly as high as $100,000 per year after you get established
Typical fees:	$40-$60 per hour or $400-$500 per day; planners handling large events such as conventions may get 15 to 20 percent of the overall projected budget for the entire event
Advertising:	Networking with convention and visitors' bureaus, caterers, and travel agents to hear about conferences and conventions, plan a civic or charitable event on a volunteer basis to gain experience, advertise in meeting magazines
Qualifications:	Excellent organizational and negotiation skills; detail-oriented; good business background; good communication and troubleshooting skills
Equipment needed:	Office and computer equipment, fax, telephone, reference books, business cards, stationery, envelopes
Staff required:	No
Handicapped opportunity:	Possibly
Hidden costs:	Phone costs could easily run higher than you budget

What You Do

If you like handling the myriad of details involved in planning formal events and if you have the organization, negotiation, and communication skills necessary to pull it off, you can have a great career as a meeting planner. There are many sources of business, from corporations and associations to conventions and trade shows. As companies become "leaner," employees can no longer be spared to handle meeting planning projects; also, meetings and events are increasingly viewed as great sales and marketing opportunities. Therefore, creative, talented meeting planners are in demand. You will need to be knowledgeable about many areas—everything from hotels to catering to travel. You may need to negotiate a block of hotel rooms, find exotic locales for company meetings, book speakers and entertainers, set up promotions, and handle all the many small and large details that make for a successful event. In return, you may get to travel and stay at exclusive resorts and hotels, you will meet interesting people from many walks of life—and you will have the satisfaction of seeing people enjoying your event.

What You Need

A computer and modem will cost from $1,000-$3,000. Software, printer, telephone, and fax will add from $900-$3,000 or more. Office equipment, reference books, insurance, letterhead, etc. will bring the total costs to $2,700-$8,500. Fees are typically $40-$50 per hour or $400-$600 per day. To get more assignments from the get-go, you should do a few "free" events to give potential clients a good idea of how spectacular your meetings really are.

Keys to Success

Meeting planning can be very rewarding, but it often requires long days and hard work. If you are good at handling details, you're halfway to success already, because all those little pieces of the puzzle are crucially important. In addition to making sure you have adequate money for your start-up, bear in mind that a meeting planner's livelihood is often tied to economic conditions, since companies may tighten their meeting budgets to cut costs. However, meetings and conventions will always be popular and productive, and the trend toward outsourcing them to professional meeting planners will continue—good news for you!

When to Hire a Consultant or Subcontractor

Your desk is piling up with unpaid bills, tax forms, and work orders. Your time is eaten up in the all-encompassing aspects of running your business entirely by yourself—and the work just keeps rolling in anyway. What can you do?

You could hire a consultant or a subcontractor to pick up the slack, help arrange your office so that it runs neatly and efficiently, or simply to offer you advice in an area where you are weakest. You can bring in such additional help on a short-term, per-project basis, by using the professional one time only or once per month.

But how do you find such a professional, and how do you know if their services are worth their price? If you're looking for an accounting subcontractor, for example, you might start in the Yellow Pages, or contact a local association for accounting professionals (they meet regularly and often have a directory of members).

You could also ask for referrals or recommendations from your own association members, as they have likely had the same needs as you and have probably used the services of a subcontractor at least once before. These folks will tell you everything you need to know about the pros and cons of hiring outside help, but be prepared to hear a lot of horror stories.

Message Retrieval Service

Start-up cost:	$15,000-$25,000
Potential earnings:	20,000-$35,000
Typical fees:	$50-$75 and up per month
Advertising:	Networking and referrals, Yellow Pages, business publications
Qualifications:	A pleasant, helpful phone voice
Equipment needed:	Computer with internal fax/modem board, word-processing and contact management software, phone headsets
Staff required:	Yes (usually 1-5 employees)
Handicapped opportunity:	Yes
Hidden costs:	Additional phone lines to handle more clients, personnel costs

What You Do

Answering services have been around for a long time, but the explosive growth in small service businesses has made them even more important than ever. You can take your pleasant phone manner and your good listening skills and create an excellent business opportunity. The latest software allows keyboard entry of caller information; pagers can connect you to the plumber or consultant who has hired you to be his "home office." A higher-tech approach is a voice mail system, with an options menu and the capability of recording and sharing long messages. This is increasingly a communications culture, and you can succeed by joining forces instead of competing.

What You Need

Equipment required depends to some extent on the level of service you plan to offer. If you're using a phone system including a switchboard with headsets, you'll spend at least $2,000 on equipment in the beginning. If you opt for the high-tech voice mail system, you'll shell out $5,000 or more. At any rate, you will be billing a healthy monthly fee of $50 or higher, so the equipment, and cost of paying your staff, could pay for itself in a relatively short period of time.

Keys to Success

You have a pleasant voice and care about people. You know how to filter out what is important from the background chatter. No one is better at keeping track of things than you. What can we say? You're a natural for this business. On the downside, this business does tie you down to your desk and phones. You will also have to work hard at marketing to develop enough customers.

Messenger Service

Start-up cost:	$40,000-$65,000
Potential earnings:	45,000-$60,000
Typical fees:	$35-$50 per delivery run
Advertising:	Yellow Pages, business publications, promotional items (such as pens, magnets, or notepads)
Qualifications:	Driver's license
Equipment needed:	Fleet of delivery vehicles, bicycles or (yes) Rollerblades
Staff required:	Yes
Handicapped opportunity:	No
Hidden costs:	Insurance, workers' compensation (this is a high-risk profession, particularly for bicyclists and Rollerblade delivery people in large metropolitan areas)

What You Do

What happens when you have an important message or document that absolutely, positively has to be there . . . well, sooner than overnight? You call a messenger service to run it over to the appropriate local business. Maybe the messenger service is made up of a small fleet of vehicles, or maybe it's comprised of a bunch of college students on Rollerblades, skateboards, or bicycles. However you determine to power your own fleet, you'll be wise to invest in safety gear and perhaps even first-aid training for each of your employees. It's a dangerous world out there, particularly in the big city, and even though it is definitely faster to deliver an envelope via bicycle as opposed to vehicle in a large, congested city, the high cost of personal injury may make this business a little more costly than you'd anticipated.

What You Need

You'll need a good fleet and lots of delivery people to make this one work profitably. Ideally, you'll have a small staff that works quickly enough to tackle several runs per hour—making your profit margin higher than most of the larger, better-known delivery services. You'll charge $35-$50 per delivery (and may have a surcharge for speedier runs), so you can expect an income potential of $45,000-$60,000 per year.

Keys to Success

Make sure your staff is physically fit, able to handle multiple tasks, and just plain quick about it. You'll make lots more money if your staff can manage to get through the streets safely.

Mobile Disc Jockey

Start-up cost:	$5,000-$10,000
Potential earnings:	15,000-$25,000
Typical fees:	$75-$150 per job
Advertising:	Classified ads, bulletin boards
Qualifications:	Knowledge of popular music, strong personality
Equipment needed:	Compact disc and cassette players, turntable, sound/mixing systems, microphone, theatrical lighting (if desired), and a larger and varied CD and cassette collection
Staff required:	No
Handicapped opportunity:	Possibly
Hidden costs:	Buying too much music at full price (try to get on record company or DJ-only promotional mailing lists)

What You Do

Because live bands cost quite a bit more than mobile disc jockey services, many party-givers book DJs to handle the entertainment needs of their party or celebration; sometimes they even ask the DJ to play "host" for a theme party. Disc jockeys have been around as long as there have been records to play, and they will continue even as equipment gets more sophisticated. For one thing, systems producing excellent sound quality are getting smaller and more portable—making it easier for DJs who travel to several locations in a given weekend. As a DJ, you'll need to develop your own style for building rapport with the audience; study the techniques of professionals you respect and try to emulate them if you can't come up with your own material. You should have a wide variety of music available—and regularly read industry publications such as Billboard and Rolling Stone to learn what's new and what's hot.

What You Need

Your start-up costs are wrapped up in equipment and your music collection itself, because advertising will cost you no more than a few hundred dollars at the outset (for classified ads). Look for used equipment and CDs before plunking down thousands of dollars extra; you could save $1,000 or more. Scour garage sales and flea markets for the unusual or obscure, and attend record fairs when you can. Since you'll be working an average of 3-5 hours per job, it's not unrealistic to set your fee at $75-$150 per event.

Keys to Success

Your work cycles will be extremely varied, with heavier loads typically in the spring and summer. Most of your work will be done on weekends, cutting into your social life considerably. If you're looking for work that's there when you want it, being a DJ is not for you. On the other hand, if you don't mind the erratic hours and enjoy being with people in a celebrative mood, you'll look forward to each new "gig."

Checklist for Success:
Can You Be a Successful
Entrepreneur?

Here are some questions you might ask yourself before embarking on a new business:

- ❏ Are you unhappy with your current situation—and ready for a change?

- ❏ Are you completely self-directed; that is, able to come up with and complete your own job requirements?

- ❏ Are you able to meet with and sell to many different types of people?

- ❏ Are you an expert planner—someone who can see not only the big picture, but every tiny line that created the big picture?

- ❏ Can you set and keep deadlines?

- ❏ Are you a clock-watcher, or someone who quickly loses track of time?

- ❏ Can you commit to projects and follow them through to completion every time?

- ❏ Are you adaptable and open to learning new ways of doing things?

- ❏ Do you have the mental and physical stamina you need to run your business?

- ❏ Are you afraid of risk?

- ❏ Do you have adequate savings to cover your first year's salary?

- ❏ Are you a positive person?

Mobile Hair Salon

Start-up cost:	$1,000-$5,000
Potential earnings:	30,000-$50,000
Typical fees:	Depends on the service (haircuts cost a lot less than perms, or hair color, but services can run anywhere from $20-$75)
Advertising:	Local newspapers, direct mail, coupons, contacts with nursing homes and hospitals
Qualifications:	Must be a licensed cosmetologist
Equipment needed:	Scissors, electric trimmers, rollers, combs, brushes, portable hair dryer, blow dryer, curling wands, towels, capes, and supplies (shampoo, etc.)
Staff required:	Yes
Handicapped opportunity:	No
Hidden costs:	Insurance, continuing education, cellular phone

What You Do

A cosmetologist who makes house calls? Without the overhead of a salon, this could be a lucrative business. However, you will have to come up with your own transportation such as a station wagon or van. Just think of all those who could take advantage of this convenient service—busy executives, stay-at-home moms, shut-ins, nursing home residents, and hospital patients. You'll have to figure in travel time. But if you plan to service a specific area on a set day of each week, you'll reduce time and travel expense. You can work with clients in their natural habitat; that can be very helpful to these clients and they will probably tip you well for your trouble.

What You Need

Spend between $1,000-$5,000 on getting this show on the road, so to speak. Mainly, you'll be covering your equipment and supply costs (and, as a licensed cosmetologist, you can buy everything wholesale, of course). Charges will vary from $25-$75, but be sure to tack on your mileage in the fee structure.

Keys to Success

You might want to hire a receptionist or answering service to take incoming calls and book appointments.

Mobile Paper-Shredding Service

Start-up cost:	$15,000-$18,000
Potential earnings:	20,000-$40,000
Typical fees:	$30-$50 per office visit
Advertising:	Local business periodicals, direct mail
Qualifications:	Marketing skills, excellent time management and scheduling ability
Equipment needed:	Van, paper shredder, computer, printer, and fax, cellular phone
Staff required:	No
Handicapped opportunity:	No
Hidden costs:	Vehicle maintenance and repair

What You Do

Mobile paper-shredding services are just now beginning to grow in major U.S. cities. As information becomes more valuable, it becomes more important to certain types of businesses to maintain security. Banks, for example, have suffered great losses when criminals obtained and analyzed their discarded paper trash. Computer codes, product information, even customer records are essential to keep confidential. The value of your service is that it guarantees security; shredding is completed on the client's premises so that no possibility exists for loss of data and information. Shredding can be done within an office, but it is time-consuming and messy. You are saving time and trouble by bringing your shredding machine to your client's site on a regular schedule to perform this necessary but tedious task.

What You Need

The van or truck is the major expense, at $15,000 or more. You, of course, will need a heavy-duty shredder as well (about $300). Charge $30-$50 per office visit; offer a monthly rate to more regular clients (attorneys and government officials, perhaps).

Keys to Success

Try to get into this business fast if you intend to do so at all, before the crush of competitors limits your opportunity to make a fair profit by your labors. Marketing will need to include considerable education so that your potential clients become aware of the advantages to their organization of the mobile shredding services

Monogramming Service

Start-up cost:	$5,000-$15,000
Potential earnings:	20,000-$50,000
Typical fees:	Varies according to items chosen and number of units/volume discounts, but generally $3.50-$100 each piece
Advertising:	Yellow Pages, local school districts, direct mail to companies
Qualifications:	Some sewing skills or ability to operate monogramming equipment
Equipment needed:	Monogramming equipment, business card
Staff required:	No
Handicapped opportunity:	Yes
Hidden costs:	Insurance

What You Do

You've seen them everywhere . . . baseball caps, sweatshirts, and jackets with company logos on them. You have a knack for knits, and for transferring a company's identity to the appropriate material. Or maybe you simply want to monogram initials onto towels, blankets, and other home accessories for the marriage-minded. Whatever your specialty area, you'll need some equipment and marketing savvy to get your business off the ground. Silk screening is a good place to start; check your local art supply shops for information and creative options. For the more advanced monogrammer, research thermal transfer devices or computer-aided sewing machines in business and trade publications before making a huge purchase.

What You Need

This business can be started on a modest budget. However, depending on the equipment you invest in, you could spend as much as $15,000 or more to get started. You will most likely need to insure any equipment purchased, plus any supplies. Expect to earn back your initial cash outlay in about two to three years, based on an income potential of $20,000-$50,000 per year.

Keys to Success

Advertising and marketing will play an important role in making this business a successful venture. Monogramming is much more than just initialing towels—and you'll need to convey that in every piece of literature you send out (particularly in your business cards).

Mortgage Loan Broker

Start-up cost:	$600-$700
Potential earnings:	15,000-$50,000
Typical fees:	Commission equal to 4 percent or less of the value of the mortgages placed, paid by borrower
Advertising:	Classified ads, real estate magazines, newspapers, referrals
Qualifications:	Extensive knowledge of real estate finance, license (in some states)
Equipment needed:	Business cards, letterhead, envelopes
Staff required:	No
Handicapped opportunity:	Yes
Hidden costs:	Advertising is necessary on an ongoing basis

What You Do

Borrowers (people and firms) who want second mortgages come to you to find a lender. Third, fourth, and even higher levels of mortgages are possible in certain cases. You may operate entirely independently or work as a subcontractor with a real estate agent or attorney. You will need to keep putting your message before the public because for the most part each transaction will be with a new client. Occasionally mortgage brokers find borrowers for lenders, rather than the reverse.

What You Need

Costs to start are very low (around $600 to start) if you already have a computer. All you'll need is a good mortgage program. You could earn your first $15,000 easily enough, charging only 4 percent of the total mortgage.

Keys to Success

Once you develop a reputation for effectiveness, you may find that repeat business from one or more lenders will bring in an excellent income. But most mortgage brokers focus on finding would-be borrowers and then linking them with the dollars. You'll need an ability to inspire confidence and to speak the language of people on both sides of the transaction. Patience and active listening are also very applicable in this type of enterprise.

Mover

Start-up cost:	$1,500-$3,000
Potential earnings:	20,000 and up
Typical fees:	$35 or more
Advertising:	Classified ads, radio spots, direct mail, flyers, community bulletin boards, referrals
Qualifications:	Physical strength, experience
Equipment needed:	Truck, pads, straps, packing materials
Staff required:	Yes
Handicapped opportunity:	No
Hidden costs:	Insurance, truck maintenance

What You Do

To set up a successful small business as a mover, you will need to carve out a niche for yourself. What can you specialize in? What type of moving service is not readily available in your community? The companies that provide enormous vans to move households across the continent are too expensive for a move within the same community, and they are too hard to schedule. Small household moves are an underserved market, and meeting these needs in a flexible, cost-effective way could allow you to fulfill your entrepreneurial ambitions and use your knowledge of how to get heavy stuff from here to there, down and up the stairs. Other local movers specialize in commercial moving: relocating businesses, office expansions, etc.

What You Need

The truck is the major expense, and locating a reliable staff will also cost you (you could start out for as little as $1,500 if you rent a truck). Your physical endurance will determine your earnings, but you should make at least $20,000.

Keys to Success

Your market may well be people who originally plan to do their moves themselves, and realize at the last moment that the task is too big. You will need to position your business so that these frustrated, desperate people can find you easily and realize that the cost of your service is far outweighed by the value they will receive: less breakage, no backaches, a faster completion of the move process, and so on. You will need to inspire confidence in your customers so that they trust you with their valuables. That way, they will recommend you to others, and word of mouth will eventually carry your business.

Multilevel Marketing

Start-up cost:	$500-$1,000
Potential earnings:	20,000-$50,000
Typical fees:	Percentage, plus bonus for new distributors
Advertising:	Networking, memberships in business and community groups, direct mail
Qualifications:	Salesmanship
Equipment needed:	Basic computer setup, phone
Staff required:	No
Handicapped opportunity:	Yes
Hidden costs:	Marketing materials like catalogs or leaflets may become necessary, membership dues

What You Do

Some products don't seem appealing unless they are demonstrated. The classic example is Tupperware, which just sat on store shelves until the company realized that buyers needed to be shown how the top is burped to create a vacuum seal. Many other products, with vitamins being an outstanding example, are sold as Tupperware is, person to person. Often, a business starts when someone develops enthusiasm for, and commitment to, a product or company. The sales process for that product then seems to happen almost naturally. If you have recognized something like a line of cosmetics that is especially effective for you, or a nutritional supplement that has made a difference in your sense of well-being, you should consider participating in multilevel marketing. You will be selling not only the product, but the opportunity for others to sell it as well. That's what sets multilevel marketing apart from direct sales—here, you're aiming to maximize your own income potential by deriving percentages from other salespeople you recruit.

What You Need

This is another business where you begin with nothing but your own energy and commitment (as little as $500 to start). Potential earnings of $20,000 and more.

Keys to Success

Do you know that you can sell? More importantly, do you love the sales process? Do you enjoy helping your customers discover products that will improve their lives? With this approach, you can make an excellent, if not wonderful, living in the multilevel marketing world. However, far more people have tried it than have made the easy millions that are sometimes promised. You really do have to work very, very hard. You can't give up when your first 74 efforts end in no sale. You will have to manage your time well, and you will have to find a company whose products are worth this much of your commitment.

Mystery Shopper

Start-up cost:	Less than $500
Potential earnings:	10,000-$20,000
Typical fees:	$25 to $50 per shopping experience
Advertising:	Personal contact with stores, hotels, corporations
Qualifications:	Knowledge of area to be evaluated, being a good actor or actress so as not to be noticed, being highly observant
Equipment needed:	None
Handicapped opportunity:	Yes
Hidden costs:	Mileage

What You Do

Mystery shoppers are used in a variety of settings: retail stores, typically where the owner is absent, hotel chains, restaurants, charitable organizations, government organizations, collection agencies, and banks. Their purpose is to observe the business from a customer's point of view and to report to management its shortcomings and strengths for the sake of improving service. A mystery shopper acts like a customer, observing the quality of the service, employee theft, plus shopping the competition for valuable information. Companies use mystery shoppers because they are less expensive than electronic surveillance.

What You Need

You won't spend very much at all launching this one, but you probably won't become a Rockefeller, either—earning $10,000-$20,000 per year would probably be as good as it gets.

Keys to Success

You might want to stick to a particular industry where you already have experience or knowledge. Chains would provide multiple sites to shop without being known as a shopper, besides providing continuing business. Provide a written and oral report of your findings. In some states mystery shoppers are considered private investigators and therefore must be licensed: look into your state's laws regarding licensing.

Nanny Service

Start-up cost:	$10,000-$40,000
Potential earnings:	$40,000-$70,000
Typical fees:	$20-$35 per hour
Advertising:	Yellow Pages, newspapers, parents' groups, business associations
Qualifications:	None
Equipment needed:	Office equipment (phone, fax, etc.)
Staff required:	Yes (about 20-30 nannies, ready and able to work)
Handicapped opportunity:	Yes
Hidden costs:	Liability insurance, personnel costs such as health benefits

What You Do

Not just your average baby-sitter, a nanny provides daily care for children in addition to helping with household chores. Obviously, then, nannies should enjoy being essentially another mom in a busy household. You need to carefully screen your nanny candidates (including running a background check with the police to make sure they have a clean record) and match them carefully to prospective households. Make sure that your client homes fill out a questionnaire detailing their preferences and exactly what kinds of work they expect to have done by the nanny. Also, since many nannies drive kids to soccer practice or other recreation activities, be sure that each nanny has a valid driver's license.

What You Need

Your costs to start a nanny service are generally quite high for a number of reasons, including liability insurance, office overhead, and benefits. Once you factor in your advertising costs (a good-size ad in the Yellow Pages and flyers or brochures for parents' and professional groups), you've spent anywhere from $10,000-$40,000. It helps if you are in a large metropolitan area, because that's where most of your clients will come from.

Keys to Success

It is a challenge to match the right nannies to each of your clients' households, but if you ask all the right questions up front, your chances of success will be high. Nannies are filling an important void in the lives of working families—and if the two-income family trend continues to rise, your service will be among the most profitable businesses to start.

Newspaper Delivery Service

Start-up cost:	$1,000-$5,000
Potential earnings:	10,000 or more
Typical fees:	Usually a flat rate
Advertising:	Cold-calling
Qualifications:	Stick-to-itiveness
Equipment needed:	Van, canvas bags
Staff required:	Yes
Handicapped opportunity:	No
Hidden costs:	Maintenance, fuel

What You Do

You will be providing newspaper delivery on a subcontracting basis within a specific geographic area. With the move toward morning newspapers in many localities, it has become more difficult for newspaper publishers to find reliable delivery people. It is very difficult for the preteenagers who used to fulfill this role to get up way before dawn, deliver papers, and still get through a full day of school. You take over, delivering one or more routes yourself and hiring a crew to complete the rest.

What You Need

You may need a van to pick up bundles of newspapers or to drop them off at your assistants' routes (could get by with just about $1,000 start-up cost). For a part-time job, $10,000 a year to start is easy money.

Keys to Success

This is another American classic: a job that depends on hard work (and an excellent alarm clock) rather than on education, social position, or good luck. You'll probably need to have others working with you to earn an adequate return on your efforts, and managing others always requires thought and effort. There's no glamour to the job of delivering newspapers, but it's good, honest work, and you'll get plenty of exercise.

Notary Public

Start-up cost:	$100-$200
Potential earnings:	6,000-$10,000
Typical fees:	$10 per requested service (average)
Advertising:	Yellow Pages, location
Qualifications:	License as Notary Public, usually upon recommendation of two lawyers
Equipment needed:	Seal
Staff required:	No
Handicapped opportunity:	Yes
Hidden costs:	None

What You Do

Notary publics usually add this service on to a related business. Witnessing signatures and administering oaths will bring you a small fee each time, but you will not become a magnate by this route alone. A surprising number of transactions must be notarized, though, so if you can draw in foot traffic or position yourself next to a business related to your services (such as a photocopy shop, license bureau, or post office), it can be well worth the trouble of obtaining the license. Check the requirements in your state, since each are different.

What You Need

Start-up costs are minimal, aside from the license fee and whatever your seal will cost you (not more than $500). A sign directing people to your location will bring walk-ins to have you witness their signatures. Fees are low, but so is the cost of providing the service.

Keys to Success

Why not? What have you got to lose? If people are going to pay notary public fees, why not have them be paid to you? Creativity in developing an associated service will enable you to make a business enterprise out of the enthusiasm for having things notarized that runs throughout American bureaucracies. Document typing is one possibility. Dreams of glory may pass you by, but the challenges are negligible, too.

On-Line Services Consultant

Start-up cost:	$4,000-$6,000
Potential earnings:	10,000-$30,000
Typical fees:	Hourly $50-$75, or per job $150 plus
Advertising:	Bulletin Board Services, flyers, publications, word of mouth
Qualifications:	Technical knowledge of hardware and software, good written communications skills, self-marketing ability
Equipment needed:	PC with high-speed modems; at least five phone lines
Staff required:	No
Handicapped opportunity:	Yes
Hidden costs:	On-line time

What You Do

As an on-line consultant, you will assist those in need of specific pieces of information or directions to a BBS or other on-line service. You will trouble-shoot for them, providing help in areas where the user is not as knowledgeable. Charges may be for the service received (employer/job searcher) or the knowledge gained (ability to use a certain piece of software). Some on-line consultants charge a flat monthly fee (average: $8-$10 per month); others have a low fee and add-on charges for time above a certain amount per month. You may need to send invoices or to obtain credit card capability to receive payments. The easiest way to be certain you're paid for your services is to obtain credit card information early in the process.

What You Need

Your initial investment is relatively high, since this is a very technology-dependent business. A computer, high-speed modem, and five phone lines—so that you can have many different on-line services running simultaneously—are the minimum equipment necessary to begin. Of course, if you are very familiar with on-line and bulletin board services, you will likely have a good start on your equipment already.

Keys to Success

Electronic links between individuals have added a new dimension to life in the '90s. You can take your enjoyment of this new way of communicating and make it into a business. Once you have found a niche, a group of potential subscribers with a strong interest in a topic and an enthusiasm for learning more, you can use your electronic communications skills to guide them on their way. BBS subscribers often expect immediate, or at least rapid, responses from their sysop (system operator), so you will need to be available several hours each day. And developing a method of charging that is competitive while bringing in enough income can be difficult.

Outdoor Adventures

Start-up cost:	$5,000-$10,000
Potential earnings:	50,000-$100,000
Typical fees:	Varied, depending on length of excursion, group size, and corporate versus individual rates (could range anywhere from $300-$1,000 per person)
Advertising:	Magazines with an outdoor or fitness focus, newspapers, public speaking on outdoor and environmental issues, direct mail
Qualifications:	Outdoor leadership skills and experience, knowledge of the natural world, first aid certificate, excellent planning ability
Equipment needed:	Outdoor equipment for yourself and group, van, basic office setup
Staff required:	Yes
Handicapped opportunity:	No
Hidden costs:	Insurance, equipment repairs and replacement

What You Do

There are almost as many ways to conduct an "outdoor adventure" as there are individual personalities. Broadly defined, your business will take groups of people into the outdoors, camping, hiking, and experiencing the vanishing wilderness as participants rather than just seeing it on TV. The popularity of the long-established organizations offering outdoor programs has not nearly met the demand, and many small organizations have been very successful in offering related services. Some focus on learning to exist with little material support in a wilderness environment. Others offer opportunities for self-development, self-reflection, or fitness. Another popular approach is to create group activities that build relationships of trust for business organizations, college freshman orientations, and similar groups.

What You Need

Your decisions about equipment will affect the cost of your start-up, and of your continuing operations. Advertising will be an ongoing requirement; expect to spend at least $5,000 on that alone. However, if you market yourself well, especially to corporations, you can really carve out a mighty fine living for yourself (to the tune of $100,000).

Keys to Success

An outdoors adventure business will rely on your love of the wilderness and your creativity in designing effective, appealing programs that allow your customers to encounter it. But not everyone who can build a camp out of hemlock twigs and catch mountain trout for dinner is also people-oriented enough to share their expertise with others. Wet, cold campers with blistered feet are not as easy to charm as day trippers on a short hike. So emphasize that experiencing and surviving the full range of challenges builds self-esteem, group solidarity, and an enduring respect for the power and beauty of nature.

Home Alone:
How to Feel "Connected"
When You're Home-Based

You work anywhere from thirty to sixty hours per week in your cozy little home office, where you curl up with a cup of coffee and enjoy the solitude of working alone. No office politics, no petty disagreements, no feeling of corporate pressure.

But too much solitude can be a bad thing. When the sound of silence gets to you, where can you go for some human interaction? Here are a few places you can start:

- A home-based business forum available through on-line services such as America Online and CompuServe

- A professional organization made up of business professionals like yourself (check with your Chamber of Commerce for listings of such groups)

- Toastmasters International—this organization offers you the chance to improve your speaking/presentation skills as well as meet with several others in your community (and from all walks of life)

- Volunteer at your local hospital, community organization, or even professional associations

- Work one day per week at your local library

- Take yourself out to lunch; you can bring along an assignment and make it a "working lunch"

- Spend at least one-half day per week networking at a function or event

- Form a "business buddy" system with another home-based worker, sharing trials and tribulations

- Form a success team with a dozen or so other home-based business professionals, where you meet once a week to discuss your business problems and offer one another some solutions

- Stop feeling alone—there are literally thousands of self-employed, home-based workers in the U.S. today

Outplacement Services

Start-up cost:	$15,000-$30,000
Potential earnings:	75,000-$150,000
Typical fees:	Retainer fees of $1,000-$3,000 per month
Advertising:	Yellow Pages, direct mail to human resource managers, trade shows, promotional items, networking
Qualifications:	A background in human resources
Equipment needed:	Computer, fax/modem, phone, letterhead, business card, corporate directories, career counseling/skills assessment materials
Staff required:	Not initially (but you may need extra help, depending on demand)
Handicapped opportunity:	Possibly
Hidden costs:	Insurance, phone bills, and time spent with each client (they'll want more of your time than is profitable for you)

What You Do

Needless to say, the late '80s and '90s haven't been exactly kind to the traditional work-force. Layoffs are coming faster, and with less warning than ever. That's why you need to promote your services, which help displaced individuals find new work elsewhere. Read the business pages daily to keep tabs on local companies. Generally, wherever there's a bad quarter, there's a layoff in the air. Your goal is to be the first (or the best) to approach these companies—at a time just before they actually need you. That way, your services can be in place before the downsizing is even announced to the employees; generally, that's the way companies prefer to do it, so that it looks like they've already got a plan for those employees caught completely off guard.

What You Need

Your start-up costs are likely to be quite high, especially because you need to have a computer system with a high-speed modem for doing on-line job searches and similar research. Expect to spend between $15,000-$30,000 getting started (detailed corporate directories alone could run as high as $6,000 per set); expect to pull in between $75,000-$150,000 per year once you've established a name for yourself. It's a business that can be lucrative for those who have a good reputation—word of mouth travels fast in industry these days (especially via E-mail).

Keys to Success

The best thing you can do in this business is stay on top of things—keep an ear to the ground (perhaps by networking closely with members of the Society for Human Resource Managers) and always get your materials in front of the vice president of operations or other key decision-makers before your competitors do.

Paging Services

Start-up cost:	$10,000-$15,000
Potential earnings:	30,000-$50,000
Typical fees:	Monthly fees range from $10-$30
Advertising:	Newspapers, radio, TV, direct mail, flyers
Qualifications:	Technical skill, organizational and sales skills
Equipment needed:	Computer paging system, office furniture, business card, letterhead, envelopes
Staff required:	No
Handicapped opportunity:	Yes
Hidden costs:	Phone bills, insurance

What You Do

No longer limited to a few types of professionals, paging services now appeal to many businesses and individuals. Parents use them to keep track of children; sales people maintain a close link to their offices. In fact, almost everyone who works away from a home office can use a pager to increase productivity and maintain the highest possible level of responsiveness to customers. Creative marketing will connect your new paging services business to these emerging markets; excellent service will keep your clients linked to you for their mobile communications needs.

What You Need

The required communications and phone equipment is quite expensive ($10,000 and up), and you may need an inventory of pagers as well. Set your monthly rates competitively to ensure maximum return.

Keys to Success

Paging is trendy, and for good reason. You can ride the crest of this trend toward a successful business. It will take determination and responsiveness to your market to make your enterprise stand out from the competition.

Party Planner

Start-up cost:	$500-$1,000
Potential earnings:	20,000-$40,000
Typical fees:	Charge a base fee of $300-$500 per party or a percentage of total cost of party (typically 15 to 20 percent)
Advertising:	Yellow Pages, direct mail, flyers, referrals/networking
Qualifications:	Resourcefulness, creative ability, exceptional organizational skills
Equipment needed:	Planning system (hand-held electronic planner or a good planning book), phone, fax, camera or camcorder (to record parties so that other potential clients can see the results of your work)
Staff required:	No
Handicapped opportunity:	Yes
Hidden costs:	Travel expenses, spending too much time on each project for the amount being paid

What You Do

A party planner tends to all the details for any given social function—from hiring the caterer, florist, and musician(s) or entertainer(s) to addressing and sending invitations. Planners should have a creative flair and be able to suggest a variety of party themes to fit the occasion. For instance, you could come up with a Caribbean theme where all the party-goers must dress in tropical attire, all the music is calypso-inspired, and giant papier-mâché palm trees sprout from various corners of the room. Or, plan a party that is a surprise for your client's family members—with a little Sherlock Holmes-style caper for guests to solve upon their arrival. Whatever your plan, you'll need to be extremely well organized to maintain a good reputation, and since your business will grow primarily based on referrals, you'll need to keep this uppermost in your mind. More than likely, you'll put in way more hours than you should for each job, but the return will be worth it if your ideas are exciting or innovative and your execution of those ideas is first-class. In other words, do your job, and do it well—the payoff will be directly related to what you put into it.

What You Need

It's a good idea to purchase some party planning guides from a bookstore (or borrow books from the library). Advertising costs will be your biggest start-up expense; be sure to get a Yellow Pages ad ($30-$100 per month, depending on ad size) since this is where many people who don't know you personally will be apt to look. You can charge either on a percentage basis (15 to 20 percent of total party cost) or a flat fee of $300-$500 per party.

Keys to Success

While getting started, you might want to plan some friends' parties for free. This will give you valuable experience and build a portfolio, so to speak, of your successes and innovations. Keep at least a photo album of your parties so that you have something to show potential clients. Nothing sells better than demonstrated success. On the downside, expect there to be difficulties in dealing with the personalities involved in planning a party. Remember, too, that your tastes (even though they may be better) will not always be the prevailing ones.

5 Steps to Better Time Management

1. **Know your company's goals** and set your own priorities accordingly. Give your tasks priority according to what must be done today, and what can be done tomorrow.

2. **Delegate wherever possible.** Invest the time at the outset to explain the task, the result you expect, and the deadline. You'll soon notice the benefit.

3. **Clear your desk each day,** at a time when you can prevent interruptions, or before they begin. You can manage interruptions by using voice mail to prioritize your calls and focusing on completing tasks by the end of each day.

4. **Make "wasted" time productive.** This may call for investment in a cellular phone or a laptop, but much of the time you spend waiting for planes or sitting in lobbies can, with preparation, become productive.

5. **Give yourself creative time.** Spend it alone with your ideas, or over coffee with an employee, but be sure it's in your schedule.

Personal Instructor/
Fitness Trainer

Start-up cost:	$100-$1,000
Potential earnings:	20,000-$65,000
Typical fees:	$50-$75 per hour
Advertising:	Business cards, brochures, flyers, bulletin boards in health clubs
Qualifications:	Experience, physical fitness, knowledge of equipment and CPR
Equipment needed:	Membership to a gym; your own equipment if you want to do it directly out of your home
Staff required:	No
Handicapped opportunity:	No
Hidden costs:	Travel time needed to meet clients where they work out

What You Do

Do you keep yourself physically fit, have a great personality, and enjoy teaching others? If you answered "yes" to all three, pull out those business cards and start a personal trainer business. You'll have to market yourself like a pro—give seminars about being fit and cover the benefits of working out to get your name and face out there in this highly competitive occupation. Experience will be on your side. Remember, you are marketing yourself and motivating others to become physically fit at the same time, so you must also be in excellent physical shape and condition. Be prepared to work out right alongside your clients if they request it, teaching them all the latest ways to get and stay in shape. Keep a couple of before and after photos of yourself and others whom you've helped tone and shape. Do a video and sell it through local health clubs.

What You Need

Start-up costs can consist solely of a gym membership; or, if you want the client to come to your home, you'll need a full set of equipment including free weights, Nautilus and weight training equipment. That could send you into the $100,000 range for start-up costs. You have the potential to stay in shape and make a decent living in the range of $20,000-$65,000 or more, depending on how affluent your clients are.

Keys to Success

How many people can say that going to work relieves stress? Not only can you have fun and stay in shape, you get to have a social life on the job. Working out has become very social and everyone can do it, but the downside is, a client may quit without warning. Some people consider working out to be seasonal, so you'll really have to go out there and establish a good client base.

Personal Shopper

Start-up cost:	$500-$1,000
Potential earnings:	10,000-$25,000
Typical fees:	$20-$40 per shopping excursion
Advertising:	Brochures, classified ads, personalized notes to busy executives
Qualifications:	An eye for a great deal and the ability to match gifts to personalities
Equipment needed:	Dependable transportation
Staff required:	No
Handicapped opportunity:	Yes
Hidden costs:	Watch your mileage and be sure that you bill on an hourly rate rather than a per-job basis; otherwise, people may try to take advantage of you

What You Do

Do you consider yourself to be the "shopping goddess of the universe?" Are you able to consistently choose tasteful and well-received gifts? If so, this business could be your dream come true. Many of today's executives are simply too busy to spend an hour or two shopping for the perfect gift, so you can do it for them by offering your services at an hourly rate. You'll need to make sure that the client provides you with some method to purchase the gifts—or arrange for the items to be held for pickup by the client. Build a strong network of places to shop; familiarize yourself with every gift/specialty store, retail store, and florist in your area. You'll need this vast resource (and plenty of catalogs) to come up with refreshingly new approaches to gift-giving. Another part of your business might be purchasing items for busy executives themselves; they could provide you with a personalized size (and preference) card, then send you off on a buying odyssey.

What You Need

Brochures and personal notes sent to managers of large corporations are a good way to introduce yourself and your services. Be sure to stress the advantages of using a shopping service (chiefly, the time-saving and money-saving factor) and be clear about the way you bill up front. Then, you'll need to start collecting catalogs, visiting malls and unusual shops, and combing the newspapers for sales. Your clients will expect you to know everything possible about shopping—so take the time to prepare!

Keys to Success

If you only want to do this job part-time for individual clients, you won't make as much as you would working full-time for large companies. Difficult situations may occur when the client isn't happy with the purchase, but you should be able to return anything you buy. All in all, the joy of spending other people's money is hard to resist—it gives you all the pleasure with none of the guilt.

Personalized Children's Books

Start-up cost:	$5,000-$15,000
Potential earnings:	20,000-$40,000
Typical fees:	$15-$30 per book
Advertising:	Business card, bookstores, preschools, direct mail, flea markets
Qualifications:	Writing capability
Equipment needed:	Computer, laser printer, binder
Staff required:	No
Handicapped opportunity:	Yes
Hidden costs:	Mistakes can add up quickly; proof your work carefully

What You Do

Customized picture books can brighten any kid's day—after all, what could be better for a kid than reading a story with his own name throughout? With these picture books, kids can actually be a character in the book they are reading—and many parents are more than willing to pay money for such a personalized item. You'll produce books using one of a few templates, and then simply drop in the child's name via computer. Then, you'll print the books out on the laser printer, bind them, and package them up for your customers. You can get the word out by advertising in community newspapers, or rent a mall kiosk during weekends or holidays to sell your services directly and in a place where you can produce products on the spot.

What You Need

Your prices will range from $15-$25, depending on the length of the book. There will be an initial investment to get the book made (around $10,000 for your basic equipment setup and paper stock). If you're not great at creating your own stories, you'll likely be buying into a franchise. Expect to shell out a franchising fee of $30,000-$50,000, but if you do, you may be thankful for the support and the ease of production that results from such an affiliation. You'll have to use mockups or prototypes to sell your services, so don't forget to include a few sample books in your start-up plan.

Keys to Success

This is a fun and entertaining venture—who doesn't love to make a child smile and get paid for doing it? The flip side of that is the frustration of working with difficult customers. It goes with the territory, since you'll likely be in a retail setting. Be prepared for little tantrums every once in a while.

Pest Control Service

Start-up cost:	$15,000-$25,000
Potential earnings:	25,000-$45,000
Typical fees:	$150-$300 per treatment for a medium-size house
Advertising:	Newspapers, classified ads, Yellow Pages, direct mail, flyers
Qualifications:	Knowledge of pesticides, insects, and rodents
Equipment needed:	Sprayer, chemicals, pager or mobile phone, vehicle
Staff required:	Not initially
Handicapped opportunity:	No
Hidden costs:	Materials, insurance, phone bills

What You Do

Almost every structure needs your pest control services, whether the owner wants to admit it or not. Needs vary in different regions, but the termites that gnaw on Louisiana plantations are happy to chew on Idaho log cabins as well. Pest control has an old-fashioned, grungy image, but you can make the buildings you treat into safer, cleaner environments. Environmental awareness has changed the world of pest control, and your selling point could be your controlled use of the least harmful agents to provide this very necessary service. Whatever you do, you'll need to have fairly extensive knowledge of chemical treatments.

What You Need

The tools of the trade can become somewhat expensive, with equipment and chemicals starting at about $15,000. Some pest control specialists manage their businesses in person, receive immediate payment of $150-$300 per job, and do not have to set up a computerized office. A pager or cellular phone will help your customers reach you.

Keys to Success

You love this work or you hate it. The advantages are that you are on the move, not tied to a desk. You are providing a service that everyone understands, and every property owner needs. It can be awkward and sometimes dirty, but it isn't really difficult once you have the knowledge. Exposure to your own chemicals may have negative health consequences. Clambering around in one dark, dirty basement after another can get you down. And there is a lot of competition, so you'll need to be creative in finding (or creating) a market niche.

Expert Advice

What sets your business apart from others like it?

"We have a real concern for the environment," says Leslie Wyman, Vice President of Marketing for EPCON, The Environmental Pest Company, in Akron, Ohio. "We rely less on pesticides and more on structural and behavioral modification."

Things you couldn't do without:

Chemicals, flashlight, stethoscope, BNG spray can, computer, and phone are all Wyman needs to keep her business running.

Marketing tips/advice:

"Get good training and state licensing first. Then, use cold call surveys to ask people what kinds of trouble they're having with pests. After that, it's pretty much: mail-call-mail-call-mail-call." You would do well, says Wyman, to pick a specialty area (such as mice) or an industry niche (such as health care).

If you had to do it all over again . . .

"I would have gotten started in this business much sooner. Also, if you've got a family-run business, you should always give your family a chance—but don't be afraid to go outside of your family network to hire additional staff if you need to."

Pet Grooming

Start-up cost:	$5,000-$10,000
Potential earnings:	25,000-$40,000
Typical fees:	$30-$60 per pet-primping session
Advertising:	Yellow Pages, direct mail, community bulletin boards, referrals from vets
Qualifications:	Experience, patience, knowledge of animal behavior patterns, familiarity with the grooming standards of different breeds
Equipment needed:	Grooming table, clippers, brushes, combs, bathing tub/shower accessories, shampoos, dryer, detangler, hair bows, business card
Staff required:	No
Handicapped opportunity:	No
Hidden costs:	Supplies could get out of hand

What You Do

You have to really love animals to consider this business. But if you enjoy working with pets—many of whom may not enjoy taking a bath—you can build a decent business providing these services. Pet ownership increases each year in this country, but people have less free time than ever. What Afghan owners can really manage to comb out their pet's entire coat every day, as the books recommend? The popular white poodles need considerable grooming to present themselves in a clean, fluffy, well-trimmed coat. Aside from the pet's appearance, good health practices dictate cleaning and brushing the coat regularly. Once you establish rapport with Rover, you are likely to have regular repeat business from his owner. Giving cats their flea baths is another popular service (to the owner, definitely not to the feline). As an add-on, consider selling pet supplies and/or specialty products for the pampered pet.

What You Need

Trying to do all this in your family bathtub is a poor idea. To make a go of the business, you'll need the setting and equipment to do a professional job without breaking your back. This may set you back around $10,000, but you stand a good chance of earning it all back in a year or so if there aren't many competitors in your area. Charge between $30-$60, depending on whether you're in the country or in a large city.

Keys to Success

You may not be the only pet grooming service in your community, but you can be the best. You can offer pickup and delivery services, you can specialize in terrier coat stripping or caring for poodles, you can leave each "patient" happy and sweet-smelling. You'll need to make your customers feel that your service is the one that they can't live without. This is hard, physical work, but each grooming session leaves a beloved pet looking better—until he can get outside again.

Pilot

Start-up cost:	$45,000-$125,000+
Potential earnings:	3,000-$5,000 per month
Typical fees:	$75 per hour
Advertising:	Yellow Pages, entertainment sections of local papers, brochures, visitor convention bureaus
Qualifications:	Federal Aviation Administration (FAA) license, 20/20 vision, 1,500-3,000+ hours flying time
Equipment needed:	Plane and appropriate safety equipment
Staff required:	No
Handicapped opportunity:	No
Hidden costs:	Fuel, maintenance

What You Do

Believe it or not, there is more to being a pilot than just climbing into the cockpit. You need to have the ability to work with words and numbers; follow procedures and read the instrument panel; be alert and ready to make decisions; and communicate accurately. If you decide that you'd like to teach others to fly the friendly skies, you must be incredibly thorough and have a great many hours in the air yourself. The more 'fly time' or experience you have the better teacher you will be. Skipping over any details could cost your students their lives, and that's a heavy amount of responsibility for anyone to take on. Still, if you have a high degree of knowledge and know how to convey that information in an accurate, concise way, you could make this business soar—particularly if you live in an area where the weather cooperates regularly.

What You Need

The plane itself is the major cause of your start-up being so high (at least $35,000). Chances are good, though, that if you are looking into this field, you already own or have access to a plane. The rest of your overhead will be wrapped up in insurance and advertising. Your typical annual earnings will be in the neighborhood of $36,000-$60,000.

Keys to Success

The good part is you're up in the sky enjoying the tranquility and breathtaking views. The bad part is you are working in a confined space and your instructions must be very accurate. A mistake in teaching could be life-threatening, and turnover could be low because of the extensive training involved.

Pool Maintenance

Start-up cost:	$15,000-$30,000
Potential earnings:	30,000-$50,000
Typical fees:	$75-$150 per total cleaning/shocking treatment
Advertising:	Flyers at pool sales and service centers, direct mail coupons, Yellow Pages, local newspapers
Qualifications:	Knowledge of maintaining and repairing inground and aboveground pools
Equipment needed:	Pool cleaning equipment (water vacuum, hose, etc.) and chemicals
Staff required:	No
Handicapped opportunity:	Not typically
Hidden costs:	Insurance, phone, transportation

What You Do

Many people like the convenience of owning and using a pool, but who really likes the maintenance that pools require? You do—and you can earn a living providing this necessary service for busy pool owners who simply don't have the time (or energy) to clean or repair pools. You'll clean, repair, chemically shock and maintain each client's pool, either on a preseason/postseason basis or perhaps at regular intervals. Simply stated, you're selling convenience and peace of mind to the luxury-minded; they'll tell you how often they need you to come out. Of course, you'll do better if you're located in a part of the country, particularly the Sun Belt, where pools are common (and almost a prerequisite). In cooler climes you may have to offer your services in a wider geographic area to support your business, and that would mean increased travel expenses to and from customers.

What You Need

You'll need the right cleaning equipment and chemical supplies to stock your van with; expect to spend at least $15,000 on all of these items from the outset. However, at $75-$150 per cleaning job, you could stand to make some decent money cleaning and maintaining pools. Spend a few hundred dollars on business cards to leave behind for repeat business and referrals.

Keys to Success

By offering excellent service, you can build a customer base. Remember to call these people back periodically for repeat business—that follow-up could reap you thousands more dollars in the long run.

Printing Broker

Start-up cost:	$1,000-$3,000
Potential earnings:	35,000-$50,000
Typical fees:	10 to 15 percent commission on sales
Advertising:	Yellow Pages, trade publications, direct mail, cold calls
Qualifications:	Printing sales background
Equipment needed:	Cellular phone, computer, printer, fax, copier, phone
Staff required:	No
Handicapped opportunity:	Yes
Hidden costs:	Insurance, mileage

What You Do

For those who are inexperienced in the world of printing and publishing, a printing bro-ker can be a godsend. Relying on an extensive background in printing sales, a printing broker can actually save the client hundreds of dollars in printing costs by shopping for the best (and most current) rates. The broker does not work for one specific printer, but represents all of them, in a sense, because he or she will offer a client the best going rate without sacrificing quality. Clients could be anyone from advertising agencies to community newspapers and book publishers. To be successful, you'll need to have a natural sales ability and the technical know-how to get printing jobs accomplished. You're servicing two sides here: the customer who needs a brochure or book printed, and the printing house itself (because you are working with them as an outside repre-sentative, and you'll need to work at preserving that relationship). If ink is in your blood, this could be a terrific opportunity for you—since most unknowledgeable folk are on the lookout for the lowest prices when they need items printed.

What You Need

Your start-up costs are low ($1,000-$3,000), because you'll only need to have a basic office setup (with computer, printer, fax, copier, and phone) and some advertising to get things off the ground (assuming, of course, that you already have a printing background, complete with contacts). With some heavy shoe action, you could make $35,000-$50,000 per year—especially if you can build a solid reputation with documented sav-ings for your clients.

Keys to Success

Your contacts will make or break you in this business; always be honest and rep-utable, and you'll reap the benefits threefold. Why threefold? Because your satisfied clients will tell at least two other contacts about your services and how much money you saved them. On the sour side, you could wind up spending a lot of your own time trying to negotiate deals that don't materialize—and that means you'll have to eat the related costs.

Private Tutor

Start-up cost:	$500
Potential earnings:	15,000-$20,000
Typical fees:	$10-$20 per hour
Advertising:	Classified ads, Yellow Pages, word of mouth (school principals would be a good group to network with)
Qualifications:	Teaching experience or degree in area of expertise
Equipment needed:	None
Staff required:	None
Handicapped opportunity:	Yes
Hidden costs:	Watch your mileage

What You Do

Since classrooms are getting larger and larger, many students' needs are getting over-looked. Your services may be needed to bring a struggling student up to speed—and the best part about this type of business is that it is recession-proof! As long as there are students, there will be a strong need for capable individuals to guide them to scholastic success. Determine where your area of expertise lies (is it in history? English? mathematics?) and meet with teachers in this subject to ask for referrals. Once you get a few clients, your word of mouth will grow quickly, and you may find that you need to net-work with other tutors to build referral systems of your own. At any rate, as a tutor you will find out the student's needs (probably in a written report from their teacher) and develop lesson plans tailored to that specific need. The opportunity to be creative is up to you, so try to make the lessons interesting and empower the student so that each success feels like their own.

What You Need

Purchase a few used textbooks (preferably with teacher's guides) and buy yourself some good books on learning challenges and motivation to succeed. To be a good inspiration to your student, you'll need to demonstrate your own willingness to learn. Your only other start-up cost will be advertising, and that will generally stay under $500.

Keys to Success

Encouraging a young student's success while fostering a thirst for knowledge can be richly rewarding if you are genuinely interested in education. Helping a student over-come what seemed like an obstacle offers you—and the rest of the world—opti-mism about our own possibilities. Aside from an occasional obnoxious child, what's there to hate about that?

Professional Organizer

Start-up cost:	$500-$1,000
Potential earnings:	25,000-$45,000
Typical fees:	$25-$40 per hour
Advertising:	Write articles for your local newspapers on time management and organizing space, Welcome Wagon, direct mail coupons; conduct seminars through local community continuing education; network
Qualifications:	You must be a highly organized person by nature, with drive for efficiency; knowledge of systems, furniture, products, supplies and accessories are a must
Equipment:	Pager or cellular phone, computers
Staff:	No
Handicapped opportunity:	No
Hidden costs:	Mileage and cellular phone bills

What You Do

Most organizers specialize in one of five areas: space planning (organizing office arrangement of furniture, traffic, lighting, noise, and leisure space); time management (setting goals, developing action plans, scheduling, and delegating tasks); paper management (organizing the steady flow of information materials by setting up filing and retrieval systems, sometimes with the aid of a computer); clutter control (finding the proper and efficient placement for things to keep clutter to a minimum); closet/storage design (organizing closet and storage space). Choose one or two and market your services accordingly. This business would thrive in highly urban areas with busy professionals who want their home life to run as smoothly as the office—and it's much more fun to organize other people's lives than to run our own.

What You Need

You'll spend at least $500 or so on business cards for networking—but that's almost negligible considering that you'll be charging $25-$45 per hour for your expertise.

Keys to Success

Look into the National Association of Professional Organizers for more information. Hook up with an organization that conducts seminars, and offer your services as an instructor. This can supplement the income of your consulting service rather nicely.

Property Management Service

Start-up cost:	$3,000-$6,000
Potential earnings:	25,000-$50,000
Typical fees:	$25 per hour or a monthly retainer of $500-$2,500
Advertising:	Classified ads, referrals, memberships in community and business real estate groups
Qualifications:	Experience in the field, related degree helpful, outstanding management skills, good ability to communicate and work with people, knowledge of basic bookkeeping, understanding of building maintenance issues
Equipment needed:	Office furniture, computer, suite software, possibly specialized property management software, printer, fax, modem, business cards, letterhead, envelopes
Staff required:	No
Handicapped opportunity:	No
Hidden costs:	Insurance

What You Do

This is the business for someone who likes juggling a thousand balls at one time, pulling many different pieces together, and keeping track of the people and data that go with the projects. If you're good, you'll become indispensable to the owners of the properties you manage, and you'll have a well-established enterprise that will keep you busy and well-rewarded indefinitely. Why are good property managers so valuable? You maintain all the financial records for each property, which include income and expenses, bills, and taxes. Skill at auditing bills is extremely valuable just on its own. The ability to keep repair and maintenance schedules up to date is essential, so you will need to be able to pay great attention to detail and also have the people skills required for relating to the individuals who carry out the work on your buildings. Collecting rents is the other central piece of this puzzle.

What You Need

Your own office needs to support you well, especially in communicating to building owners, repair personnel, and tenants. The computer is the tool used most for tracking all the financial information related to the properties (around $3,000 to start). Depending on your location, you should make at least $25,000 annually.

Keys to Success

The owners of properties—your prospective clients—will need to place great responsibility on your shoulders. Things can degenerate very quickly in a poorly managed building, and once the financial records become tangled, it can be very difficult to bring them into order, or even to learn if the expenses are exceeding the income. You are asking your clients to have a large amount of confidence in you, and marketing these services successfully may depend on how well you can engender that sense of trust. It may be, however, that you will only need a few clients. This is one small business where constant marketing may not be necessary.

Understanding Your Cash Budget

For those business owners who are "mathematically challenged," here is a quick breakdown of the items that should appear on your cash flow projection statements. Basically, you need to look at what's coming in and what's going out on a regular basis.

"In" column:

- Cash sales
- Accounts Receivables
- Funds from sales of assets or equipment
- Refunds (such as tax refunds)
- Collections (outstanding accounts)

"Out" column:

- Inventory/stock purchases
- Operating expenses
- Fixed expense payments
- Credit payments on long-term debt
- Tax payments (most often quarterly)
- Shareholder/stock payments

Taking a look at these items and how they change over a period of a year can provide you with a Profit and Loss statement that clearly shows you what your business is earning and spending.

You can use this information to build your following year's budget, by making educated assumptions based on what happened the previous year. For instance, if you had a bad winter quarter because your business is somewhat dependent on good weather, you'll know to build sales up in the fall to cover your winter operating budget and make sure the bills get paid.

Public Pay Phone Services

Start-up cost:	$5,000-$10,000
Potential earnings:	20,000-30,000
Typical fees:	Income dependent on usage (high-traffic areas generate as much as $50 a day for each telephone installed)
Advertising:	Flyers, bulletin boards, location
Qualifications:	Communications technical skills, marketing ability
Equipment needed:	Pay phones, installation equipment
Staff required:	No
Handicapped opportunity:	No
Hidden costs:	Insurance, repairs

What You Do

In many locations across the U.S. it is extremely difficult to find a pay phone. Small businesses are finding this niche in the huge telecommunications market. If you have telephone-industry experience, you may be able to ride this trend and create a viable business enterprise that fills in the gaps. An extremely refined marketing sense and skill at linking your callers to the network of major phone company services will define your ability to make a go of this. Some franchises are available.

To set up a public pay phone service, you need to first contact manufacturers of the phones to secure inventory. Equally important is your contact with the public utilities commission in your state. There may be regulations for you to comply with, so do your homework ahead of time.

A growing related service is prepaid phone cards, which can be imprinted with an advertiser's information. For instance, many drugstores now offer prepaid calling cards with their logo printed on the card; it's a good way for many companies to keep their name in front of their customers. You can market the same capability to as many companies as you can think of, then contract with a specialized card production house to finish the work.

What You Need

Costs may be relatively high for a small business, depending on the type and configuration of services you plan to offer. Plan to invest at least $5,000 in this start-up; and, if you decide to buy into a franchise, expect to pay an up-front fee of $10,000 or more. Earnings are dependent upon phone location and usage; prepaid phone cards generally retail for $5 and up.

Keys to Success

This business will allow you to express your marketing agility to the utmost extent. It can be a real high to play the game that most people think is available only to telecommunications giants. The risks are significant, though, and there are a large group of businesses out there offering alternative types of communication services, from pager services to computer bulletin boards.

Public Relations

Start-up cost:	$5,000-$10,000
Potential earnings:	35,000-$75,000
Typical fees:	$50-$75 per hour, a bid-per-job basis, or monthly retainer
Advertising:	Networking and personal contacts, speeches before business or community groups, volunteer work for non-profit organizations, telemarketing
Qualifications:	Strong communication and telephone skills, assertiveness and persuasiveness, ability to deal effectively with abstract concepts, high energy level
Equipment needed:	Computer with modem, printer, and fax, desktop publishing software, telephone headset, multiple phone lines with call-forwarding and conferencing features, office furniture, business card, letterhead, envelopes
Staff required:	No
Handicapped opportunity:	Yes
Hidden costs:	Slow starting time; expect two years before profit

What You Do

As with so many other fields, the demand for PR is growing. At the same time, corporations are cutting their public relations staffs (usually the first to go in the age of downsizing). The work is definitely being farmed out, so public relations is ideal for a home-based business. Relationships with clients take time to develop, though, and depend in part on your network of contacts in the media. When a small company has a breakthrough new product, when advertising is too expensive, when an organization needs to get its message across to the public, or when a negative situation occurs that needs a positive spin, your PR services can be invaluable. To attract media attention and interest, you will need outstanding writing and speaking skills, a healthy dose of creativity, awareness of what the different types of media (trade journals, the nightly news shows) are hungry for, and an ability to put all the pieces together. It's fun, yet tough to do well unless you're an animal at networking with influential media types.

What You Need

A very well-equipped office is a must, and you will need to present yourself and your business at the level of polish and professionalism you are selling for your clients. Expect to spend at least $4,000 on your office and equipment; bill at least $50-$75 per hour for your expertise.

Keys to Success

For creative, dynamic, and above all energetic people, public relations is a wonderful field. If you thrive on relationships with many different individuals and organizations and love the stimulation of constant change, you should consider making PR your business. As a solo practitioner, you'll start with small projects and gradually expand your network and contacts to take on more complex projects. Not everyone has the skills and attributes to make a success of PR, although many people are out there trying. You will need to produce results; recognize that your business will take tremendous time and effort to grow. Marketing your own services must be a priority even as you complete one project after another for your clients. Media representatives can be fickle; getting publicity for your clients will require new angles and ideas each time to catch the media's attention.

Expert Advice

What sets your business apart from others like it?

Connie Delehanty, owner of a Sir Speedy Printing Center franchise in Fairlawn, Ohio, says: "A knowledgeable staff that asks the right questions and is able to get the job done right as a result. We have a commitment to customer service and quality."

Things you couldn't do without:

"We couldn't do without our staff and up-to-date technology such as interfaced computers with digital color output devices and laser printers."

Marketing tips/advice:

"Location, location . . . you need to be in a highly traveled path." Delehanty's print shop is located in a small shopping plaza near a major thoroughfare.

If you had to do it all over again . . .

"I'd start with more capital," says Delehanty. "Equipment costs can skyrocket in this technology-driven business."

Rare Book Dealer

Start-up cost:	$5,000-$10,000
Potential earnings:	20,000-$40,000
Typical fees:	$10-$15 plus a percentage of sale on book (based on your markup)
Advertising:	Yellow Pages, book industry publications, referrals from bookstores
Qualifications:	Good organizational skills and excellent follow-up ability
Equipment needed:	Computer, printer, fax/modem, phone with 800 number, on-line services
Staff required:	No
Handicapped opportunity:	Yes
Hidden costs:	On-line services and phone bills

What You Do

Some avid readers will go to extraordinary lengths to find a used or rare book that they'd relish having in their private collection. Whether you're providing this service in addition to running a bookstore (as many searchers do) or running it as a separate business, you'll need to be highly detail-oriented and well-organized to make this business profitable. The good news is, there are plenty of publications that you can subscribe to, and these provide monthly listings of what books are currently available through other dealers. Sometimes, you'll be lucky enough to work out an even trade (and maximize your own profit on the book you're selling to the customer). Most often, however, you'll derive your income from a search fee ($10-$15 in some areas) and a sales commission on the book itself (which you will have priced accordingly to suit your bank account's needs). The older and more rare the book, the harder it is to locate—but if you can manage to drum up one yellow-paged copy, your earnings could be quite high on just one book.

What You Need

It will take between $5,000-$10,000 to get you started with your computer and on-line searches; expect to spend $1,000 or so on advertising in your first year. If you are good at what you do, you can see income potentials of $20,000-$40,000 per year.

Keys to Success

The stress level is actually quite low in this field, and you can pretty much search for a book at your own pace. However, you don't get paid as much for looking as you do for finding—so use computer on-line services to expedite your searches.

Real Estate Agent

Start-up cost:	$500-$1,000
Potential earnings:	25,000-$100,000
Typical fees:	Commissions of 30 to 40 percent are common
Advertising:	Yellow Pages, memberships in local business and charitable organizations, local newspapers, penny savers, referrals from agencies
Qualifications:	Real estate license
Equipment needed:	Phone, computer, printer, fax/modem and copier, business cards, letterhead, envelopes
Staff required:	No
Handicapped opportunity:	No
Hidden costs:	Travel, marketing

What You Do

You will be focusing here on one part of the residential real estate agent's job. You will be doing the basic research rather than carrying out the entire process through to closing. You will develop a range of choices based on the buyer interview. This gives the agent and the buyer an opportunity to plan, clarify wants and needs, and consider the financial implications. It is reassuring for a family making a transcontinental move to know what choices are available to them within their price range, general preferences for neighborhood type, and so on. Your job, essentially, is to match your clients to their "perfect" home; you're different from a relocation specialist in that your territory is limited to your own immediate community. You provide information on the homes in your geographic area as opposed to helping clients relocate elsewhere around the country.

What You Need

Start-up costs are low (could get by for $500), but marketing efforts will be ongoing unless referrals or subcontracting can bring you adequate business. You could earn $25,000 annually.

Keys to Success

You will need to prove, consistently, that your services add value, don't threaten agents, and make sense to transferees. Keeping good records of your effectiveness will support your marketing efforts. Projecting an enthusiasm for your local area, its different communities, and its varied attractions, will enhance your work. This is a good choice for someone who loves houses and enjoys thinking about what type of family would choose each one, but who finds the "sale" process unappealing. Not everyone wants to spend all weekend showing picky buyers house after house, only to see the sale evaporate. As a home researcher you can create a service that suits you as well as it does your clients.

Relocation Consultant

Start-up cost:	$3,000-$6,000
Potential earnings:	15,000 and more
Typical fees:	$25-$35 per hour
Advertising:	Trade publications, networking, memberships in real estate and general business organizations, referrals
Qualifications:	Real estate experience, close knowledge of your area's neighborhoods, attractions, amenities, schools
Equipment needed:	Office furniture, computer, printer, fax, modem, business cards, letterhead, envelopes
Staff required:	No
Handicapped opportunity:	No
Hidden costs:	Telephone bills, membership dues, entertainment

What You Do

Your ideal market will probably be companies that do some relocations but are too small to provide much assistance in-house to the executives they are transferring to your community. Moving is a challenging experience for almost all families, and enlightened employers will see the value of your assistance in making the transition go as smoothly as possible. You will provide advising as the transferees begin to make decisions: What neighborhood will we like best? Where can we find eldercare or child care? What sports are played at local high schools? Can we find a house with enough land for trail riding? Your relocation consulting service will assist transferees with questions like these. You work with the employees before they are ready to choose a real estate agent.

What You Need

Equipping your office will be the main expense (about $3,000). You will do some work by computer and fax, but most of your time will probably be spent driving to the different areas of your city, or having a restaurant meal with a transferee. Annual wages of $15,000 is realistic for part-time work.

Keys to Success

You're doing two kinds of marketing here, first, for your own service, and second, for your community. Many organizations use relocation consultants to help persuade a prospective employee to take the job with that company. How the prospect and his family feel about moving to your area can be a major factor. Your services can offer an unprejudiced look at what the locality has to offer. Hospitals recruiting a certain physician and companies recruiting someone for an upper-management position will both value your service highly.

Resume Service

Start-up cost:	$1,000-$5,000
Potential earnings:	20,000-$50,000
Typical fees:	$150-$500 per resume (depending on your demographics)
Advertising:	Yellow Pages, newspaper classifieds, referrals
Qualifications:	Writing ability, attention to important detail, strong organizational ability
Equipment needed:	Computer, printer, fax/modem, paper, extra computer disks
Staff required:	No
Handicapped opportunity:	Yes
Hidden costs:	Insurance, spending too much time with one client

What You Do

Thousands of people are looking for new work these days, and they all have one need in common: they simply must have a dynamic resume. Those who really want to put their best foot forward with a trend-setting (yet somewhat traditional-looking) resume and cover letter will come to you for a package that looks visually appealing yet businesslike enough to get even a stuffed-shirt hiring professional to glance twice. Your resume service needs to reflect the trends of the future in order to survive, because the small typing service-variety resume service simply can't keep up with technological demands and self-promotional waves of the future. Some folks are even posting their resumes on the Internet, and you could offer additional services such as this if you choose. Regardless, your days will be spent meeting with a wide variety of clients from all walks of life (from foundry supervisors to attorneys), writing down specific job histories, and adding pertinent skill information that will make a potential employer jump with glee. It's a time-consuming job, but it gets easier the more you work at it.

What You Need

Your start-up is relatively low ($1,000-$5,000) because all you really need is a good computer setup and a small advertising budget to get the word out. You can expect to earn $20,000 or so in most medium-size markets; in New York City and other large metropolitan areas, you'll be charging much more for your services (up to $500) and could easily make $50,000 per year.

Keys to Success

If you're a writer, this is a pretty easy way to make a living (or an additional income to support your quest for the Great American Novel). However, you do need to enjoy working with people: they will hound you day and night until their project is finished, and possibly even afterward. If you don't like to be hounded, stick to novel writing.

Expert Advice

What sets your business apart from others like it?

Katina Z. Jones has a nontraditional resume service called Going Places Self-Promotions, Inc., in Akron, Ohio. She says that her business is unique because it breaks many of the traditional rules of resume writing. "We do resumes that are not only eye-catching, but also go beyond providing a mere rundown of a client's job history. We like to add a sense of not only what a person has accomplished in their career, but also who they are and how they might fit into an organization. We have a 98 percent success rate in helping clients secure interviews because of that personalized approach."

Things you couldn't do without:

"I couldn't do without my computer, laser printer, phone, pager, and fax. My clients want fairly quick turnaround, and these items help me to accomplish that. Also, I need to have plenty of paper catalogs on hand, as I use a ton of specialty preprinted stationery to produce resumes on."

Marketing tips/advice:

"Set yourself apart from the people who are glorified typists . . . recognize that the resume industry is changing rapidly, and the resumes of the past (with cookie-cutter objectives and meaningless buzzwords) are just not getting people results anymore. After you've got your niche, network like crazy. Anywhere you go, introduce yourself; you're bound to meet someone who either needs a resume or knows someone who does."

If you had to do it all over again . . .

"I would have started networking much sooner and would also have put together a more meaningful marketing plan; I don't think I strategized nearly enough in the beginning."

Retirement Planner

Start-up cost:	$1,000-$2,000
Potential earnings:	20,000-$40,000
Typical fees:	Set fee of $150-$1,000 (depending on scope of project)
Advertising:	Newspapers, publications of local interest groups, membership in community organizations, word of mouth, direct mail
Qualifications:	Expertise in financial planning (certification helpful), experience in a related field
Equipment needed:	Computer, printer, fax, phone, copier, marketing materials, business cards, letterhead, envelopes
Staff required:	No
Handicapped opportunity:	Yes
Hidden costs:	Conferences for continuing self-education

What You Do

We're an aging population in this country, and the baby-boom generation is notorious for its poor planning for retirement. It used to be something that people just didn't want to think about, but the tide is changing. Now, with widespread fears about the future of Social Security, retirement planners are finding a rising demand for their services. You will be distinguishing yourself from the hundreds of "financial planners" searching for customers in every community by your focus on this one vital piece of the financial puzzle. As with lawyers, accountants, and other professionals who operate as small businesses, your challenge will be to gain the confidence of your clients so that they prefer your excellent personal service over the security of dealing with a large institutional business that claims to offer the same type of advice. You'll sell them on how meticulous you are at developing financial strategies tailored to their own unique financial situations (instead of a grid in a book). You'll take a good look at their plans for retirement and work out a sensible budget based on that information. You may also suggest financial products or options, such as mutual funds.

What You Need

Minimal (about $1,000)—you just need adequate materials to present the image of reliability that will make people feel confident in your knowledge and expertise. If you travel to your clients' homes, you do not need an elaborate office setup.

Keys to Success

The difficulty in selling retirement services is that, while almost everyone needs them, they're afraid to contemplate the reality that they should be saving more, spending less, and keeping to a budget. Your "hook" for this market may be to find a way to send a reassuring message, to plan for retirement without taking all the fun out of today.

Reunion Organizer

Start-up cost:	$2,000-$3,000
Potential earnings:	15,000-$50,000
Typical fees:	$5-$10 for each classmate who attends
Advertising:	Word of mouth and warm calling
Qualifications:	A big network of friends and acquaintances in your community, patience, determination, organizational ability
Equipment needed:	Computer, database and suite software, fax, copier, office furniture, business cards, letterhead, envelopes
Staff required:	No
Handicapped opportunity:	Yes
Hidden costs:	Telephone bills

What You Do

Changing life patterns are making reunions seem more appealing to many kinds of groups; more women in the workforce leaves fewer people with the time to pull such events together. High school reunions are a major focus of this business and finding the "lost" members is an important part of the process. Your persistence and sheer determination need to be applied to the search process, which usually starts one year before the event. Former employees of some organizations also occasionally hold reunions, and there is a niche market in putting together reunions for today's far-flung families. Once you discover the whereabouts of the people, you may turn your attention to the event itself, arranging the catering, photos, band, decorations, and mementos.

What You Need

Basic office equipment ($2,000-$3,000) should get you started, but you will need to get the database program ($175-$300) as soon as possible. Set your charges different-ly for the time involved and the number of people you're expected to locate; many charge between $5-$10 per attendee, but others charge a flat rate commensurate with an hourly fee of $10-$15 per hour.

Keys to Success

Most communities are excellent markets for this service, but they don't know it yet. Reunion organizing is an obvious service to offer, but people won't be expecting it to be available. Consider the organizations and groups in your locale that have reunions, such as schools and colleges. Get a foothold, do one excellent job, and you will find that the referrals will begin to roll in. Your success will depend to some extent on the material and information you have to work with, but once you refine your people-searching skills, you should have a service to offer that can't be matched by amateurs. One tip: Use on-line phone books or the new telephone directories on disk or CD-ROM; these can help you locate nearly anyone in the country.

How to Stay Positive

Let's face it, the best thing about owning your own business is that it is your own business. But, it has also been said that the worst thing about owning your own business is that it is your own business. When things are going great, it's easy to be positive, but what can you do when you have some slow times?

- **Take inventory of all the good things that have happened in the last month.** Write them down, and really appreciate them.

- **Put a "plus" sign over your desk.** At eye level, so you remember to try and remain positive at all times (especially when on the phone with customers).

- **Concentrate on the opportunities you still have.** So often, we expend all of our energy on negative things that happen. Focusing on the future will keep you from ignoring potentially great opportunities that you might have missed while wallowing in your sorrow.

- **Surround yourself with positive people.** If you've got friends in business, try to support one another in times of despair. Offer positive advice and encouragement—but, most of all, learn to accept it when it's given to you.

- **See, then be.** Picture yourself succeeding again, and your chances of success will nearly double. Never underestimate the power of creative visualization.

- **Don't give up.** Even the most successful entrepreneurs have experienced setbacks, so you're not the only one. Have the courage to go on.

Roommate Referral Service

Start-up cost:	$500-$1,000
Potential earnings:	10,000-$25,000
Typical fees:	20 to 50 percent of a month's rent
Advertising:	Yellow Pages, flyers at apartment complexes, coin-operated laundries, and supermarkets, newspaper classified ads
Qualifications:	Excellent organization skills
Equipment needed:	Database management software, computer modem, printer, phone, credit card processing equipment
Staff required:	No
Handicapped opportunity:	Yes
Hidden costs:	Insurance

What You Do

With the rising cost of living in many major cities, and the rise in displaced folks who need to share rent with the ideal roommate, you could make a fine living playing match-maker for live-ins. Ideally, you would have a method for screening each of the candidates (police checks at the very least) and a method for securing your payment ahead of time (credit card processing equipment would be helpful). Advertise in places where people generally look for a place to live, and you'll have found your special niche. Develop a good questionnaire that really asks the kinds of questions a potential room-mate would want answered. To double your income potential, you could add on other services such as mediation between rumblin' roomies or budget development assis-tance. The best advice is to focus on one area first, then branch out your services as you move successfully along.

What You Need

Your costs are incredibly low when compared to most other businesses, mainly because you can create your own flyers to post in noticeable, highly trafficked areas. That's why your income potential, while seemingly low, is actually somewhat appealing—you have such low overhead, most of your income ($10,000-$20,000) will be sheer profit.

Keys to Success

The only advice is to be sure you carefully screen your applicants—bad matches are sure to strike you if you don't.

Rubber Stamp Business

Start-up cost:	$5,000-$10,000
Potential earnings:	40,000-$60,000
Typical fees:	Anywhere from $5-$15 per stamp
Advertising:	Mail order, direct mail, newspapers
Qualifications:	None (you can be trained by a printing professional)
Equipment needed:	Computer with laser printer, photopolymer system (you can subcontract the larger orders that need to be made of rubber)
Staff required:	No
Handicapped opportunity:	Yes
Hidden costs:	Materials can run high (as much as $1,000 per year)

What You Do

The rubber stamp business gets the stamp of approval from many entrepreneurial resources. Why? Because it's a relatively easy way to make steady money from a simple product. The variety of stamps you can produce is mind-boggling; think of the last time you went into a retail store and saw literally hundreds of choices (from frogs to stars to computers). Now think of the possibilities in the business world: small businesses need to have return address stamps; they're cheaper in the long haul than labels and more readily available as well. You can sell wholesale, retail, or mail order with this business, and expect to generate immediate interest if you introduce your company with introductory specials and discounts for new customers. You'll work with printers and graphics people who can provide you with all the background and technical information you need . . . so what's to lose from a product line so easy to produce?

What You Need

You'll need to invest in some equipment ($3,000-$5,000) at the outset. If you're buying a franchise version of this business (which could provide you with all the training you'll need), expect to spend another $10,000 minimum on licensing fees. But, since you'll be marketing your inexpensive ($3-$15 each) product to the masses, you stand a good chance of making a go of this one.

Keys to Success

The investment's not too high, the income potential is high . . . what more could you ask?

Sales of Novelty
and Promotional Products

Start-up cost:	$1,000-$5,000
Potential earnings:	30,000-$60,000
Typical fees:	Each product sells anywhere from a few dollars to several hundred
Advertising:	Trade publications, business periodicals, direct mail, catalogs
Qualifications:	Sales ability
Equipment needed:	Computer, suite software, modem, fax, laser printer, business cards, letterhead, envelopes, marketing materials
Staff required:	Probably
Handicapped opportunity:	Yes
Hidden costs:	Inventory, reprinting of catalogs and other sales materials

What You Do

This is the business for you if you know what will amuse people (namely, your clients' customers) and catch their attention. You are providing one facet of the activity that is essential to every business: marketing. Novelties and promotional materials put the name and message of a business out before the public. They can be an enormously effective way of reaching out for customers. In this process, you are far more than just a writer of orders. You present ideas for the new and different. Promotional materials can take many forms, and fitting the object to the message takes a special kind of business insight. You'll need to have an enthusiasm for sales and marketing in your blood. You need to be as creative and off-beat as possible to attract the attention of companies who want to attract attention to themselves.

What You Need

Your relationship with your distributor will control your need for inventory, which ideally will be kept to a minimum. Demonstration samples and catalogs may be quite expensive, though. Try to secure a good arrangement with your manufacturers and their reps before trying to produce your own. You can earn a living selling these types of products; just look at how well companies such as Successories are doing and you'll know that the market is profitable.

Keys to Success

Your devotion to the needs of your clients will make you stand out from the crowd. There is quite a lot of competition in this field, but many of the other businesses just throw a catalog at prospects and expect them to do the creative work. You, on the other hand, develop a presentation focused on each client's distinctive needs and expectations. You give them several appealing options, and you carry out the detailed ordering and delivery process. It is work, but it's also fun.

Expert Advice

What sets your business apart from others like it?

"We have not only created a specialty product, but something that has a life and character all its own," says Mark Juarez, President and CEO of Tender Loving Things, Inc., in Oakland, California, which produces tiny wooden creatures with massage capability.

Things you couldn't do without:

"Birch or maple wood, drilling machine, glue, smiley-face brander and office equipment to run shipping, production, art, marketing, customer service, and administrative departments."

Marketing tips/advice:

"We turn profits into social responsibility; we donate 10 percent of our product to non-profit organizations and other groups that might benefit from the caring touch."

If you had to do it all over again . . .

"One of our biggest external challenges has been combating knockoffs and copycats." Juarez suggests protecting yourself as early as possible within federal trademark regulations.

Seamstress

Start-up cost:	$1,000-$5,000 (depending on whether you have to rent space)
Potential earnings:	20,000-$40,000
Typical fees:	Varied, but charges normally start at $5 and go all the way to $75, depending on what needs to be done
Advertising:	Newspapers, bulletin boards, fashion shows
Qualifications:	The ability to create fashions and apparel without patterns would be useful
Equipment needed:	Sewing machine and materials
Staff required:	No
Handicapped opportunity:	Possibly
Hidden costs:	Remakes could take up more than an inch of your time; make sure your work meets even the toughest standards

What You Do

If all you need is a needle and thread to design a business you feel comfortable in, then the alterations/sewing business is a perfect match. In this recession-proof business, you will repair or alter clothing that belongs to your client—but you can also offer custom-sewn clothing to busy executives who appreciate fine threads designed expressly for them. Creativity and the desire to make good clothes even better are the only requirements you'll need, and the higher the quality of your work, the more people will hear about your service. Word of mouth is nearly always the best way to grow the alterations business, although you may want to consider posting your business card on all the bulletin boards you can find in your community. Also, leave some extra cards for owners of dress shops—they often refer their customers to good tailors or seamstresses.

What You Need

Your biggest up-front cost will be a good sewing machine (up to $1,000 or more); you might look into buying a used commercial sewing machine, because they are more durable and can be purchased for as little as $400. Be sure to invest in professional-looking business cards, because you'll need a lot of them to spread the word about your service. Use a rate card to keep track of what you're charging per job; some alterations are simple and inexpensive ($5-$10), while others are time-intensive and require you to charge $75 or more.

Keys to Success

If you like to work sparingly with people and spend much of the time by yourself, you'll love this type of work. However, the hours can be long and the rewards not as frequent as you might like. Sewing is tedious work except to those who truly enjoy it—so make sure that you enjoy it enough to spend 65 percent of your workday doing it.

Secretarial Service

Start-up cost:	$3,000-$5,000
Potential earnings:	20,000-$40,000
Typical fees:	$10-$20 per hour (depending on size of the company you're working for)
Advertising:	Classified ads, Yellow Pages, phone contacts
Qualifications:	Good typing and clerical skills
Equipment needed:	Computer or word processor, paper
Staff required:	No
Handicapped opportunity:	Yes
Hidden costs:	Invest in a freelance proofreader or proofreading software, as mistakes could cost you repeat business

What You Do

The executive stretches in his chair, puts his feet up on his desk, and calls for his secretary . . . only, in the age of downsizing, he's likely to be kept waiting—because he's sharing with ten others who are already in line with their requests. The old days where everyone had a personal secretary are gone; many functions have been replaced by small secretarial pools or computers. But the need for personalized service has not gone away, and often a beleaguered company, its small administrative force stretched to the max, needs to farm out work. That's where you come in. You can assist them for a short period of time, typing letters or producing manuals that would be simply too costly to employ a full-timer with benefits to do. Training and/or experience as a secretary will help you understand the types of skills that you need and an idea of who to offer them to (dictation, shorthand, filing, and form typing are just a few). There is a lot of flexibility possible with this type of business: after-regular-hours work for out-of-towners to temporary fill-ins for local companies to contracting overflow and everything in between.

What You Need

A computer is the recommended choice for running a secretarial service since it has greater versatility and a variety of available programs (compatible, of course, with your client's), but a word processor could work in a beginning pinch. Computers will cost anywhere from $1,000-$3,000, while a simple word processor can be bought for as low as $500. Whichever you choose, buying used models only a year or two old will help keep start-up costs down. Advertising in the Yellow Pages for $50-$100 per month, in the classifieds for $10 per week, and leaving flyers at hotels where businesspeople from out-of-town might need some help are some easy, inexpensive ways to get word out about the services being offered. Remember, the amount of time it will take to finish one assignment will vary and is generally unknown at the start, so charging an hourly fee of $10-$15 will prove more profitable than working for a set price per task.

Keys to Success

Since it's likely that this job will involve working with many different people, tolerance of personality quirks will make jobs—and time—go more quickly and smoothly. The hours will be varied, which could become stressful for you (and your bank account) at times. This business needs a high-energy, go-getter type of person; do you have what it takes (and can you take the orders placed upon you by others)?

Expert Advice

What sets your business apart from others like it?

"I'm incredibly fast, accurate, and affordable," says Jana McClish, owner of Paragon Word Services in Akron, Ohio. "I can offer a quicker turnaround than most of my competitors."

Things you couldn't do without:

McClish needs a computer, answering machine, and a 10-key adding machine to run her business effectively.

Marketing tips/advice:

"You have to be persistent and market almost constantly. You must be confident and be able to sell that confidence in order to get in the door. You really need to have a special skill that sets you apart, too."

If you had to do it all over again . . .

"I'd research my equipment purchases better. I needed to buy new equipment a year and a half into my business because I did not purchase wisely. Also, I would've started with a much bigger base of prospects . . . I got kind of discouraged in the beginning because I didn't have huge amounts of work."

Seminar Service

Start-up cost:	$5,000-$10,000
Potential earnings:	30,000-$50,000
Typical fees:	$125-$500 per speaking engagement; service earns 25-40percent of this
Advertising:	Press releases to newspapers, radio, business/civic organizations
Qualifications:	Managerial and marketing skills, expertise in planning and promotion
Equipment needed:	Computer and printer, tape recorder and transcription equipment, business card, letterhead, envelopes
Staff required:	No
Handicapped opportunity:	Yes
Hidden costs:	Transcriptions and tape reproduction costs

What You Do

If you have a sense of what trends are catching the attention of the public, you may be able to create a business by arranging for speakers on these topics. If you can organize appealing seminars and publicize them effectively, you can make a good living in this area. You can make some of the presentations yourself, but in order to be very successful you will need to have a list of speakers available who can make amusing or captivating presentations that stay with the audience long after they leave the meeting. Enjoyable seminars have a sense of give and take, with a lively speaker and active participation from the audience. These satisfied customers will be your best advertising; they will return with their friends for future sessions. An add-on business is sales of presentation tapes or transcripts. If you are a bit of a showman yourself, combine those skills with a good event planning skills and this business may be expressly for you.

What You Need

Each seminar requires extensive planning and advertising. You will need a computer ($1,500-$2,500) to prepare materials and flyers, and to keep track of your database of effective speakers and satisfied customers. Mailings will cost you $500 and up for each event. Your speakers can earn $125-$500 or more for each speech they deliver, and your percentage of that could be as low as 25 percent and as high as 40 percent.

Keys to Success

Bringing together a group of people for an enjoyable seminar is almost like putting on a play. There is a sense of excitement when a presentation goes well. You can get satisfaction from enabling people to learn something they need or want to know. You are also providing a service to your speakers, who rely on you to organize and support their work. Not all seminars are well-attended, though. You may have chosen the wrong topic, or bad weather may interfere with the success of the meeting. It takes a very detail-oriented person to make all the pieces come together in an event-promotional business like this one.

Silk Flower Arranger

Start-up cost:	$500-$1,000
Potential earnings:	20,000-$40,000
Typical fees:	$25-$300
Advertising:	Yellow Pages, newspapers, bridal salons, restaurants
Qualifications:	Some training with flower arranging, creativity
Equipment needed:	Phone, floral accessories (vases, baskets, floral tape, access to a wide variety of silk flowers)
Staff required:	No
Handicapped opportunity:	Yes
Hidden costs:	Watch materials costs

What You Do

There's nothing in the world like fresh flowers, but they only last a short while. That's why silk flowers are the mainstays of interior decorating; all you've got to do is dust them every once in a while and they retain their beauty forever. You'll always have plenty of customers if you choose to work in this field, from brides who don't want to worry about wilting flowers, to mourners who want to give the bereaved family a lasting token of their remembrance. You'll work many hours in your office, putting together the arrangements that have been ordered by your customers. The only problem is, you'll have to work hard to get some business, since there are plenty of others like you. Think about what makes you different, and let your customers know exactly what your unique marketing point is. Finally, network with funeral homes, churches, and wedding shops for cross-marketing opportunities.

What You Need

Obtain a vendor's license (approximately $25) and buy your supplies at a wholesale store. Check with local craft stores to see if they offer additional discounts if you have a vendor's license. When starting the business, invest a few hundred dollars in floral supplies and silk flowers so you can make arrangements to sell at craft shows. Also, set aside money for booth space rental ($25-$100). Your products will sell anywhere from $25-$300.

Keys to Success

Gain experience by working with florists or taking classes at craft stores. Once you have some knowledge of floral arranging, sign up to sell your goods at holiday craft fairs. Always have plenty of business cards/brochures to accompany each sale, and keep an album with pictures of your work to show clients.

Small Business Consultant

Start-up cost:	$5,000-$15,000
Potential earnings:	50,000-$150,000
Typical fees:	$900-$2,000/day
Advertising:	Word of mouth, referrals, presentations made to business groups, audiovisual materials, professional organizations
Qualifications:	Experience and expertise in all forms of marketing, management sense, communication skills, research, and planning ability
Equipment needed:	Office furniture, computer, suite software, printer, fax, business card, letterhead, envelopes
Staff required:	No
Handicapped opportunity:	Yes
Hidden costs:	Make sure you get paid ASAP, as many of your clients who launch small businesses have little money to begin with

What You Do

As a small business consultant, you are the one with the knowledge and expertise to assess and solve many of the difficulties facing today's small businesses. Between complying with growing government regulations, integrating new technologies, and competing in a tightening economy, most small businesses are looking for consultants who have proved their ability to solve problems. This position offers variety, challenge, and respect—you are the bottom line.

What You Need

A sizable time investment (and at least $5,000) is necessary to identify and approach your clients. Do research, send letters, do lunch. You should make at least $50,000 your first year.

Keys to Success

You must know what you are talking about at all times. While you are selling your experience, companies are buying concrete solutions to their problems, even though the benefits from your work will not always be immediately apparent. Be able to apply your skills to your own business as well as to your clients'.

Snow Plow Service

Start-up cost:	$5,000-$15,000
Potential earnings:	25,000-$35,000
Typical fees:	$25-$40 per job
Advertising:	Yellow Pages, seasonally in newspapers
Qualifications:	Must have a driver's license
Equipment needed:	4-wheel-drive truck, snow blower, shovel, snow plow for truck; pager or cellular phone may be helpful
Staff required:	No
Handicapped opportunity:	Not typically
Hidden costs:	Liability insurance

What You Do

There's nothing like the convenience of having a snow plow service remove the mountain of snow on your driveway—or your roof—in blizzard conditions—and convenience is the main reason you'd decide to be in this business in the first place. After all, if you've already got a heavy-duty vehicle that needs only a plow attachment, your start-up would be relatively small and the potential for earning quite high. You would be on-call for homes and businesses the majority of your winter time, and if you advertise in the right places, you could be in the enviable position of having to farm out some of your work to another service like yours. Obviously, you should only consider this business opportunity if you live in a climate with cold, snowy winters—since this business is dependent upon the white stuff. Still, you could intentionally make it a seasonal business, and paint houses in the summer. Many folks do exactly that.

What You Need

You can start your operation small by investing only in a shovel and snow blower at a cost of approximately $500. However, you won't be able to clear anything larger than an average driveway or sidewalk with this equipment. To clear larger parking lots, you'll need a truck and a snow plow. Don't forget to set aside money for vehicle upkeep and repairs. Bill your services by the size of the job.

Keys to Success

It's a great and necessary service you provide . . . and it can be profitable if you don't mind being out in Ice Station Zebra. However, this is a seasonal business, so be sure to make enough to stretch you through the warmth of summer!

Standardized Test Preparatory Services

Start-up cost:	$1,000-$5,000
Potential earnings:	30,000-$45,000
Typical fees:	$75-$175 per client
Advertising:	Yellow Pages, direct mail to students/parents
Qualifications:	Familiarity with all standardized tests (including SAT, ACT, GED, LSAT), teaching degree helpful (and required in some states)
Equipment needed:	Practice tests, pencils, timers
Staff required:	No
Handicapped opportunity:	Yes
Hidden costs:	Insurance

What You Do

Thousands of students each year must take standard tests for entry into college, and they usually must spend weeks preparing for these all-encompassing tests. There are sections on math and language usage in most of these tests, and you can help students prepare for each by presenting them with similar questions or problems as practice guides and answering their questions. Perhaps you'll choose to work with a more specialized test such as the LSAT that undergraduates must pass before being accepted to law school. Whatever area you choose to specialize in, you'll need to work with groups of students at one time to make it truly profitable.

What You Need

Your start-up costs will be low, because you'll only need some workbooks, pencils, and timers to start with—and, since your clients will be paying up front for your services, you needn't worry about maintaining an inventory prior to accepting clients. You may want to spend $35 or so per test prep session on space rental (check with local schools for their after-hour rates). At $75-$175 per student, you can easily see an income potential of $30,000-$45,000.

Keys to Success

If you enjoy repetition, this could be a relaxing and comfortable way to make a living; all you have to do is provide the same services over and over, and collect your checks as you do. On the other hand, it could become too repetitious, and therefore less challenging than most entrepreneurs would like. You decide what your comfort level is.

Systems Integrator

Start-up cost:	$1,000-$5,000
Potential earnings:	37,500-$100,000
Typical fees:	$150+ per hour
Advertising:	Referrals, direct mail, publications, networking
Qualifications:	Technical knowledge and expertise in systems, time-management skills
Equipment needed:	Computer, software, modem, fax, office furniture, letterhead, envelopes
Staff required:	No, but subcontracting may be required depending on project needs
Handicapped opportunity:	Yes
Hidden costs:	Time and expense of staying current in this demanding field

What You Do

Computers are wonderful business tools; few organizations can begin to operate without them today. Yet no one would disagree with the premise that the design and planning of computers, both hardware and software, has a long way to go. Operations and compatibility problems are enormous, and as businesses grow, they must resolve issues related to the necessary growth in their information systems. If you have the expertise to be a systems integrator, nearly every growing company in the U.S., possibly the world, needs your services. One successful project should enable you to easily move on to another. You will need some people skills to work with the employees involved with information systems at your client's office. Your principal offering will be your detailed understanding of how the current systems work, what the needs are, and how to move the systems into effective integration.

What You Need

Most of your work will be carried out at your client's premises and on their equipment, so you needn't spend too much on your own office and equipment. However, keep in mind that you'll need to be familiar with many different types of equipment, some of which you'll own and some of which you can lease. You'll need to be billing at a rate of at least $100 per hour.

Keys to Success

Many businesses need your service, so if you live within commuting distance of an urban area, you ought to be able to create an excellent and profitable business of your own as a systems integrator. A longtime commitment to one client, necessary to complete most projects in this field, can limit your contacts—but it also should provide you with an excellent referral base. This is an extremely challenging field; however, one problem is that the people making the decision to hire you often have little understanding of what their information system needs. Education, then, is a major part of each sales effort. Systems integration is often carried out under high pressure. Bidding jobs is challenging as well.

Tax Preparation Service

Start-up cost:	$5,500-$15,000
Potential earnings:	40,000-$100,000
Typical fees:	From $25-$50 per hour; more if complex
Advertising:	Referrals, networking, ads in local publications and Yellow Pages, direct mail
Qualifications:	An interest in people and their situations, patience, excellent math skills, thorough understanding of tax laws and calculations
Equipment needed:	Computer, phone, fax, office equipment (including copier), specialized tax software, reference manuals, insurance, business card, paper
Staff required:	None
Handicapped opportunity:	Yes
Hidden costs:	Time and money for continuing education, if needed

What You Do

Income tax regulations and their associated forms are often too complicated for the average person to comprehend. Making heads and tails of tax forms, then, is a much-needed service and one that people often don't mind paying for (remind them that income tax preparation fees are tax-deductible, and you'll sell them even more on your service). You obviously need to have a thorough knowledge of tax law, tax preparation, and forms to succeed, but you don't need to study for a license unless you want certification as a CPA or other designation. This is complicated, detailed work; our tax laws are cumbersome and confusing. It would be quite beneficial to take a training course before you begin. This would not only ensure that your skills are adequate, but would give you a feel for whether this work is for you. Tax preparation can earn a talented, detail-oriented business owner a very nice income.

What You Need

In addition to the usual computer and office equipment, detailed tax guides, special software, errors and omissions insurance, and a good quality printer and copier will be required. Depending on what you need, your office can be set up for as little as $3,500. Charge at least $25-$50 an hour for your services; more if the job looks complex.

Keys to Success

Since people will always have to pay taxes, you will never run out of potential clients. IRS guidelines are complex and confusing to most citizens, so knowledgeable tax preparers are in great demand. To be a good preparer, though, requires constant upgrading of skills to meet the changes in forms and regulations. Tax preparation is seasonal, which means cash flow can be uneven; you might add other services to fill in the slower months.

Telemarketing Service

Start-up cost:	$6,000-$10,000
Potential earnings:	40,000 or more
Typical fees:	$30 an hour
Advertising:	Yellow Pages, direct mail, business publications, membership in local business and civic groups
Qualifications:	Experience, persistence, ability to market your own service, writing skills for preparing script and reports
Equipment needed:	Telephone with headset, ergonomic office furniture, computer, suite software, printer, fax, modem, business card, letterhead, envelopes
Staff required:	No
Handicapped opportunity:	Yes
Hidden costs:	Utility bills, marketing time and materials

What You Do

Telemarketing is a specialized and very focused form of marketing. No business can survive without effective marketing, and your challenge will be to reach the organizations that need to develop their customer base and show them how your service can help them grow. Telemarketing can be informational—a way of doing market research—but the major proportion will be focused on sales. As a small business, you may choose to offer a specific type of telemarketing: pharmaceuticals, commercial photography, wedding services, etc. This specialization will help you focus on your own marketing.

What You Need

You'll need excellent telephone equipment and reasonably sophisticated computer equipment to track results and produce reports (about $6,000 to start). Once you get the hang of it, you can make $40,000 annually.

Keys to Success

People skills are even more important to success as a telemarketer than they are in other types of small businesses. Listening well, speaking convincingly, and tuning the message to the receiver are all essential. You'll need experience writing effective scripts, and you'll need patience and persistence. It will probably take some time to develop the client base for your business. You can distinguish yourself from the run-of-the-mill telemarketers because you're not someone just hired off the street. You have experience, you're creating a proven track record, and you have an unquenchable enthusiasm for your clients' projects.

Expert Advice

What sets your business apart from others like it?

"While there are many marketing and advertising agencies, public relations firms, and telemarketing organizations, my company is a one-stop agency that has the capability of coordinating any and all aspects of a marketing plan," says Cheryl D. Cira, owner of Columbus, Ohio-based Marketing Dimensions. "I cannot stress how important it is to be honest and up front with your customers. Marketing Dimensions looks at each project and account as a long-term relationship."

Things you couldn't do without:

"Essentials include telephone equipment and office furniture. It also helps to have computers in order to enter large lists, track calls, pull up records, and run reports. Computers are also used for simple design work, database management, and mail merges," says Cira.

Staffing tips/advice:

"Telemarketing projects depend on the work and devotion of employees. And, because people are people, there are some aspects that cannot be controlled, such as employees quitting without notice, coming in late, and calling in sick time after time. My office manager is very good at juggling schedules and maintaining a strong pool of telemarketers, but it can get crazy at times."

If you had to do it all over again . . .

"I don't think there is any one thing of great importance that I would change or do differently. In general, however, I wish that I had had more hands-on experience in managing a large staff and more working knowledge related to personnel issues."

Temporary Employment Agency

Start-up cost:	$60,000-$150,000+
Potential earnings:	200,000-$450,000
Typical fees:	$1,000-$1,500 per employee per project
Advertising:	Yellow Pages, direct mail, newspaper ads, billboards, referral
Qualifications:	Previous employment agency experience would be helpful; business background and ability to match candidates successfully is paramount
Equipment needed:	Computers (four to six) with printers and fax/modems, phone system, scheduling/billing software (image is everything, and your office shows your success)
Staff required:	Yes
Handicapped opportunity:	Yes
Hidden costs:	Workers' compensation

What You Do

It used to be that temporary agencies specialized only in clerical types—but the age of corporate downsizing has led to an increase in professionals entering the "temp" field, from marketing communications professionals to product designers and even attorneys. It's a $33-billion-dollar industry, mainly because the large companies that employed thousands a few years ago are now using help only as they need it. After all, from their point of view, why pay the huge benefits packages and salaries for work that can be done on a project-by-project basis? From your standpoint, this philosophy makes perfect sense; you're making your money on the fact that both workers and corporations are seeking less permanent commitment; workers are beginning to see the positive side of nonpermanent employment (they can freelance, launch businesses of their own, etc.) and the companies see the obvious benefit of saving money where possible. It's a win-win . . . all you have to do is match the right temp to the right assignment, and make sure that all of your employees are trained and able to work on short notice. You'll do an extensive background check and intake (including typing tests, computer aptitude assessments, etc.) and ensure that each temporary employee has sufficient credentials and/or experience to do a fine job. Then you'll sit back and reel in the money—particularly if you choose to specialize in a specific, in-demand area (such as nursing or engineering).

What You Need

You'll need $60,000-$150,000 to buy into a franchise; possibly more if you decide to go it alone (because you'll need a comprehensive benefits plan, several computers, and the placement staff or account executives to manage each account thoroughly and professionally). This is an extremely lucrative field, and you can make anywhere from $200,000-$450,000 if you develop enough contacts and build a fine reputation.

Keys to Success

You can dig yourself an early grave if you don't spend enough time preparing; know that your competitors are out there, that they have just as many good candidates as you, and that all you have to do is set yourself apart by advertising the uniqueness of your service. That's why a niche would work wonders for you financially—it gives potential clients a way to pigeonhole you in a positive way, so that they associate your company name with whatever specific need they have (i.e., Acme Personnel = engineering specialists).

Expert Advice

What sets your business apart from others like it?

"We have a personal approach and a high level of applicants to choose from; in that sense, we're a cut above the rest," says Fran Doll, President of Superior Staffing, Inc., in Akron, Ohio, and recognized Ohio Entrepreneur of the Year.

Things you couldn't do without:

Doll says her business thrives on a telephone system, a computer, and fax machine. "If our phones go down, we're dead," she says.

Marketing tips/advice:

"You need to have worked in this industry for a while before embarking on your own. It's not as easy as it looks. Also, be sure you have enough capital or you'll have cash flow problems because you're underfinanced."

If you had to do it all over again . . .

"I would be more careful about the accountants I chose to work with. I had two accountants who really messed me up."

Ticket Broker

Start-up cost:	$15,000-$35,000
Potential earnings:	25,000-$35,000+
Typical fees:	5 to 40 percent of each sale; it varies depending on whether you're selling nationally
Advertising:	Industry trade publications, newspapers
Qualifications:	Knowledge of state licensing requirements
Equipment:	Computer with specialized software program/hookup, 800 number phone line
Staff required:	No
Handicapped opportunity:	Yes
Hidden costs:	Make sure you have in the contract that you're not liable for any unsold tickets

What You Do

How many times have you wanted to buy tickets for an event or a show, to find that it has been sold out? For those who simply can't get to the big tickets, ticket brokers provide a welcome relief by offering tickets, often at a discounted rate, and the convenience of purchasing by phone. Organization and responsibility are key to this business. Your job includes assigning seat locations, providing ticket sales information, making recommendations about ticket pricing according to the area or event, soliciting group sales, and keeping a customer ticket list. You'll need to purchase specialized software that allows you to search on-line for ticket availability and accept credit card orders over the phone. An accounting or bookkeeping background would prove especially helpful, as there are a million little details that need to be managed on a daily basis to keep this one up and running.

What You Need

Computers are a way of life for this occupation. You have to be able to hook up to the ticket distribution center. Your fee will depend on the event and place. Typically you get a 5 to 40 percent cut of each sale.

Keys to Success

You may need to hire a staff to run this from your home; it all depends on how big you want to get. There may be some travel involved and you'll want to attend all of the trade shows so the industry knows you are out there. Most of the big ticket brokers have been in business a long time and have a good reputation. Get to know them; you may need to network with them sometime.

Time-Management Specialist

Start-up cost:	$1,000-$6,500
Potential earnings:	20,000-$40,000
Typical fees:	$75-$100 per hour or a set fee ($100+ per person) for classes you offer
Advertising:	Free workshops/seminars and other public speaking, word-of-mouth referrals, networking, news releases, written articles
Qualifications:	High level of organization, analytical ability, punctuality, ability to deliver on your commitments, an open mind
Equipment needed:	Computer with fax/modem, printer, phone, time-management software, handout materials
Staff required:	No
Handicapped opportunity:	Yes
Hidden costs:	Preparation time if you are not already using a previously written program, licensing fees if you are

What You Do

Bringing relief to people under inordinate stress is just one of the many benefits of being a time-management specialist. In addition to making the workplace a little less of a sweatshop, you'll be assisting clients in goal-setting, developing action plans, defining priorities, and scheduling/delegating tasks and activities. You may decide to work as a consultant, identifying problems for harried company executives in search of an answer in the pursuit of higher productivity. But you may also decide to add on additional services, such as seminars for large groups or individual personal productivity training. The opportunities to make money from time are there, you just need to send the message out to the people most in need of your services (and they are nowhere near as limited as you at first might think). Quick profitability is a definite possibility with this low overhead business—but you need to charge appropriately for your time and expertise. One last tip: Don't forget to offer periodic refresher courses for repeat business; you'd be surprised how many customers say they'd benefit from another session.

What You Need

Word-of-mouth advertising keeps initial costs low in this business, because it is based on credibility and trust of the specialist. To present a professional image, allow a minimum of $250 for business cards, letterhead, and brochures. Computer costs can range from $1,500-$5,000. Remember that organizational dues will be necessary to continually network and prospect for clients; set aside at least $250 per year for this valuable lead-generator. Charge at least $75 per hour for corporate consulting; more ($1,000 per day is typical) if you're conducting seminars for groups of professionals.

Keys to Success

The art of timeliness and organization is relatively new to businesses. Hence, competition may not be a significant problem. If you enjoy leading others to dramatic results in a short period of time, this career can be extremely enjoyable. But you should be advised that this work demands a lot of your own time and energy to get started; are you able to practice what you preach? It may take as much as a year or two before you are able to make a full-time income; hopefully, you have been gifted with patience yourself.

Expert Advice

What sets your business apart from others like it?

Jennifer Annandono, Managing Partner of the Kent, Ohio-based Progressive Leadership Center, says her business is unique because she is. "I greatly enjoy demonstrating to others how to have a more balanced work and personal life. My feeling is that time management is about setting goals, and the implementation of new tools, which will promote achievement."

Things you couldn't do without:

Annandono says she could not do without a second telephone line with answering or voice mail capability. "My computer and laser printer allow me the convenience of professional correspondence."

Marketing tips/advice:

"It is always more effective to market your service as the 'benefit' customers will receive rather than focusing on various features you might offer. Much of my marketing success is based in community interaction and word-of-mouth referral. The best advice is: always be a product of the service you provide!"

If you had to do it all over again . . .

"I would have spent the months preceding the opening of my business selecting centers of influence. If you are not already established in the community, it is never too early to identify and communicate with those individuals who know and trust you and clearly understand what service you provide."

Trademark Agent

Start-up cost:	$1,000-$1,500
Potential earnings:	40,000-$65,000
Typical fees:	Usually a flat fee of $175-$250 (more for larger corporations)
Advertising:	Business publications, direct mail, referrals, networking
Qualifications:	Extensive experience in field, familiarity with computer searches, residence near Washington, D.C.
Equipment needed:	Computer with fax/modem, business cards, letterhead, envelopes
Staff required:	No
Handicapped opportunity:	No
Hidden costs:	Insurance, on-line time

What You Do

The business cliché of today is that perception is reality. Whether you agree with that idea or not, the image of a product or service is undeniably a factor in its value. Since medieval times, a trademark has been a way of protecting an essential element of that image, the name. Since medieval times, however, an incredibly large number of names have been trademarked, and your clients need to know if they can call their stunt act Angelic Skydiving Service or if someone in Hawaii has already used that name. You will discover if the name has already been used by conducting a search of the paper records at the Trademark Office in Washington, D.C. Database information such as records from all 50 Secretaries of State is proprietary—owned by your giant competitors—so as a small business person, you must rely on manual searches. Many trademark agents specialize in a field they know well, such as tire names.

What You Need

Costs are relatively low, especially if you already have a computer (add $2,000 if you don't). The outlay of your own labor, however, will be high for each search; if you are an attorney, you'll likely use a computer database, but if you're not, you'll have to do it all manually—and time is money. Charge $175-$250 per search/registry; more if working for a larger corporation (although many of these companies already have in-house or on-retainer attorneys who would accomplish the same work).

Keys to Success

Skill and sometimes intuition are required to establish the validity of a given trademark. Finding the proper trademark files is an art. You can't simply look up a name, like "sword," in an index. Instead, you must consider all words with similar meanings, like "rapier and "saber," as well as the words with similar sounds, like "sod" and "sore." Then you must consider designs that might include swords. It all becomes quite complicated, so be sure you enjoy minute details before embarking on this one.

Translation Services

Start-up cost:	$1,000-$2,000
Potential earnings:	20,000-$30,000
Typical fees:	$25-$35 per hour
Advertising:	Trade journals, Yellow Pages, referrals, personal contacts
Qualifications:	Proficiency in a foreign language, excellent writing and communications skills
Equipment needed:	Computer, modem, fax, printer, software, office furniture, business cards, letterhead, envelopes
Staff required:	Yes, for languages you cannot translate yourself
Handicapped opportunity:	Yes
Hidden costs:	Telephone costs, marketing

What You Do

Thousands of languages are spoken across the globe, and even within the U.S. texts often need translation into French or Spanish. For most business communications in the global marketplace, a translation service can be useful to develop, among other things, a glossary of terms to use in the translation process. Additional services can relate to development of icons and illustrations that are effective across cultures. You can specialize in a business field such as medical instrument sales, or you can focus on one particular language. Producing effective, accurate results under deadline will enable you to build your translation business into a very successful enterprise.

What You Need

Reference materials and the normal office equipment are the major start-up costs. You'll need a printer that can produce all of the characters and accent marks used in your specialty languages. Grand start-up total should be somewhere from $1,000-$2,000; earnings will come from $25-$35 per hour fees.

Keys to Success

The market for translation services is growing rapidly and will continue to do so in the future. English is by no means a universal language, and few Americans are fluent enough in a foreign language to produce their own translations. You'll be learning as you translate while providing a very significant service to your clients. Problems can result from lack of awareness, though. Translating is not a question of simply plugging words into slots (e.g., one foreign word for one English term). It's a creative and challenging activity to communicate the total meaning of a sentence or paragraph accurately, and your pricing needs to reflect the time needed to do this.

Travel Agent

Start-up cost:	$2,000-$5,000
Potential earnings:	25,000-$45,000
Typical fees:	Commission of 10 percent is fairly common on each sale; some airlines have been cutting those commissions considerably, however
Advertising:	Travel, meeting/hotel magazines, Yellow Pages, direct mail, location
Qualifications:	Knowledge of the travel industry and particular destinations; often, certification is required through an accredited travel school; training on the customized computer systems most travel agencies use.
Equipment needed:	At minimum, a computer and phone
Staff required:	No
Handicapped opportunity:	Yes
Hidden costs:	Phone expenses

What You Do

Would you find satisfaction helping others fly the friendly skies to exotic places? Have you always been a travel nut? If you answered yes to both questions, you could potentially succeed as a travel agent. As an outside travel agent, you would associate with a travel agency willing to work with you. You can refer business to them (for perhaps a 10 percent commission) or actually arrange travel bookings for which the agency will cut the tickets (because restrictions on ticketing won't allow you to do it). For the latter work, you can make as much as 60 to 70 percent of the commission. There are also networked travel agencies that rely almost solely on home-based agents, so your options are many if you decide to embark on this exciting and interesting business. The best part is, many travel companies offer incentives and special perks for agents like you—and you could wind up doing some sightseeing yourself.

What You Need

You need a budget for advertising, the appropriate computer and office equipment, software, and phone, and may have to pay small fees (such as $50) to use your associate's name and ticketing number.

Keys to Success

The travel business is huge—and still growing by leaps and bounds. Many opportunities exist to make money in this field. The cost of running a travel business is modest if you are working as an outside agent; little more than computer and office equipment is required. Opening your own agency is an expensive proposition; it also takes time to get established, and competition from larger agencies capable of booking large corporate accounts can be daunting.

Expert Advice

What sets your business apart from others like it?

"My agents and I have traveled to almost every destination in the world, so I would say that personal experience set us apart from other travel agents," says Helen Meek, owner of Helen Meek Travel in Fairlawn, Ohio.

Things you couldn't do without:

Computers with specialized reservation programs (leased from airline companies) and telephones are the primary pieces of equipment needed to run this travel agency. "We also couldn't do without our experienced, wonderful staff."

Marketing tips/advice:

"You need to look at location and market demographics; I knew my area would grow, and now I'm an established leader in my geographic location." Meek also advises entrepreneurs to get their names out there any way possible while building credibility.

If you had to do it all over again . . .

"Nothing. It's worked for thirteen years, and if you can get past those first five, you are probably going to make it."

Trophy/Engraving service

Start-up cost:	$40,000-$75,000
Potential earnings:	40,000-$65,000
Typical fees:	Can be as low as 40 cents and as high as $100 or more per piece
Advertising:	Direct mail, Yellow Pages, networking with business and civic organizations as well as schools
Qualifications:	None (but you will need initial training on the engraving equipment)
Equipment needed:	Engraver, molds, and stencils
Staff required:	No
Handicapped opportunity:	Yes
Hidden costs:	Insurance, workers' compensation

What You Do

For nearly every school, association, or organization, there is a trophy or an award to be given to its members. For every business, there are name badges to be made for the employees. Think of the potential, then, for your engraving business—it's a bottomless cup, isn't it? You'll need to be a strong networker, as much of this business has already been soaked up by those established much earlier than you. But, to compete, you can set yourself apart by offering unique products to engrave—or even by reselling recognition products from other sources, such as the retail shop and catalog outfit, Successories. Sell people on your exceptional eye for detail and customer service abilities—and, if you can, throw in quick turnaround. Often, your clients will need an award or trophy to be made on a tight deadline—so you can reap an additional fee for 48-hour service, if you think you can handle it.

What You Need

You could spend anywhere from $40,000-$70,000 or more on your engraving equipment, depending on how high-tech you get and how large a company you'd like to be. Your best bet is to seek out good used equipment first. In terms of earning power, you could make between $40,000-$65,000 if you work hard and build the right contacts.

Keys to Success

You'll be singled out as a winner yourself if you can keep up with your orders in an accurate, timely manner. The best thing you can do is to send samples to folks with their names or company logos already printed on it—nothing appeals more to a person than a little ego boost (wasn't it Dale Carnegie who said that there is no sweeter sound than the sound of one's own name?).

Tropical Fish Servicing

Start-up cost:	$1,000-$2,000
Potential earnings:	10,000-$20,000
Typical fees:	$25-$35 per job (depending on tank size)
Advertising:	Flyers, bulletin boards, Yellow Pages
Qualifications:	Knowledge of aquarium maintenance
Equipment needed:	Cleaning equipment, business cards, letterhead, envelopes
Staff required:	No
Handicapped opportunity:	No
Hidden costs:	None

What You Do

This is a business opportunity for a person with patience and enthusiasm for the under-water world and self-marketing ability to go with it. Tropical fish aquariums can require a surprisingly high level of maintenance, and your challenge will be to make your services known to the businesses and individuals who would appreciate being relieved of this tiresome, ongoing chore. The tanks must be cleaned regularly and replenished with fresh water and chemical treatments to ensure that the fish remain healthy. Experience caring for your own fish will help you to recognize what is needed by each aquarium that you service.

What You Need

Costs are minimal for a maintenance service but will increase if you decide to move into sales of aquarium equipment or the actual fish. You should charge $25-$35 per clean-ing job, and remember to include your mileage as overhead.

Keys to Success

This is a nice part-time job for a self-starter. Many people are simply happy with the opportunity to make a hobby into a business. You must plan your service deliveries so you don't spend too much time traveling between clients. Remember, too, that mar-keting your services can be quite demanding of your time.

Used Computer Sales

Start-up cost:	$5,000-$15,000
Potential earnings:	5,000-$100,000
Typical fees:	Used computers sell anywhere from $250-$3,000; your percentage could be a 50/50 split with the previous owner
Advertising:	Telephone marketing, word of mouth, networking
Qualifications:	Sales ability; energetic pursuit of buyers, sellers, and equipment
Equipment needed:	Computer, fax, modem, printer, office furniture, business card, letterhead, envelopes
Staff required:	No
Handicapped opportunity:	Possibly
Hidden costs:	Building up inventory can be costly; be sure to figure in reconditioning costs if necessary

What You Do

There's definitely a market for used computers, but it's not an obvious one. To succeed in this business you will need to be the connection. You will be advertising in both directions, as a buyer of used equipment, and as a seller. Rapid changes in technology mean frequent upgrading of hardware by large organizations and even by many individuals. The "old" equipment may still function as well as it did when new, but need for a larger hard drive or more memory has made these machines seem obsolete. The previous generations of computers are very desirable to organizations that operate on a shoestring, to third-world companies, and to individuals who don't want to pay a lot to jump on the latest technology bandwagon. Your business opportunity arises from your ability to bring the used equipment together with its hidden market.

What You Need

A great deal of advertising is required, and can cost you anywhere from $1,500-$5,000 per year. Inventory will be a variable but can lead to a considerable additional cost: where are you planning to store all of these units? Add rent if you build up too much inventory for your basement. In this field, you could make a nice percentage of each sale—your negotiation skills, however, will determine whether you can make a living doing this.

Keys to Success

If you love a bargain and can attract the attention of others who share that view, you can take advantage of the technology whirlwind that is costing the rest of us so much money. As businesses upgrade, they will appreciate the opportunity you present to sell their previous hardware rather than just junking it. And you will enable canny buyers to obtain the computers they need at a fraction of the price for the glitzy models hot off the retailers' shelves. Time and effort is needed to educate both sellers and buyers. Finding exactly the equipment a customer wants can be very time-consuming and require you to have a network of sources. You will need to manage inventory costs carefully.

Vacuum Cleaner Repair

Start-up cost:	$5,000-$15,000
Potential earnings:	25,000-$40,000
Typical fees:	$45 per hour is the usual rate; often, it's a set fee for the estimate and a negotiated fee for repair
Advertising:	Yellow Pages, local newspapers, supermarket and community bulletin boards, direct mail
Qualifications:	Strong technical knowledge and hands-on ability
Equipment needed:	Parts from a variety of manufacturers, including central vacuum systems (look for places that sell old vacuum cleaners for parts)
Staff required:	No
Handicapped opportunity:	Not typically
Hidden costs:	Shipping costs for overseas parts

What You Do

How many times has your beater bar been completely filled with animal hair—to the point where it won't move anymore? The fact is, we've all experienced difficulty with our trusty vacuums from time to time. You'll have no shortage of customers, because every home has a vacuum cleaner and they all need service and parts from time to time. The problem is, your customers won't be thinking about your services until they definitely need them—so be aware of that in your advertising or marketing plan. Be where most customers will look for you, such as the Yellow Pages or in coupon books. You could, in fact, offer a free six-month checkup for early problem diagnosis and bring in instant business. Diversify as much as you can, too; by stocking replacement bags and commonly used parts you can make a tidy side profit.

What You Need

From the start, you'll need to set up shop in a comfortable place with adequate lighting and a sturdy workbench. You can do this in your home, or spend $300 or more per month renting shop space. Whichever you choose, you'll need to advertise ($1,500-$3,000) and keep a fairly complete parts inventory. Charge at least $45 per hour for your time to be sure you're covering overhead and expenses.

Keys to Success

Supplement that business by installing and servicing central vacuum systems, a feature in many new homes. Cultivate contacts among local developers and builders.

Vacation Rentals Broker

Start-up cost:	$500-$1,000
Potential earnings:	45,000-$60,000
Typical fees:	Usually a percentage (10 to 15 percent)
Advertising:	Advertising in real estate magazines and real estate section of newspaper, Yellow Pages, referrals
Qualifications:	Experience in real estate rentals, good organizational skills
Equipment needed:	A basic office setup for record keeping
Staff required:	No
Handicapped opportunity:	No
Hidden costs:	Insurance, vehicle maintenance

What You Do

A vacation rentals broker keeps track of all the details related to renting property for distant owners. Many people with second homes rent them for the better part of the year, reserving a week or two for themselves and their families. Renting helps with the costs of this additional residence, but it also creates a number of headaches and problems that are very difficult for someone who lives far away to deal with. Your service finds renters, writes the rental contract, and makes sure that the agreements are carried out. You collect the rent, check for any damage, answer the million and one questions renters always have, and generally keep an eye on things.

What You Need

Costs are minimal; you just need an effective way to keep track of information and money. Since your business depends directly on how much time you put into it, expect to earn as much as you work for (and that could be anywhere from $45,000-$60,000 or more).

Keys to Success

Consider becoming a vacation rentals broker if you live in an area that has a high appeal for renters and a large stock of available summer (or winter) homes to rent. Once you develop a reputation for dependability, referrals will bring other homeowners to you. The amount of advertising you will need to do will vary depending on your area and the presence or absence of competing services.

Vending Machine Owner

Start-up cost:	$1,000-$20,000
Potential earnings:	Depends on the machine location and type; a possible annual potential income of $20,000-$35,000
Typical fees:	Can be as low as $100 per month and as high as $500 per month (per machine)
Advertising:	Direct mail, Yellow Pages
Qualifications:	Excellent sales ability
Equipment needed:	Vending machines and the product to fill them
Staff required:	No
Handicapped opportunity:	No
Hidden costs:	An average of 10 percent on what you earn from each machine is given to the property owner

What You Do

Although they seem to be everywhere, some research will be required to determine what type of vending machine is needed and exactly which spots might be most profitable for you. Without a doubt, you'll need good marketing and sales skills for this occupation. For example, solicit large factories to find out if they have round-the-clock shifts and need 'real food' such as soup and sandwiches—or, if it's a small firm, will only soda and candy machines do? Once you've obtained a client, that customer should be able to tell you what to stock, but ask to tour the facility so you can get a good idea of where to actually place the machine. If you go with soda and candy, make sure your client company will place your machine in a high-traffic area.

What You Need

Start-up costs depend on what type of vending machine you will want to use. Bubble gum machines cost as little as $100 and cappuccino machines can run as high as $1,000 or more. Whatever machine you decide to go with, it should be a winner if you market correctly, and you could earn $20,000-$35,000.

Keys to Success

Our recommendation is to hit the big factories and large businesses. They usually pay you to come to them and don't require the 10 percent fee. You will also have to follow up on your machines; every day in a large business and a minimum of once a week for smaller-volume vending machines. This can pretty much be a five-day-a-week job, since most businesses close for the weekend.

Web Site Developer

Start-up cost:	$2,000-$3,000
Potential earnings:	15,000+ (it's an emerging market, so the true ceiling isn't known yet)
Typical fees:	$500+ per creation
Advertising:	Word of mouth, bulletin board services, trade journals, on-line account
Qualifications:	Marketing skills, computer graphic skills, experience in cyberspace
Equipment needed:	Computer, modem, office furniture
Staff required:	No
Handicapped opportunity:	Yes
Hidden costs:	Be sure to watch your connect time with on-line services

What You Do

This is about as cutting edge as you can get in the world of marketing. Industries of almost all types are exploring the Internet; many have found that a home page connects them with their customers in new ways. An effective full-color home page works much better than a dull list of products available with their specs. Producing an effective home page is an entirely different experience from developing an old-fashioned paper brochure; if you can make the Web come alive for a client by designing a home page that is visited often, you can be one of the first in this emerging field. Businesses need to understand that surfers will spend time at a location on the Internet that offers something they want: an interesting, informative home page that engages their imaginations and offers them products related to their needs.

What You Need

Power up your modem and go. On-line time will probably be a significant cost and you will want to advertise on-line as well; these rates will vary according to carrier but run $8-$10 a month for basic services and an average of $4 per hour on extended services. Set your fees according to what the market will bear—check out what competitors are charging by visiting their Internet site.

Keys to Success

This business depends on several kinds of creativity at once. The process of making home pages isn't something you can follow step-by-step out of your old college textbooks. You're covering new ground here. It will take creativity to market yourself as well, because the whole idea of computerized marketing is so new. Learning about your client companies so you can represent them creatively and effectively will keep you on your mental toes. You'll find it takes quite a bit of time to find clients creative and futuristic enough to understand the advantages of your service.

Window Treatment Specialist

Start-up cost:	$1,000-$5,000
Potential earnings:	25,000-$35,000
Typical fees:	$20-$30 per hour or a per-job basis
Advertising:	Personal contacts with interior decorators, fabric and drapery stores, Yellow Pages, local newspapers
Qualifications:	Basic sewing skills, ability to accurately measure
Equipment needed:	Heavy-duty sewing machine
Staff required:	No
Handicapped potential:	Yes
Hidden costs:	Materials can get costly; buy wholesale

What You Do

You can provide a year-round service with a heavy-duty sewing machine, space to create, and an interest in interior decorating. With the continuing influx of housing developments and condominium complexes, you should have no shortage for customers in need of fine window detail such as curtains, valances, or swags. Network with condo associations and apartment complex owners; they may provide you with regular referrals and a steady flow of business. Cultivate contacts with local fabric stores and interior designers. Remember, accuracy is a must because mistakes in measuring can get expensive if you have to replace fabric.

What You Need

Even with your equipment costs considered, you'll still be in the $1,000-$5,000 start-up range with this business. The biggest cost, really, is your advertising—you'll need to get the word out in community newspapers, the Yellow Pages, and through coupon books, so expect to spend $3,000 or more on advertising alone. Your hourly rate should be somewhere near $20-$35 per hour.

Keys to Success

Make a portfolio with photographs of samples of your work to show prospective clients. Display some of them in fabric stores, and make business cards available to store owners and interior designers.

Word-Processing Service

Start-up cost:	$5,000-$15,000
Potential earnings:	30,000-$45,000
Typical fees:	Many in this field charge $5-$10 per page
Advertising:	Yellow Pages, focus advertising in a 5-10-mile radius of your business location, direct mail, university bulletin boards, networking with business and professional organizations
Qualifications:	Fast and accurate typing skills (at least 65 words per minute), customer-oriented attitude
Equipment needed:	Computer hardware and software, laser printer, modem, copy machine, fax; optional: transcribing machine and scanner.
Staff required:	None initially
Handicapped opportunity:	Yes
Hidden costs:	Equipment and software upgrades

What You Do

Despite the abundance of personal computers, demand for off-site word-processing services has steadily increased. Essentially, word-processing is a fancier (and more technically correct) phrase for typing service. You'll be doing all the same kinds of work, only you'll be using a computer instead of the great typewriter dinosaur. Customers will come to you with everything from reports and term papers to resumes and technical documentation. The ability to produce an attractive product with quick turnaround will ensure your success in this fairly competitive field. Remember that just about any Joe with a basic computer system and printer thinks of getting into this type of business; you'll have to be able to set yourself apart from these folks as well as the hundreds of secretarial services out there (who perform services that go beyond your own). Position yourself close to a university or in a downtown area, and you'll increase your chances of success by at least 50 percent.

What You Need

Your start-up costs are going to be quite reasonable if you already own a computer and laser printer. Most of your initial expense will result from advertising and appropriate software purchases (set aside at least $3,000 for these). Charge a per-page rate of $5-$10 or an hourly fee for the larger jobs; it'll take you a while to get a feel for which projects are more labor-intensive.

Keys to Success

Beware of underpricing your service. Consider adding a surcharge for handwritten or hard-to-read documents and materials that include charts or tables. If you can stand the repetitive motion of using a keyboard, and of typing other people's work, your income is limited only by your speed and the number of hours you want to work.

Workers' Compensation Consultant

Start-up cost:	$5,000-$7,000
Potential earnings:	45,000-$60,000
Typical fees:	Monthly retainer fee of $1,500-$3,000 (depending on the size of the company)
Advertising:	Business periodicals, networking, referrals
Qualifications:	Ability to locate best rates for companies and ways to keep costs down
Equipment needed:	Computer, printer, office furniture, business card, letterhead, envelopes
Staff required:	No
Handicapped opportunity:	Yes
Hidden costs:	Insurance, membership dues

What You Do

A workers' compensation consultant is an outside contractor who works with companies to reduce the incidence of workers' compensation claims, find better rates, and innovative ways to save money. You will investigate the circumstances of the manner in which the employer deals with these problems. You might even administer the claims process for a period of time, instead of having a company employee do it. Typical strategies to reduce claims include: 1) more thoroughly investigating the claim to determine whether it is indeed valid; 2) conducting regular reviews of workers' compensation benefits packages; and 3) recommending changes in the workplace to reduce injuries. The bottom line is, your nose for trouble can prevent a company from being taken advantage of—either by invalid claims or high rates.

What You Need

Investigative tools and the equipment to write reports are what you will need; spend at least $4,000 equipping your office with computer and printing equipment. Your reports will need to be clear and easy to understand (after all, they hired you to clear up the red tape, right?), so buy a decent software package for all of your major communications. Most disability consultants work on a retainer (typically $1,500-$3,000 per month).

Keys to Success

This is quite a lively field. To establish yourself you will probably need the experience gained from having been a workers' compensation specialist for an employer, or at least another consulting firm. If you show that you can conduct excellent investigations, write effective reports, and make productive recommendations for improvements in processes, you can build a very successful enterprise. You will not be everyone's favorite person as you uncover cheaters, but you will be improving your clients' bottom line.

Expert Advice

What sets your business apart from others like it?

"We're based in the fundamentals of advertising and design," says Larry Rosenthal, President of Cube Productions, Inc., in New York City. "We are also on the cutting edge; if it's new technology, it's been in here for an experimental run. Our clients appreciate the fact that we try everything out first."

Things you couldn't do without:

Rosenthal says he couldn't do without a computer and modem, Internet lines, software tools, and external, peripheral equipment such as scanners.

Marketing tips/advice:

"Get yourself a home page, and make it a well-constructed, easy-to-use one with a clear point of view. Also, use e-mail to market directly to those who might be interested in your services."

If you had to do it all over again . . .

"I would have started working on the Web even earlier. I would've also e-mailed Mark Andreeson from Netscape and ask to work with him!"

Listing of Businesses by Category